Social Theory in the Twentieth Century

To Julia

Social Theory in the Twentieth Century

Patrick Baert

NEW YORK UNIVERSITY PRESS
Washington Square, New York

Published in 1998 in the U.K. by Polity Press

First published in the U.S.A. in 1998 by
NEW YORK UNIVERSITY PRESS
Washington Square
New York, N.Y. 10003

Library of Congress Cataloging-in-Publication Data
Baert, Patrick, 1961–
    Social theory in the twentieth century / Patrick Baert.
        p.   cm.
    Includes index.
    ISBN 0–8147–1340–8. — ISBN 0–8147–1339–4 (pbk.)
    1. Social sciences—Philosophy.   2. Sociology—Philosophy.
3. Functionalism (Social sciences)   I. Title.   II. Title: Social
theory in the 20th century
H61.15.B34   1998
300′.1—dc21   98–18650
                                                                      CIP

Printed in Great Britain

Contents

Contents

Acknowledgements

I wish to express my gratitude to Catherine Alexander, William Outhwaite, Nigel Pleasants and Alan Shipman for their detailed comments on earlier drafts. My special thanks go to Anthony Giddens, who followed the progress of the book very closely, and whose suggestions proved to be extremely valuable. The staff at Polity Press showed remarkable patience and expertise, and I am particularly indebted to Julia Harsant, Petra Moll, Gill Motley and Pamela Thomas. I am also extremely grateful to Sarah Dancy for her constructive copy-editing. Finally, I wish to thank all the students whom I taught in the Faculty of Social and Political Sciences at the University of Cambridge during the past five years. Teaching them forced me to clarify my thoughts and, on several occasions, to reconsider my views.

Some ideas of the book were first introduced at conferences. My perspective on Foucault (chapter 5) was presented at the World Congress of Sociology in Bielefeld (1994), the conference 'Einstein meets Magritte' in Brussels (1995), and a workshop on methodology at the University of Rome (1996). Some aspects of my critique of rational choice theory (chapters 7 and 8) and of realism (chapter 7) were presented at a workshop on realism and economics in King's College, Cambridge (1995/6). I appreciated and incorporated comments by participants at these meetings. Chapter 5 is partly based on my article, 'Foucault's History of the Present as Self-Referential Knowledge Acquisition', to be published in *Philosophy and Social Criticism* (1998).

I am grateful for permission to reproduce the following copyright material:

Figure 1.3, 'The culinary triangle', from Claude Lévi-Strauss: *The Origin of Table Manners: Introduction to a Science of Mythology: 3*, translated by John and Doreen Weightman (Cape, 1978), copyright © 1968 by Librairie Plon; English translation copyright © 1978 by Jonathan Cape Limited and Harper & Row, Publishers, Inc, reprinted by permission of Random House UK Ltd, and HarperCollins Publishers Inc.

Figure 1.4, 'Structure of the Oedipus myth', from Claude Lévi-Strauss: *Structural Anthropology*, Volume 1 translated by Claire Jacobson and Brooke Grundfest Schoepf (Basic Books, 1963/Allen Lane, The Penguin Press 1968), English translation copyright © 1963 by Basic Books, Inc, reprinted by permission of Basic Books, a subsidiary of Perseus Books Group, LLC, and of Penguin Books Ltd.

Table 2.2, 'How people adapt to the state of anomie', from page 194 'A Typology of Modes of Individual Adaptation' in Robert K. Merton: *Social Theory and Social Structure* (revised and enlarged edition, The Free Press, 1957), copyright © 1967, 1968 by Robert K. Merton, reprinted by permission of The Free Press, a division of Simon & Schuster.

Introduction

This book aims to be a critical overview of the various contributions to social theory this century. I take a social theory to be a relatively systematic, abstract and general reflection upon the workings of the social world. However elementary this definition might be, a number of consequences follow from it. First, I will only discuss theories which reach a high level of *abstraction*. This is certainly not to say that social theories are necessarily independent of the empirical study of society. Of course, some theories have hardly any bearing on empirical research, while others very much rely upon or inform empirical sociology. But whether they are empirically grounded or not, the main purpose of social theorists is obviously to theorize, and there is thus a clear distinction between the abstract nature of social theory and the practical orientations of empirical sociology. Second (and relatedly), I will explore theories which reach a high level of *generality*. That is, they aim to cover various aspects of the social realm, across different periods and across different societies. For example, they would deal with the question how social order is brought about in *any* society – rather than in *a* particular society. Third, there is the *systematic* nature of social theories. Compared to mere opinions and beliefs, they exhibit a high level of internal consistency and coherence. Even recent attempts to move away from grand theory-building are systematic endeavours; they are not mere amalgams of opinions.

I cover social theory in the twentieth century, but this is not to suggest that coherent views on the subject had not previously emerged. Numerous ancient and pre-modern political philosophers based their political agenda on highly sophisticated views about the social realm. Furthermore, social theory was central to the emergence of sociology as a separate discipline in the course of the nineteenth century. Auguste Comte, Émile Durkheim, Max Weber and Karl Marx (to name only a few) developed extremely elaborate views about the mechanisms of the social world. Nevertheless, twentieth-century social theory is, at least in some respects, quite distinct from its predecessors. Let me, for the sake of clarity, mention three differences between the position of nineteenth-century social theory and its contemporary status. First, although Comte, Durkheim and others made great efforts to establish sociology as a separate discipline, they did not pursue an institutional dividing line between theory and empirical research. By contrast, in many countries, social theory has increasingly become a separate academic field – clearly distinct from empirical sociology. Second, social theory has become professionalized. In the nineteenth century it was practised by people who were educated in aligned fields (philosophy or political theory). Few occupied academic positions which would have allowed them to train others. Neither Comte, Alexis de Tocqueville, Marx, Herbert Spencer nor Georg Simmel occupied permanent posts in universities. In the late twentieth century there are numerous graduate schools where a formal training in social theory is provided. Third, social theories are now less clearly tied to political action than they used to be. They used to be tools for dealing with political problems. For example, Comte (and to some extent Durkheim) wondered how social order could be reinstated following the political and economic turmoil of the time. Tocqueville tried to ascertain how equality of opportunity and freedom could be reconciled, and Marx aimed to develop a more equal and less alienating type of society. For all of them, social theory was not an aim in itself; it was considered to be a necessary medium for dealing with current political issues. The intricate link between social theory and the reality of political life has diminished in the course of the twentieth century.

Let me briefly elaborate the main presuppositions of each school of thought. Most twentieth-century perspectives are influenced by some nineteenth-century precursors. Both structuralism (see chapter 1) and functionalism (see chapter 2) have a lot in common in that they adopt Durkheim's holistic picture of society. According to the doctrine of holism, society is to be studied as a whole, and this whole cannot be reduced to a mere sum of its components. Like Comte, Durkheim emphasized that society is an entity *sui generis*; that is, an entity with its own complexity. Society can therefore not be seen as a mere aggregation of people pursuing their individual interests. Likewise, both structuralism and functionalism are interested in the extent to which different parts of a social system are interrelated, and how they contribute to that system. Structuralists search for those underlying social structures which constrain and determine people's action and thought. The individuals themselves are not necessarily aware of the existence of the structures, and they are *a fortiori* rarely conscious of the constraining effects of the very same structures. In addition, structuralist social theorists often employ analogies with language in order to make sense of non-linguistic, social phenomena. They do so, often, by relying upon the work of Ferdinand de Saussure, a Swiss linguist and founding father of structural linguistics.

Functionalists, instead, believe in the existence of so-called universal functional prerequisites. That is, they hold that for any social system to survive, a number of functions or needs must be fulfilled. For example, for a system not to disintegrate, a minimum level of solidarity is needed amongst its members. Functionalists thus pay attention to how various social practices fulfil (or might fulfil) the central needs of the wider system in which these practices are embedded. Just as structuralism pays attention to the underlying structures of which people are rarely aware, so functionalism focuses on functions of which the individuals involved tend not to be conscious. Like structuralism, functionalism became especially dominant in the 1950s and 1960s. Many theorists then adhered to both perspectives, and tried to integrate the two in a 'structural-functionalist' framework. Functionalism became highly unfashionable in the 1970s, but there has been a revival of functionalist reasoning in the 1990s. Compared to its forerunner, 'neo-functionalism' is a broad church in that it attempts to integrate functionalist notions with insights from rival theories.

For a long time so-called 'interpretative sociologies' (see chapter 3) were the main alternatives to the hegemony of structural-functionalism. These include symbolic interactionism, the dramaturgical approach and ethnomethodology. Both symbolic interactionism and the dramaturgical approach draw upon the work of the American philosopher G. H. Mead. Like Mead (but unlike structuralism and functionalism), they emphasize that people have selves; that is, individuals have the ability to reflect upon their (imaginary or real) actions and upon the actions of others. In opposition to structuralism and functionalism, people's actions are not seen as merely the product of social structures imposed upon them. Instead, these 'interpretative schools' stress that people actively interpret their surrounding reality, and act accordingly. The same emphasis on human agency and reflectivity is present in Harold Garfinkel's ethnomethodology and related theories. Both ethnomethodology and structuration theory (see chapters 3 and 4) are heavily influenced by Alfred Schutz's social phenomenology and the later Wittgenstein. Garfinkel and other ethnomethodologists investigate the extent to which people actively (though unintentionally) reconstitute social order in their daily routine activities. Structuration theory (see chapter 4) relies upon both Erving Goffman and Garfinkel to demonstrate that order is indeed a practical accomplishment by knowledgeable individuals who know a great deal about social life. That knowledge tends to be tacit (where the understanding is unspoken), rather than discursive (where the understanding can be put into words). These interpretative schools came to the surface especially in the 1960s; structuration theory emerged in the late 1970s and early 1980s.

Neo-functionalism (see chapter 2, final section), Pierre Bourdieu's genetic structuralism (see chapter 1, final section), Anthony Giddens's structuration theory (see chapter 4) and Jürgen Habermas's critical theory (see chapter 6) came to the forefront in the 1970s and 1980s. These theories have two features in common. First, they all attempt to integrate opposing philosophical and theoretical traditions. For example, they aim to integrate structuralist notions and insights from interpretative sociology, and they seek to transcend the opposition between determinism and voluntarism. Second, they all wish to overcome previously held dualisms. For example, they try to move beyond the opposition between the individual and society. Besides these two features, genetic structuralism and structuration theory have other characteristics in common. Both reject mechanistic views of the social world in which structures are seen as imposed upon people. Instead, people are portrayed as active agents – their behaviour being constrained, but not determined. Both Bourdieu and Giddens argue that people's daily routines are rooted in a taken-for-granted world. In general, people know how to act in accordance with the implicit, shared rules which make up that world. They draw upon these rules, and in so doing they unintentionally reproduce them.

Bourdieu and Giddens acknowledge that sociology and social theory have a critical potential. Social theory especially can help us to reflect critically upon society. Nevertheless, the task of developing the foundations of a critical theory is very much that taken on by the Frankfurt School and particularly by Habermas (see chapter 6). I will focus on Habermas, since his version of critical theory is highly sophisticated. It is extremely elaborate, and it integrates a wide variety of philosophical and sociological traditions. Like other liberal rationalists, Habermas promotes the implementation of procedures of an open, unrestrained debate amongst equals. His notions of 'communicative rationality' and 'ideal speech situation' are situated around this vision. Habermas's utopia looks suspiciously like an academic seminar: society is to be organized so that people are able to criticize openly what others say. Likewise, everybody should be able to defend their viewpoint against the criticisms of others. For Habermas, this vision of an open, unrestrained debate underlies Enlightenment philosophy.

French structuralism eventually led to post-structuralism in the course of the 1970s and 1980s. Structuralism and post-structuralism have quite a lot in common. For example, the modern concept of the individual is not prior to society. It emerges out of time and space-specific structures or discourses. But post-structuralists differ from their predecessors in that, for example, they abandon the scientistic pretentions of structuralism. Post-structuralists flirt with Friedrich Nietzsche's perspectivism, according to which there is no absolute standpoint from which to make statements regarding what is or what ought to be. They are often inclined to adopt some kind of relativism: different epistemological frameworks bring about new meanings, and each framework is accompanied by novel standards of rationality and truth. The most well-known post-structuralists are Jacques Derrida, Gilles Deleuze and Michel Foucault. Derrida had an enormous influence on literary theory and literary criticism, Deleuze on philosophy. For our purposes, Foucault's work (see chapter 5) is especially relevant. Although a historian by training, his writings have had an enormous impact on social theory. I will focus on his historical methodology, since doing so sheds light on the highly original nature of his project. I think that most secondary sources on Foucault fail to acknowledge the distinctive nature of his methodology.

Most social theorists believe in the inapplicability of economic logic to social phenomena. Rational choice theorists (see chapter 7) argue otherwise. They hold that it is possible to explain and predict social and political phenomena by drawing upon the notion of a rational, self-interested agent. So, like Weber and Tocqueville, they account for social life by referring to the fact that people act intentionally, and produce numerous effects some of which are intended, some unintended. However, they also assume a constant rationality. There is a vast amount of literature on what rationality consists of. It means, *inter alia*, that people have a clear ordering of preferences, that they gather information about the costs involved in obtaining the preferences, and that they act accordingly. The model suggested is basically derived from economics, hence some rational choice theorists refer to their view as the 'economic approach'. They attempt to show the usefulness of their theory to areas which are traditionally not associated with economics. Take, for example, marriage patterns, rates of fertility or criminal behaviour. Rational choice theorists feel that the more a practice is *prima facie* irrational, the greater their accomplishment in showing that the practice is rational after all. Rational choice theory became more popular in the 1980s and 1990s.

Social theory and philosophy of the social sciences are closely related. Any theorizing about the social world relies upon some implicit philosophical assumptions, for example, regarding the differences between the social and the natural realm, or regarding the nature of causality. I have therefore included a chapter which deals solely with the history of the philosophy of the social sciences in the twentieth century (see chapter 8). In particular, I will show how positivist epistemology was superseded by falsificationism in the course of the 1950s and 1960s, and how, more recently, realism has come to the forefront. Positivist philosophy deserves our attention, since, with the notable exception of rational choice theory, most social theories of the twentieth century have distanced themselves very clearly from a positivist notion of social science. The inadequacy of positivism has, indeed, been a starting point for numerous contributions to modern social theory. Broadly speaking, positivism attributes epistemological priority to science over metaphysics or religion. Positivists are naturalists in that they believe that the social and the natural sciences employ the same method. From this follows the suggestion that sociologists, political scientists and psychologists ought to emulate the practices of their colleagues in the natural sciences; that is, they are all to infer general laws from observed regularities. These laws allow one not only to explain, but also to predict. Positivists are willing to acknowledge the existence of entities, if and only if the latter are immediately accessible to observation. To refer to hidden structures or powers is considered to be an illegitimate metaphysical leap.

Like positivists, falsificationists believe that scientific theories ought to be testable. But whereas positivists argue that statements are scientific if they can be *confirmed* on the basis of empirical evidence, falsificationists believe that statements are scientific if they can in principle be *refuted* empirically. For falsificationists, scientific progress occurs through trial and error: scientists come up with bold conjectures which eventually get refuted, and then a new theory emerges. With this picture of science in mind, falsificationists are highly critical of both Marxist sociology and Freudian psychological theory. They regard Marxism and psychoanalysis as 'non-falsifiable' because both are immune against empirical refutation: neither is scientific precisely because neither can be refuted. Falsificationists tend to be sympathetic towards 'methodological individualism', propounders of which oppose Durkheim's holistic view of society, and believe instead that the social world ought to be seen as the (partly intended, partly unintended) outcome of individuals pursuing their goals. People's motives are the causes of their action, and the latter leads to effects, some of which are intended, some unintended. The economic approach (see chapter 7) is perfectly in line with a falsificationist conception of social science.

Realists mostly share with falsificationism and positivism a belief in naturalism; that is, the doctrine that the method of the natural sciences is applicable to the social sciences. But realists adopt a very different notion of what this method consists of. For realists, to explain is not merely to identify regularities. To explain is to account for *how* regularities are brought about, and this can only be accomplished by referring to underlying structures or powers which are not immediately accessible to observation. Various structures are simultaneously at work, they occasionally cancel each other out, and structures are thus not necessarily visible at a surface level. The result of all this is that, contrary to positivists and falsificationists, realists downgrade the importance of empirical verification and falsification. It is no surprise that many realists feel affinities with structuralist-inspired social theory. But, like Giddens and Bourdieu, they wish to link structuralist notions to insights from interpretative sociology. As with Giddens and Bourdieu, they wish to move beyond both holistic views of society and methodological individualism. Similar to Habermas, they see their philosophy and social theory as having a critical potential. It is ultimately directed towards people's self-emancipation.

Underlying this book is a particular view of what is a fruitful way of thinking about social theory. This view also has consequences for how social theory should be taught. I can contrast this view with the way in which numerous (introductory or advanced) books on the subject tend to proceed. First, some commentators commit what I call the 'fallacy of perspectivism'. By 'perspectivism' I mean here the (often implicit) view that no independent yardstick exists which would enable one to judge and compare between rival theories. Very few explicitly adhere to this, but many more actually practise it. One recognizes perspectivists by the way in which they describe differences between theories. They seem to believe that what distinguishes various theories is merely that they shed light on different aspects of social life. For example, one theory focuses on power, another one on daily interaction and yet another on values and norms. None of them is regarded as superior to any other; they simply *do* different things in that they highlight different features of the social realm. Underlying this book is the strongly held conviction that differences between social theories cannot be reduced to mere differences in emphasis or subject-matter. There are indeed a number of yardsticks by which social theories can be judged and compared, the main ones of which are intellectual depth, originality, analytical clarity and internal consistency. Without explicitly referring to these criteria, I employ them throughout what follows.

Second, some commentators on social theory commit the 'fallacy of externalism' in that they present *external* criticisms of the authors discussed. That is, social theories are often criticized for failing to accomplish something which the theorists did not set out to pursue in the first place. For example, many have criticized Garfinkel for not sufficiently taking into account broader social structures. This, in isolation, is obviously an external criticism because the issue of wider structures falls outside Garfinkel's project. I consider external criticisms (at least in isolation) generally to be less desirable, and I try to avoid them in what follows. Nobody can accomplish everything. To criticize a theory for ignoring something is unlikely to be particularly informative. In general, it is more appropriate to evaluate theories from within – to evaluate their internal consistency. This is not to say that all projects have the same value. Some theoretical assumptions or aims are indeed more plausible or interesting than others. Neither is it to say that external criticisms are always inadequate. As a matter of fact, there are at least two ways in which they might be useful: they can be a stepping-stone towards an internal critique – for example, it might be shown that taking broader structural issues into account undermines some of Garfinkel's propositions; and they can be used as a medium for developing one's own social theory – for example, Giddens's structuration theory rests upon a series of external criticisms. The concluding chapter of this book suggests a theoretical frame of reference which is partly based on external criticisms of earlier theories.

Third (and related to the previous point), some commentators commit what I call the 'political fallacy'. They criticize theories for their potential or actual *effects* on socio-political matters. For example, a common criticism of functionalist social theory has been that it maintains or reinforces the political status quo. Now, I do not doubt that some publications in social theory *might* affect society. Neither do I wish to argue that it is impossible to ascertain or predict the likely effects of a given theory. For example, it is probably true that, compared with some other theories, functionalist theory can be used more effectively as a justification for the (or any) existing socio-political order. But the identification of possible or actual consequences of a theory should *not* normally interfere with the intellectual appreciation of that theory. I can see only a few exceptions to this rule, one of which refers to the phenomenon of the so-called self-denying prophecy. That is, in some cases, once a theory becomes public knowledge, people start to act in ways which lead to the erosion of that theory. Here, the identification of effects of the theory are crucial to one's judgement regarding its validity. Generally, however, this is not the case. In what follows, I will be concerned with the intellectual validity of social theories, not with their intended or unintended effects on society.

With all this in mind, I wish now briefly to outline the structure of the book. Besides chapters 3 and 8, all chapters deal with a particular school or viewpoint in social theory, namely: structuralism (chapter 1), functionalism and neo-functionalism (chapter 2), Giddens's structuration theory (chapter 4), Foucault's post-structuralist view (chapter 5), Habermas's critical theory (chapter 6) and rational choice theory (chapter 7). Chapter 3 discusses three theories which deal with more social psychological issues: symbolic interactionism, ethnomethodology and the dramaturgical approach. Chapter 8 deals with three theories in the philosophy of the social sciences: positivism, falsificationism and realism. Every chapter follows a clear temporal sequence. For example, chapter 1 starts with the predecessors of structuralism (Durkheim and Ferdinand de Saussure), then moves on to Claude Lévi-Strauss's structuralist anthropology, and finally discusses recent attempts to link structuralism with some insights from Heidegger and the later Wittgenstein. A less strict temporal logic applies to the sequence of the chapters.

This book should normally be accessible to undergraduates and postgraduates in the arts and humanities. Some sections of chapter 8, such as the critical evaluation of realism, are more difficult, and are directed towards postgraduates and specialists. Each chapter can be read independently of the others.

1
A Timeless Order and its Achievement
Structuralism and Genetic Structuralism

St Augustine argued that he knew what time was until he was asked. One interpretation of this enigmatic statement is that time is so essential to being human that knowledge of it cannot be put discursively. In a sense, structuralism has occupied a similar role in twentieth-century intellectual life. It is indeed virtually impossible to conceive of social theory without taking on board structuralist notions. Yet it is equally difficult to provide an accurate definition of structuralism precisely because it is so much intertwined with current ways of theorizing about the social. The task of defining structuralism is even more complicated because of the wide range of subject-matter that it covers. Its area of application is not restricted to social theory, and it is at least equally prominent in a wide variety of other disciplines. Structuralism incorporates Saussure and Roman Jakobson's linguistics, Lévi-Strauss's anthropology, Jean Piaget's contributions to the psychology of development, François Jabob's biology and Louis Althusser's reading of Marx.

Being aware of the above reservations and focusing solely upon the social sciences, I think that nevertheless four features can be distinguished. First the most obvious characteristic of structuralism is that it advocates a 'holistic view'. Holism suggests that the various parts of a system should not be investigated independently of each other. The parts can only be understood in terms of their interrelations, and, eventually, in terms of their connections to the whole. Holism is often accompanied by a holistic theory of meaning. According to the latter, the meaning of signs, concepts or practices depends on the broader structure or context in which they are embedded. For example, the meaning of an utterance depends on which language is spoken; the meaning of any scientific term is dependent on the scientific theory in which it is employed; and the meaning of gestures or practices depends on the broader culture in which they take place. It follows that the same utterance might mean something different if spoken in another language; that the meaning of a scientific term might change with a new theory; and that the same gestures or practices could mean something else in a different culture.

The second feature of structuralism is that, like Plato and Parmenides, it tends to prioritize the invariant over the transient. Structuralism downgrades the flux of actions and events, and looks instead for social structures that are more stable across time. Structuralism assumes that these relatively unchanging social structures are either the 'real' causal powers behind actions and events, or that they are crucial in attributing meaning to these observed phenomena. Owing partly to its search for invariant structures, structuralism has a distinctive and controversial method of enquiry. Structuralism has affinities with 'synchronic analysis'. Synchronic analyses merely take a snapshot of society, as opposed to diachronic analyses which look at developments over time. Structuralists tend to downgrade the flow of time, some of them go as far as holding that a snapshot will do. Yet even if they embark upon diachronic analysis, they do so in a distinctive manner. Structuralist historians, for instance, are not particularly interested in the minutiae of historical events. Instead they search for those factors which, although not immediately visible to the people involved, play a central role in the shaping of their destiny: climate, geography, cultural frameworks, to name a few.

The third characteristic of structuralism is that it opposes positivism. Positivist philosophy will be discussed in detail at a later stage (see chapter 8). It will suffice to say here that positivists prefer to explain things only in terms of entities that are immediately observable. For positivists, to explain is to invoke causes, and causes are to be derived merely from observed regularities. In contrast, structuralists acknowledge the existence of a deeper stratum of reality far below the surface level of observed phenomena. The underlying structures are not immediately visible to the people subjected to them, nor to an observer. It is the task of the social scientist to uncover these latent structures in order to explain the surface level. Structuralists also distance themselves from a positivist notion of causality. First, they often refuse to commit themselves to statements regarding causality; they prefer to talk about 'laws of transformation'. Second, even if structuralists do employ causality, their notion is radically different from a positivist one. For structuralists, causality cannot be derived simply from observed regularities. Causes are not immediately available to sensory observation; social structures are latent, but nevertheless exercise causal power.

The fourth characteristic, which most structuralists have in common, is that they acknowledge the *constraining* nature of social structures. That is, structuralists tend to hold that people's actions and thoughts are heavily constrained and determined by underlying structures. It is possible to distinguish both a weak and a strong version of this structuralist position. The weak version is basically a methodological dictum. It suggests that the social researcher needs to search for those parameters which set limits to people's choices. This methodological position leaves open whether or not, in spite of the existence of structures, people really have choice and freedom. The strong version is a philosophical statement with far-reaching consequences. It does not simply say that structures are constraining, but that they are constraining to the extent that they preclude the possibility of the individual's agency. That is, although people might be under the impression that they are in control of their own destiny, they never really are. In its strong version, structuralism should be seen as a reaction against some philosophical currents of the 1940s and 1950s. The assumption that the individual cannot help but be free was indeed a central starting point of existentialist philosophy; structuralism set out to show otherwise.

Most self-declared structuralists would subscribe to the above four features. But in spite of these similarities, it would be a mistake to conceive of structuralism as simply a unified doctrine. There are at least two strands in structuralist thought: one goes back to Durkheim's sociology, the other to Saussure's structuralist linguistics. The first strand emphasizes the extent to which social structures impose themselves and exercise power upon agency. Social structures are regarded as constraining in that they mould people's actions or thoughts, and in that it is difficult, if not impossible, for one person to transform these structures. The second strand draws upon semiology, a general science of signs. Authors within this tradition borrow insights from and analogies with the study of linguistic activities for understanding non-linguistic, rule-governed behaviour. Culture is then conceived of as a 'system of signs'. Ferdinand Braudel was a clear example of the Durkheimian version of structuralism, Roland Barthes of the Saussurean strand. Lévi-Strauss incorporated both Saussure and Durkheim.

In this chapter I will first deal with the founding fathers of both versions of structuralism: Durkheim and Saussure. I will then elaborate upon Lévi-Strauss's structuralist anthropology, which will allow me to explain some of the deficiencies of structuralist thinking. This will subsequently lead me to Bourdieu's work, which is one of the major attempts to overcome these inadequacies.

Durkheim's contribution

Émile Durkheim (1858–1917) studied at the École Normale, a selective institution in France for the training of teachers and academics, where he developed a keen interest in social and political philosophy, and an equally keen dislike of what he saw as the humanistic, non-methodical and literary nature of the Parisian intellectual scene. He subsequently spent some time in Germany, where the cultural climate was somewhat more to his liking. On his return to his homeland, he was soon to receive a post at the University of

Bordeaux, and fifteen years later he returned to Paris. The irony is that this man, who devoted his whole life to the foundation of the discipline of sociology, never officially held a post in his favourite subject until late in his life. Sociology was still associated with Auguste Comte (1798–1857), whose ideas, it was thought, matched his disreputable personality. Durkheim was supposed to teach educational science, but this was hardly a deterrent for a man with such a zealous devotion. He took every opportunity to smuggle sociology into the bastions of the French academic establishment.[1]

A useful way of introducing Durkheim's sociology is by showing how he relates to two other icons of nineteenth-century thought: Comte and Herbert Spencer (1820–1903). This is not to suggest that either Comte or Spencer's influence on Durkheim exceeds the impact of any other author. As a matter of fact, the effect of neither should be overrated; Charles Renouvier, Émile Boutroux and Wilhelm Wundt, for example, were at least as influential. But the advantage of focusing upon Comte and Spencer is that they enable one to locate Durkheim within the broader intellectual spectrum of the nineteenth century.

Through his teacher Boutroux, Durkheim came across Comte's hierarchical division of various domains of reality, where the higher levels are irreducible to the lower ones. Hence the social domain cannot be seen as an aggregate of its psychological components. As society has *sui generis* features, a holistic view is called for. From Comte, Durkheim borrowed the notion that, as in other realms of reality, society can be studied according to rigorous scientific methods. Like Comte, he called this study sociology, and believed it to be not only possible, but also desirable; it would enable one to steer society rationally and to eradicate 'pathological' forms. Also like Comte, Durkheim thought that, given the current crisis of society, steering was not just desirable, but necessary. But like J. S. Mill, Durkheim thought that Comte's sociology was still too speculative and dogmatic. Consequently, Durkheim's theories have a more solid empirical foundation, and he tried to use methods that were as rigorous as possible. Hence he expressed more admiration for the detailed, methodological research conducted by Alfred Espinas and Albert Schaeffle. On the same theme, whereas Comte made sweeping generalizations about 'humanity' in general, Durkheim was more sensitive to differences between societies.[2]

Evolutionary theory, and especially Spencer's version of it, was another source of inspiration. Durkheim was attracted to Spencer's sophisticated use of social analogies with biological evolution. Like Spencer and many other theorists at the time, Durkheim introduced a dichotomy to portray the evolution of society. Spencer wrote about a transition from military to industrial societies, Ferdinand Tönnies saw a shift from *Gemeinschaft* to *Gesellschaft* and H. S. Maine was struck by the demise of a society based on status and the emergence of a society based on contract. Durkheim preferred to talk about the replacement of mechanical by organic solidarity. Whereas the former is a type of solidarity based on similarities, the latter is based on division of labour and mutual dependency.[3] As with Comte, Durkheim did not find Spencer's writings empirical or detailed enough.[4] He also disagreed with Spencer (and with Maine and Tönnies) that modernization goes together with the weakening of social bonds. One of the main propositions in *Division of Labour* is that, with the advent of industrial society, a new type of solidarity is formed. He distanced himself from Spencer's (and Maine's) view that in modern society people engage in free contractual relations devoid of any moral basis. Contracts presuppose, rather than create, a social order.[5]

Partly because of the wide variety of influences on Durkheim's thought, his work does not always present a unifying picture. Equally compelling arguments can be presented for reading him in radically different ways; indeed, authors with different theoretical outlooks have found inspiration in his writings. For instance, it is possible to see Durkheim as the founding father of modern positivist sociology, as can be inferred from a glance at his methodological pamphlet, *Rules of Sociological Method*, and its application in *Suicide* (see also chapter 8).[6] It is equally plausible to regard some aspects of his work (notably the underpinning theoretical framework of his doctoral dissertation in *Division of Labour*, and sections of his *Rules of Sociological Method*) as foreshadowing modern functionalism (see also chapter 2).[7] Finally, there are undoubtedly structuralist tenets in his work. Some argue that these features only appear in his later work on religion, but this is to ignore the more subtle, though equally strong, structuralist claims in his *Rules of Sociological Method*. Be that as it may, it is true that his commitment to structuralism is nowhere as clearly stated as in his *Elementary Forms of Religious Life*.[8]

I will now select those aspects of Durkheim's work which are relevant to the history of structuralism. The Durkheimian concept which deserves our attention is the notion of a 'social fact', of which Durkheim insisted that the subject-matter of sociology consists. He defined the latter as 'any way of acting, whether fixed or not, capable of exerting over the individual an external constraint . . . [and] which is general over the whole of a given society whilst having an existence of its own, independent of its individual manifestations'.[9] One of Durkheim's methodological dictums is that social facts have to be treated as 'things'. By this he meant that they have to be studied like natural objects. That is, social facts exist independent of one's framework or one's perception, and can only be found through empirical research.[10] An example of a social fact is a 'collective representation'. Being a state of the collective consciousness of a group, collective representations show how that group envisions itself and its surroundings.[11] Collective representations are social in two ways. They have social origins (they emerge out of social associations) and they deal with social phenomena.[12]

Durkheim's definition of social facts, as outlined, is not exactly what one would call an elegant formulation, but it does reveal three of their most important characteristics: they are external, constraining and general. By the externality of social facts Durkheim meant that they are prior to the individual, and, more controversially, that their functioning is independent of the individual's use of them. For instance, the individual does not define the duties which he or she has to perform; these obligations are prescribed in law and custom which are external to the individual.[13] By the constraining nature of social facts Durkheim meant that they have 'compelling and coercive power' through which they exercise control over the individual. People tend not to recognize this as coercion because they generally comply with the social facts out of free choice. Durkheim demonstrated this coercive power by imagining what would happen if the individual were to decide not to acquiesce – it would lead to punishments and result in failure.[14] Finally, generality indicates that social facts are beliefs and practices which are neither individual nor universal attributes, but which refer to those feelings, thoughts and practices that would have been different if people had lived in other groups. Social facts take public-collective forms, as opposed to their individual applications.[15]

Like Boutroux and Comte, Durkheim argued that every scientific domain needs to be understood according to 'its own principles'. Just as the biological realm cannot be reduced to physico-chemical forces, society is not an aggregate of psychological phenomena. Through social associations emergent properties occur which transcend and transform the individuals involved, similar to the numerous 'creative syntheses' in the bio-chemical realm. Advocating a strict methodological holism, society is considered to be an entity *sui generis* and therefore subject to its own laws. More precisely and polemically, social facts are only to be explained by other social facts.[16]

Durkheim's later work dealt particularly with the sociology of knowledge and the sociology of religion.[17] Whereas his earlier work aimed at demonstrating that it is erroneous to conceive of moral codes in a social vacuum, he continued his sociological crusade by attempting to show the social nature of the Kantian elementary categories of thought. Even the concepts of number, space and time do not escape Durkheim's vigorous campaign. The exact nature of his 'sociological Kantianism' is not entirely clear. It has been shown convincingly that he conflated four separate claims.[18] First, Durkheim argued that basic categories are shared by members of the same society. Second, he claimed that these Kantian categories are caused by the underlying social conditions. Third, he argued that the very same categories demonstrate a structural homology with the social conditions out of which they emerge. Fourth, he maintained that the categories fulfil essential functions for the social conditions out of which they evolved. Durkheim's attempt to use sociology in order to rectify Kant's apriorism inspired structuralist anthropology. Like Durkheim, Lévi-Strauss searched for the latent structures by which people categorize the external world.

It should be obvious from this brief survey that Durkheim's work adumbrated the development of structuralist thought in a number of ways. Let me recapitulate why he was a structuralist *avant la lettre*. First, he drew attention to those features of social life which cannot be reduced to a mere aggregate of its component parts. In structuralism one finds a similar commitment to holistic types of explanation. Second, the notion of constraint was essential to Durkheim's concept of social facts. He was trying to demonstrate the extent to which society moulds and penetrates the individual. Likewise, structuralism allocates coercive power to social structure. Third, Durkheim often relied upon a structuralist two-level world view, opposing a superficial level of self-mastery to a deeper, more real level of unconscious structures. Fourth, he attempted to eradicate those explanations which refer to subjective states of individuals (intentions, motives, purposes). This shows striking affinities with the 'objectivist' ambitions of structuralist sociology and anthropology in the course of the twentieth century. Fifth, Durkheim's rejection of Kantian apriorism culminated in an attempt to demonstrate the social nature of the basic categories by which people order and classify the surrounding world.

Saussure's approach to linguistics

Having studied at Leipzig and Berlin, Ferdinand de Saussure (1857–1911) taught Sanskrit, Gothic and Old High German, first at the University of Paris and subsequently in Geneva. An obviously gifted man, at the age of 21 Saussure wrote a splendid dissertation ('Mémoire sur le système primitif des voyelles dans les langues indo-européennes'), which already anticipated pivotal features of his mature thought. But with age Saussure wrote less, and by the time he died he had not published more than six hundred pages. His ideas only became widespread through the posthumous publication in 1915 of his *Course in General Linguistics*, which was based on his lectures at the University of Geneva.[19] For almost half a century the readership of this work was limited to linguists, but once the structuralist bandwagon was well on its way, other social scientists became fascinated with it.

It is, first, important to compare Saussure's structuralism with that of Durkheim. Three differences are worth mentioning here. First, whereas Durkheim's *oeuvre* is Janus-faced, Saussure's is not. I have already referred to the fact that various theoretical research programmes can be attributed to Durkheim; structuralism is only one of them. This is not the case for Saussure, whose theoretical contribution forms much more of a unity. Second, whereas Durkheim's structuralism was meant to be a contribution to sociology, Saussure's was not. Saussure was concerned with linguistic matters and only occasionally explored the possibilities of extending his ideas beyond the boundaries of the study of language. It was the accomplishment of others to demonstrate the wider sociological significance of his insights into linguistics. It also follows that, whereas Durkheim's propositions for sociology are clear-cut, the implications of Saussure for the social sciences remain open to discussion. Third, one of Durkheim's main concerns throughout his life was to explain social facts as *caused* by other social facts, similar to the way in which physico-chemical forces operate. Drawing upon analogies with thermodynamics and electricity, structuralist notions are subordinated to a causal analysis. As will be shown shortly, the purpose of a Saussurean approach to language was to reveal the underlying 'syntagmatic' and 'paradigmatic' relations. In this structuralist theory of semiotics there is hardly any place for a fully developed notion of causality.

Linguists today argue that the importance of Saussure's *Course* lies in the fact that the author distanced himself from two established opinions on language. First, there was the view, initially introduced by Claude Lancelot and Antoine Arnauld as early as the seventeenth century, that language is a mirror of thoughts and intrinsically rational. Second, there were the *Junggrammatiker* (the 'neogrammarians') such as Franz Bopp and Karl Brugmann, and Saussure's teachers Hermann Osthoff and August Leskien. According to their view, very much in vogue in the nineteenth century, the history of a language informs one about its current form. Sanskrit was believed to be the oldest language, and knowledge of it made it possible to trace back the history of other languages and to reveal their mutual roots. These two views had two features in common. First, both assumed that it could be established why, within any language, a particular name or pattern of sound is used to express a certain idea or concept. The further back one goes in history, the less arbitrary is the relationship between naming and concepts. Second, both conceived of language as a nomenclature. That is, both took it to be a set of names attached to universal concepts which are unchangeable and which exist independent of language.

With the appearance of Saussure's *Course* this picture was changed altogether. First, contrary to the atomistic nature of these earlier beliefs, Saussure introduced a holistic view of language. Whereas his predecessors conceived of language as nothing but the sum of its component parts, Saussure insisted that it needs to be seen as a structure in which the meaning of individual concepts is dependent on their relationship within a larger whole. Second, in contrast with, for instance, Bopp's bias in favour of diachronic analysis, Saussure's view of language attributes more importance to the synchronic investigation of language.[20] Third, Saussure demonstrated successfully that language is not a nomenclature. If it were, translation would be an easy task, but it is not, and this can be explained by the fact that different languages structure the world differently. Likewise, the boundaries and semantics of concepts continuously change through time, and this again shows that languages organize the world differently.

Central to Saussure's theory is his distinction between '*langue*' and '*parole*'. Saussure introduced this distinction in his attempt to identify the object of linguistic investigation.[21] What Saussure called *parole* or the 'executive side of language' alludes to actual utterances. *Langue* refers to the shared set of structural properties underlying language usage. Saussure insisted that the major concern of linguistics should be with *langue*, not *parole*. Similar to Durkheim's notion of the externality of social facts, Saussure argued that the simultaneous system of *langue* precedes *parole*, and that the former is the *sine qua non* for the latter. What people say or write makes sense because of the pre-existent structural properties of language. Language is a shared, social experience: people can speak and write because of the intersubjective nature of language usage.

Equally important is his distinction between 'sign', 'signifier' and 'signified'. The sign refers to both the signifier and the signified.[22] Whereas the signifier is the utterance or trace, the signified is the concept attached to it. If I say 'horse', the utterance or trace 'horse' is the signifier, the concept 'horse' is the signified, and the sign refers to both. These distinctions are relevant for understanding his notion of the 'arbitrary nature of the sign'.[23] The arbitrariness refers to the bond between the signifier and the signified. Saussure's use of 'arbitrary' calls for further explanation here. What he meant is that a different signified could have been attached to a particular signifier, were it not for the relationship between the sign that links them and other signs within that language. Now, I mentioned earlier that, in Saussure's view, language is not a nomenclature and that there are thus no unchangeable universal signifiers. Hence, his notion of the 'arbitrary nature of the sign' not only designated the 'unmotivated' bond between sound-image and concept, but also the arbitrary nature of both the signified and the signifier in themselves.[24]

Still regarding Saussure's concept of the arbitrary nature of the sign, there is a potential misunderstanding, which I briefly wish to point out. The notion of an arbitrary nature of the sign could well be understood to mean that the individual speaker can decide which signifier to use. But Saussure insisted that he did not mean this at all.[25] As a matter of fact, he very much denied individuals that power. Reminiscent of Durkheim's reflections upon the constraining features of social facts, Saussure went to great lengths to show that, because of its public-collective features, language is 'necessary' in that no individual is able to choose different signifiers from the ones in use. This particular view of language, as both arbitrary and necessary, is sometimes referred to as 'conventional'.[26]

Closely related to the notion of the arbitrary nature of the sign is the principle of difference. Saussure's famous analogy between language and a chess game is useful here.[27] The meaning of a piece is not derived from its material form in itself, but depends on how that piece can be distinguished from the other pieces. Likewise, in language, identity is a function of differences within a system. This applies to both signifier and signified. The meaning of the utterance 'man' is dependent on its difference from the utterances 'can', 'gen', 'mean', 'mess', etc. Likewise, the meaning of any colour, say green, is dependent on its differences from the other colours currently in use: blue, yellow, red, etc. Another way of expressing this insight is by saying that identity depends on difference from an 'absent totality'. For instance, when I refer to the colour green, the meaning of green is derived from its difference within a *system* of colours, which is currently in use and which, although not uttered, is nevertheless *implied*. Notice that the principle of difference operates at several linguistic levels, say from phonemes to grammatical facts. The phoneme (for instance, *c* in the word 'cat') is defined by its opposition to other phonemes which can potentially replace it and still make sense (in this case: 'bat', 'mat', 'sat', etc.). Grammatical facts comply with the very same notion of the relational nature of the sign: for instance, the future tense of a verb is dependent on its opposition to its present tense.[28]

Saussure's distinction between synchronic and diachronic analyses of language is well known. Initially he used the terms 'static' and 'evolutionary' linguistics, but then opted for synchronic and diachronic analysis.[29] Whereas the former takes a snapshot of language, the latter follows its evolution through time. Although critics of Saussurean linguistics tend to portray it as simply 'ahistorical', Saussure's own position was more subtle. Contrary to what the textbooks say of him, he recognized the historicity of language. The arbitrary nature of the sign implies that there are no essential, universal features to meaning, and meaning is thus constantly in flux. Now comes the interesting twist in Saussure's argument. Whereas most scholars would conclude from this the priority of diachronic over synchronic analysis, for Saussure it meant exactly the opposite. The arbitrary nature of the sign not only makes for the historicity of language, but also for the necessity of analysing language synchronically. From a Saussurean perspective, the explanation for this paradox is rather straightforward. The arbitrary nature of the sign means that the sign does not possess any essential features of its own. In structuralist parlance, there are no positive, self-defined signs in language. Every sign is entirely defined by its relationship with other signs which are currently in use, and it must therefore be taken to be a relational entity. Now, if the meaning of a sign is dependent on its relationship with other signs at a given time, it follows that a synchronic analysis is called for.[30]

I finish the exposition of Saussure's thought with a brief note regarding the distinction between paradigmatic and syntagmatic relations. Whereas the former refer to oppositional relations between replaceable items, the latter refer to combinatory relations between signs. Hitherto, I have only dealt with relations of paradigmatic contrast. Regarding syntagmatic relations, 'I love', for instance, can be followed by 'you', 'flying', 'them', 'Bruges', 'that film', etc. It cannot be followed by 'underwent', 'she', etc. There is thus a group of words which, according to the rules of syntagmatic relations, can follow 'I love'. Each two members of that group are in paradigmatic opposition to one another. Saussure's bold conjecture is that, at any level (i.e. whether one is dealing with phonemes, morphemes or 'grammatical facts'), language can be reduced to a combination of paradigmatic and syntagmatic relations.[31]

Saussure's impact on the development of social theory has been considerable. First, his distinction between *langue* and *parole* (and his prioritizing of the former over the latter) struck a chord with those who were disenchanted with the positivist pursuit of regularity conjunctions (see also chapter 8). The relevance of the distinction between *langue* and *parole* indeed extends beyond the realm of language. It can be seen as derived from a more general opposition between underlying structures on the one hand, and their particular instantiations on the other. From that general dualism follows, for instance, the hierarchical opposition between social structure and behavioural patterns. With this model in mind, the positivist preoccupation with statistical regularities was in vain: it was a mere search at the superficial non-structural level. Second, various social scientists became aware that, like language, other systems of discourse could be studied semiotically. Whether scientific theories, hairstyles, restaurant menus, or ancient myths, they can all be studied as systems of signs.[32] For example, there are clear rules regarding appropriate combinations of meal courses and *vis-à-vis* potential substitute courses. The meaning of each course depends on its difference from alternative choices. Compared with a light course, heavy and filling courses might suggest (in some social circles) a lack of delicacy or sophistication.

Durkheim and Saussure set the stage for a structuralist movement in the social sciences. Three Frenchmen were essential to the further development of structuralist thinking. First, Ferdinand Braudel introduced Durkheimian notions in history.[33] As opposed to a mere history of events or 'small-scale science of contingency', Braudel searched for what he coined the *longue durée*. This refers to underlying structures which are relatively stable and which stretch over long periods of time. These geophysical, climatological or demographic structures constrain people's action and thought. Braudel was one of the founders of the highly influential Annales School; most of its members carried out historical research in a similar vein.[34] Second, Louis Althusser argued that there is an epistemological break between the early and the later Marx.[35] Whereas the former was still indebted to German idealism and classical political economy, the latter went further and developed a structuralist 'science of history'. Against existentialist readings of Marx, Althusser argued that the later Marx rejected any *a priori* conceptions of human needs. Individuals are not the real subjects of history any longer;

the hidden relations of production are. Others soon followed Althusser in the pursuit of structuralist Marxism; Étienne Balibar and Nicos Poulantzas were probably the best known amongst them.[36] Third, by drawing upon Roman Jakobson, Sigmund Freud and Durkheim, Lévi-Strauss developed a structuralist anthropology. With the help of the structuralist method, he analysed diverse social phenomena, ranging from myths to kinship systems. Compared with Braudel and Althusser, Lévi-Strauss has been the most influential. His structuralist method was emulated by Edmund Leach and many other anthropologists. Given the abstract nature of his work, his influence went far beyond anthropology. I will therefore pay special attention to his work.

Lévi-Strauss's anthropology

The name of Claude Lévi-Strauss (1908–) is closely associated with the structuralist tradition. Born in Belgium, Lévi-Strauss moved to France as a child, and studied philosophy at the Sorbonne. During his studies in Paris he became acquainted with French sociology, notably Comte, Durkheim and Marcel Mauss. His interest soon shifted to cultural anthropology when he moved to Brazil, first in a teaching capacity at the University of São Paulo, then on a research expedition funded by the French government. During the Second World War he fled to the States, and taught at the New School of Social Research in New York. It was there that he met the linguist Jakobson – an encounter which would lastingly shape Lévi-Strauss's intellectual development. In his later life he moved back to France, first to the École Pratique des Hautes Études, subsequently as Professor of Anthropology at the Collège de France. Back in France he established himself as one of the leading figures of the structuralist movement.

It has occasionally been asserted that Lévi-Strauss's structuralist analysis of culture is very much indebted to Durkheim. Although there is some truth in this claim, it certainly requires further qualification. As a matter of fact, a brief comparison of the intellectual projects of Durkheim and Lévi-Strauss will help in elucidating the latter's. In so far as there has been an appropriation of Durkheim's thought by Lévi-Strauss, it has been a highly selective one. He distanced himself from the functionalist or positivist readings of Durkheim which were prominent at the time (see also chapters 2 and 8). Not that these readings were necessarily false depictions of Durkheim's thought at certain points in his life. Yet for Lévi-Strauss these aspects of Durkheim's work were less attractive, probably erroneous and largely to be ignored. More worthy of attention, but seriously in need of a contemporary reassessment, were Durkheim's earlier propositions regarding social facts and collective representations. Finally, the most important contribution to Lévi-Strauss's intellectual development are Durkheim's later writings on religion.

Lévi-Strauss's selective appropriation of Durkheim is symptomatic of the significant differences between the two men. First, whereas especially the earlier work of Durkheim is still very much embedded in the *Weltanschauung* of the nineteenth century, Lévi-Strauss's work is, in many respects, a reaction to this intellectual tradition. In *Division of Labour* Durkheim drew upon analogies with biological evolution to explain the transition from 'mechanical' to 'organic' types of solidarity. In contrast, Lévi-Strauss has always been hostile to evolutionist types of explanation. The early Durkheim was mainly concerned with those theoretical principles that only reveal themselves across longer temporal spans. *Ex adverso*, Lévi-Strauss focused upon those mechanisms that reveal themselves across cultures. Durkheim was aware of the problems which accompanied industrialization and modernization, but he nevertheless defended the cultural and structural transformations which the West was undergoing. Certain adjustments needed to be made, but the overall trend was one of progress. By contrast, Lévi-Strauss's *oeuvre* can be read as a fierce critique of the western project of modernity.

Second, in some respects the aims of Durkheim and Lévi-Strauss are diametrically opposed. To clarify this, it is useful to consider the not uncommon view that anthropologists belong to either of two categories. On the one hand, there are those who are struck by and sensitive to the enormous cultural differences between societies. Underlying their work is an inclination to focus on the more malleable features of people's personality or practices, or, more strongly, a tendency towards an outright *tabula rasa* conception of the individual. On the other hand, there are those who find these differences superficial, and who are overwhelmed by that which all human beings have in common. They dedicate their life to a search for the universal features of humankind. However crude this distinction, it is a very useful one within the context of our discussion, for whereas Durkheim is very much representative of the former, Lévi-Strauss is an almost archetypal example of the latter. Durkheim was sensitive to the differences between various cultures. The existence of these differences (which can be ascertained empirically) was, for instance, central to his refutation of any *a priori* moral theory. Lévi-Strauss's project could not be more different. Normally, one would expect a collection of ethnographic details about numerous foreign cultures to back the insight that cultures radically differ from each other, but Lévi-Strauss used that information to convince the reader about the similarities between human beings. For him people cannot help but structure the world in the same way.

Third, some of the ideas of Durkheim reached Lévi-Strauss through his reading of the work of Durkheim's nephew, Mauss. This is not to suggest that Durkheim did not exercise any direct influence on Lévi-Strauss. But Mauss's influence is at least as important, and whenever he deviated from his uncle's path (a rare occurrence indeed), Lévi-Strauss was likely to follow the nephew. In particular, Lévi-Strauss seemed very much taken by Mauss's notion of a 'total social fact'. Through that notion, both Mauss and Lévi-Strauss purported to transcend the opposition between atomism and holism. They followed Durkheim in his critique of individualist forms of explanation, but deplored the reifying tendencies in his notions of a collective mind or collective consciousness. In an attempt to avoid the deterministic pitfalls of Durkheim's idea of a collective consciousness, Mauss outlined the concept of a total social fact as embedded within actual patterns of social interactions. This seemed attractive to Lévi-Strauss, who also attributed to Mauss the uncovering of unconscious structures underlying the surface level of ethnographic results. For Lévi-Strauss this was remarkably similar to the way in which linguistics reveals structures underneath the immediately accessible level of speech patterns.[37]

Fourth, Durkheim and Lévi-Strauss were different personalities, involved in different kinds of practice. To put it bluntly: Durkheim was a scientist at heart, and Lévi-Strauss was not. Although Durkheim contemplated following in the religious footsteps of his father (who was a chief rabbi) and although there are some obvious traces of a religious upbringing in his work, his outlook on the world was, from an early age onwards, a rational-scientific one. I have already briefly sketched Durkheim's antagonistic attitude to the literary 'brilliance' of his Parisian contemporaries, and how his life was devoted to the development of a scientific approach to society. Durkheim aimed at applying as much scientific rigour as was employed in the natural sciences, and he tried to achieve this by rigidly adhering to the rules of logic, and by putting his theories through severe empirical tests.[38] Lévi-Strauss is very different indeed. Although he (and structuralism in general for that matter) aimed at a science of society, he regularly broke the most elementary rules of scientific investigation. We are dealing here with a very different mind: a man with great sensitivity, but surely not a scientist. For anybody who is acquainted with Lévi-Strauss's writings, it will come as no surprise that his home background was artistic, and that he himself was an accomplished musician. Leach was not far from the truth when he referred to Lévi-Strauss as a 'visionary'. We are dealing with a highly imaginative, artistic mind, which *expresses* intuitions about the world, rather than *examining* their validity.

If Durkheim's influence on Lévi-Strauss is ambiguous, the impact of structuralist linguistics is less so. Whilst lecturing in New York during the war, Lévi-Strauss developed a friendship with the Russian linguist and folklorist Jakobson. Jakobson introduced Lévi-Strauss to Saussure's work, the linguistics of the Prague School and, obviously, his own contributions. Jakobson was very much influenced by Saussure's notion that the meaning of a linguistic item depends on its *difference* from other items currently in use. With this Saussurean framework as his starting point, Jakobson conceived of language in terms of binary oppositions. That is, people are able to distinguish a consonant from a vowel, an acute sound from a grave one, and a voiced sound from an unvoiced sound. By extending Jakobson's theory to non-linguistic domains, Lévi-Strauss became one of the first to investigate social life by systematically employing analogies with linguistic systems. He analysed kinship and myths in terms of binary oppositions, correlation, inversion and permutation, similar to Jakobson's treatment of the phoneme on the phonological level. What is important, however, is Lévi-Strauss's systematic attempt to go beyond the conscious level, looking for those universal, unconscious features of the mind which uniformly force a particular structure onto the world. As I suggested earlier, from Lévi-Strauss's perspective this search for the universal, unconscious level is loyal to both Mauss and structural linguistics.

Lévi-Strauss deplored the fact that Freud and Marx had been excluded from the syllabus when he was a student. He did become acquainted with the writings of both later in his life. Here again, his readings of these authors deviated from the prevailing interpretations of his time. During the 1940s and 1950s, an attempt was made to merge existentialist philosophy with Marxism, and to interpret the latter in terms of the former. Lévi-Strauss's understanding of Marx could not be more different. He saw in Marx a structuralist *avant la lettre* who constantly searched beyond the surface level for economic structures. The same applies to his reading of Freud. Freud was initially introduced into the social sciences by members of the Frankfurt School (e.g. Theodor Adorno and Max Horkheimer) and theoreticians with close affinities to critical theory (e.g. Wilhelm Reich and Erich Fromm). Most of them attempted to integrate Freud (and Marx) with a humanist tradition, and they interpreted the work of Freud along these lines. Lévi-Strauss's reading was different indeed. What was appealing for him was Freud's attempt to develop a scientific explanation of psychological phenomena by moving beyond the conscious level and searching for the underlying structure and power of the unconscious. The merging of structuralism and psychoanalysis became prominent in Lévi-Strauss's analysis of myths, to which I will turn shortly.

First, I need to outline Lévi-Strauss's overall scheme. His starting point is that human beings have certain features in common, one of these being the way they construct and divide up the external world. The surrounding world is potentially open to many categorizations, but human beings employ particular ones. They interpret their surroundings by reducing them to discontinuous units. Lévi-Strauss came to this conclusion through generalizing from Jakobson's structuralist treatment of language. According to this theory, people have an in-built ability to discriminate vowels from consonants. The former have high noise energy, whilst the latter are less loud. People are also able to distinguish compact sounds (*a* or *k*) from diffuse sounds (*u*, *p*, *i* or *t*), and acute sounds (sounds with a high frequency pitch, such as *i* or *t*) from grave

Figure 1.1   Jakobson's primary vowel (and consonant) triangle

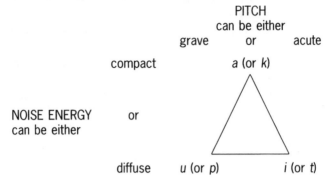

Figure 1.2   Lévi-Strauss's primary culinary triangle

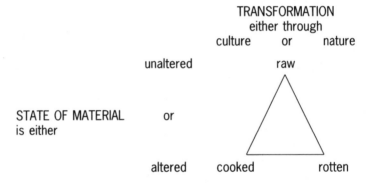

sounds (sounds with a low frequency pitch, such as *u* or *p*). So one arrives at Jakobson's primary vowel (and consonant) triangle (see figure 1.1).

According to Jakobson's triangle, people unwittingly process linguistic information through binary oppositions. Lévi-Strauss used this simple idea to analyse non-linguistic cultural phenomena. Take, for example, food and culinary activities. Simple binary oppositions ('nature versus culture' and 'altered versus unaltered') are at work here. It is obvious that ordinary raw food has not undergone any transformation, whereas cooked or rotten food has. But there is a difference between cooked food and rotten food. The former has been altered through cultural means, whereas the latter has been transformed through nature. So Lévi-Strauss arrived at a primary culinary triangle (see figure 1.2), which allows him to distinguish and analyse the main types of culinary activity. Boiling, for instance, is similar to rotting, because it also leads to the decomposition of food. But it is different from rotting in that it can only take place through the medium of water plus

Figure 1.3 Lévi-Strauss's developed culinary triangle

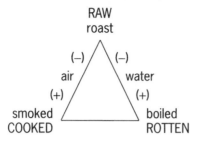

Source: Lévi-Strauss (1978, p. 490)

cultural means (one needs a container). Smoking leads to complete cooking, with the medium of air, but without any cultural means. Roasting leads to only a partial transformation, and it is accomplished without the medium of air, water or any cultural means. Lévi-Strauss thus arrived at his *developed* culinary triangle (see figure 1.3). This example gives some indication of how, through simple binary oppositions, Lévi-Strauss tried to tackle elaborate cultural procedures.

Let us now move to Lévi-Strauss's treatment of myths, which, amongst other things, will give some indication of the extent to which both structuralism and psychoanalysis have influenced his work. He started off by pointing out a particular ambiguity in the study of myths. That is, on the one hand, a myth is one amongst many linguistic manifestations, and, on the other hand, it belongs to a more complex order than other linguistic expressions.[39] Indicative of the fact that myths are both 'part of and above language' is that, contrary to other linguistic phenomena, they employ a dual time referent. On the one hand, they allude to reversible time in that they refer to events which have taken place a long time ago. On the other hand, they operate outside time in that they inform us not only about the meaning of the past, but also about the present and the future. Now, this means that in order to understand myths they need to be analysed at both temporal levels. Lévi-Strauss invoked the example of an orchestra score to support his method of analysis. In order to find harmony, one needs to read the orchestra score both 'diachronically' and 'synchronically'. The former means that it is read as if it were a book: from left to right and top to bottom, starting with page one, then page two, etc. The latter means that one tries to conceive of the notes along each axis as one bundle of relations. Now, Lévi-Strauss invited us to 'read' myths in a similar fashion.[40]

Take, for example, the Oedipus myth, which Lévi-Strauss transformed as a chart (see figure 1.4). If one wanted to tell the story, one would read from left to right, and from top to bottom. But if one wants to understand the myth,

Figure 1.4   Lévi-Strauss's treatment of the Oedipus myth

Cadmos seeks
his sister Europa,
ravished by Zeus

Cadmos kills the
dragon

The Spartoi kill
one another

Labdacos, Laios'
father = lame

Oedipus kills his
father, Laios

Laios, Oedipus'
father = left-sided

Oedipus kills the
Sphinx

Oedipus = swollen
foot

Oedipus marries
his mother,
Jocasta

Eteocles kills his
brother, Polynices

Antigone buries
her brother,
Polynices despite
prohibition

Source: Based on Lévi-Strauss (1993, p. 214)

Lévi-Strauss argued, one would read column by column.[41] The columns are constructed such that each one involves events which have something substantial in common. For instance, the events included in the first column indicate blood relationships which are too intimate or too close, whereas events in the second column imply the underrating of blood relationships. The third column refers to the killings of those monsters who are a threat to the coming to life or the living of human beings. The fourth column concerns the names of Oedipus and his ancestors, and all indicate problems with walking or standing up.[42]

Now, whereas the first and the second columns are rather straightforward, the third and the fourth are obviously not self-explanatory and necessitate further interpretation. Here the interpretative abilities of the structuralist researcher become important. Partly drawing upon psychoanalytic accounts of symbols and partly inferring from his general knowledge of other myths, Lévi-Strauss suggested that the events in column three symbolize the denial of the autochthonous origin of human beings, whereas column four symbolizes the continuance of that very same autochthonous origin. It follows that column four is to three as column two is to one. That is, 'the overrating of blood relations is to the underrating of blood relations as the attempt to escape autochthony is to the impossibility to succeed in it'.[43] So, the myth deals with the contradiction between the belief that human beings are authochthonous and the knowledge that they are born from the union of man and woman.[44]

This example is indicative of Lévi-Strauss's structuralist analysis of myths, and it allows me to summarize the main features of that analysis. First, there is no intrinsic or invariable meaning to any 'mytheme' or 'gross constituent unit'. Their meaning depends on their opposition to other symbolic units within that myth. Second, myths should not be conceived of in isolation from each other. A closer look shows the extent to which, through necessary transformations like symmetrical inversion, one myth is related to another. Whether we study Oedipus, Antigone or Phaedra, myths express the basic polarities such as 'nature versus culture', 'gods versus man' or 'life versus death'. Third, myths enable people to articulate and come to terms with the basic contradictions of human existence. The contradictions at stake are those between people's unconscious wishes or anxieties on the one hand, and their conscious experience on the other. Myths have an existential value in that they enable people to transcend these contradictions, somehow to reduce these in-built tensions.

Lévi-Strauss's analysis of myths shows most effectively that his work meant a radical break with nineteenth-century ways of theorizing about the social. Against nineteenth-century unilinear evolutionism and its attendant notion of progress, Lévi-Strauss argued for the importance of synchronic analysis through which foreign cultures, *prima facie* very different, end up remarkably similar to ours. Through an in-depth comparative analysis of different cultures, he attempted to demonstrate the universal, innate properties of the human mind which bring the old and the new together, and which show distant societies to be much closer to us than was once believed. There is, no doubt, a political or ideological message to Lévi-Strauss's anthropology. Whereas for decades armchair anthropologists had somehow assumed the West to be the ultimate outcome of a necessary, linear process, Lévi-Strauss's notion of a universal mind looks for that which necessarily links us all together.[45]

Attempting to capture the innate properties of the human mind, Lévi-Strauss's work is one of the most ambitious and challenging attempts to develop a grand theory about culture. But it is evidently not devoid of problems, and two arguments, which have been held against him, are especially worth mentioning. First, it has been pointed out correctly that, contrary to what Lévi-Strauss believed, not all cultural forms are reducible to the logic of binary oppositions. Second, it has been argued (again convincingly) that, rather than attempting to put his theory to the test, Lévi-Strauss seemed to *select* empirical evidence in order to support his argument. Both are valid points, but it seems to me that there are more severe problems with his project. First, his work exhibits a remarkably closed, circular form of argument. He always seems to have a set of tools at hand (inversions and permutations) which turn those myths that do not *prima facie* fit his scheme into transformations of ones that do. There is an uncertainty regarding which potential or real myths would, within the parameters of his structuralist theory, be potential falsifiers of that very same theory. Second, an aura of mystery surrounds his choice of the basic dichotomies, and the reader is expected to accept uncritically the 'superior' intuition of the *maître-penseur* in these matters. It is perfectly possible, without deviating from the structuralist cause, to account for the same phenomena by invoking a different set of universal dichotomies from the ones used by Lévi-Strauss. It is not clear which criteria should be employed to judge and compare between these distinct structuralist readings. Third, from the perspective of evolutionary biology, there might be grounds to support Lévi-Strauss's assumption that there are innate, universal structures of the human mind. More contentious, however, is his belief that he can have access to these innate structures as they are. If innate universal structures of the human mind did exist, any attempt, including Lévi-Strauss's, to get access to them would only be possible by drawing upon the very same innate structures. These universal structures are both the object of research and the medium through which that research becomes possible. It is obvious that the dual nature of this type of knowledge formation (as both medium and object) is not unproblematic, and calls for more epistemological foundation than provided in Lévi-Strauss's work.

By the end of the 1960s, structuralism had developed into two different schools. Both criticized central features of the structuralist project, but both also shared a lot in common with structuralism. First, there is post-structuralism, associated with the work of Jacques Lacan, Jacques Derrida and Michel Foucault.[46] Post-structuralists build further upon the work of Friedrich Nietzsche, Martin Heidegger and Ludwig Wittgenstein. The theory shares with structuralism an anti-humanist and anti-Cartesian stance. But whereas structuralists aimed at a science of signs (and a science of society), post-structuralism purports to undermine notions of truth and scientific objectivity. Post-structuralists tend to commit themselves to conceptual or epistemological relativism. A more radical version of the post-structuralist position is taken up by some feminist authors, such as Hélène Cixous, Luce Irigaray and Julia Kristeva.[47] I will deal with Foucault and post-structuralism in chapter 5. Second, there is Pierre Bourdieu's genetic structuralism and Anthony Giddens's structuration theory. Both feel uneasy with the reifying tendencies of structuralist reasoning and its neglect of social praxis. Both also feel uncomfortable with the structuralists' exclusive emphasis on the constraining nature of structure. This explains why structuralism fails to account sufficiently for how structures are reproduced through time. Whilst accepting some structuralist notions, both Bourdieu and Giddens attempt to link these with insights from social phenomenology and hermeneutics. The reproduction of structure is then seen as a continuous practical accomplishment by competent individuals. Bourdieu is clearly embedded in the French structuralist tradition, whereas Giddens is more eclectic. This explains why I leave Giddens for a separate chapter (see chapter 4), and why I will turn to Bourdieu now.

Bourdieu's genetic structuralism

Pierre Bourdieu (1930–) is currently Professor of Sociology at the Collège de France in Paris. He initially studied philosophy at the École Normale Supérieure, but subsequently moved in the direction of social anthropology and sociology. He became well known firstly in anthropological circles because of his critique of Lévi-Strauss and because of his meticulous anthropological analyses of Algeria. His work on the sociology of education in the 1960s introduced him to a wider audience. Meanwhile, he had worked out a sophisticated theoretical frame of reference which enabled him to develop a perspicacious analysis of his collected data. By the late 1960s Bourdieu had introduced many of the key notions of his framework: *habitus*, *doxa*, field, capital, etc. His empirical analyses already adumbrated his subsequent conceptual endeavours to connect structuralist notions with social phenomenology. These theoretical attempts were summarized in his highly influential *Outline of a Theory of Practice* and later in his lucid *Logic of Practice*. The very same theoretical considerations also underlie his more recent empirical writings, which range from studies of culture and symbolic power to the intricacies of higher educational establishments and similar elite formations.

This résumé allows me to introduce a number of features of Bourdieu's work. First, there is his relationship to theory. It is obvious from the above that Bourdieu is not merely a theorist in that he has carried out numerous empirical researches. But there is a more fundamental way in which he distances himself from what he sees as the Anglo-Saxon notion of social theory; that is, a coherent, abstract project independent of any empirical basis. For him theory should grow out of research, and it should be directed towards that research. In this view, theory is a set of tools or directives, which suggest to the reader which questions ought to be asked. Without an empirical base, social theory becomes a pointless and empty enterprise.[48]

Second, there is Bourdieu's relationship to other French intellectual traditions. During his formative years at the École Normale Supérieure, he came across three philosophical strands: French Marxism, Jean-Paul Sartre's existentialism and Lévi-Strauss's structuralist anthropology. Of these three,

Bourdieu seems to be most sympathetic towards Lévi-Strauss. He strongly distances himself from the economic determinism of French Marxism. Although he agrees with Marxist sociologists that power struggles are central to social life, he insists that they are not exclusively economic; they often operate on a symbolic level. Bourdieu is equally critical of Sartre's philosophy. Sartre's writings were still embedded in a Cartesian philosophy of consciousness, whereas Bourdieu draws upon social phenomenology, Heidegger and the later Wittgenstein, learning from them the importance of shared, practical knowledge. Existentialist views are justified in emphasizing the pivotal role of agency, but they fail to acknowledge the objective constraints of the social world. Bourdieu saw Lévi-Strauss's anthropology as a systematic attempt to reveal these structural constraints, and this accounts for why he was initially favourably disposed to Lévi-Strauss. However, Bourdieu soon became dissatisfied with the structuralist neglect of social praxis. Rather than opting for either structuralist or agency-orientated views, Bourdieu's conceptual frame of reference aims at transcending that opposition.[49]

This brings me to one of the *idées maîtresses* of Bourdieu's viewpoint: to transcend the antinomy between what he coins 'subjectivism' and 'objectivism'.[50] By objectivism, Bourdieu means a search for underlying structures independent of people's knowledge, concepts or purposes. Subjectivism tries to capture how people experience or conceptualize the world, and then how they act in accordance with it. By ignoring one vital aspect of social reality, each viewpoint inevitably distorts its complexity. Subjectivism tends to conceive of the social world as created *de novo*, failing to take into account the extent to which people's mental framework and their practices are adjusted to social constraints. Contrary to the premisses of subjectivism, social life is not created from nothing. People's hopes, expectations and goals are in tune with the social environment in which they have been brought up. However problematic subjectivism may be, one cannot find rescue in objectivist accounts either. By abandoning insights from hermeneutics altogether, objectivism erroneously adopts a mechanistic view of human conduct, ignoring the extent to which social life is a practical achievement by skilful actors.[51] Objectivism reduces the complexity of social life to, for example, a mere role-playing or a following of rules. It fails to take seriously the ability of people to cope with novel situations and their capacity to improvise whenever necessary.

Bourdieu's attempt to transcend the opposition between the objective and the subjective culminates in two methodological notions. First, his research aims at what he calls 'participant objectivation'. That is, the researcher first objectifies the object of research, then scrutinizes the validity and presuppositions of that objectification, and finally takes into account people's improvizations and skilful achievements. Second, Bourdieu attempts to break with the distinction between the researcher and object of research. That is, given that the social sciences are embedded in structural conditions and power struggles themselves, the researcher needs also to take up a critical attitude to his or her own practices. Hence his appeal for 'reflexive sociology' which aims at just such a critical distance.

From social phenomenology, and from Heidegger, Wittgenstein and Goffman, Bourdieu learns the importance of people's *practical mastery* of the complex logic of everyday life. He insists that this practical mastery should not be reduced to conscious intervention or theoretical knowledge. Nor should people's practical sense be conflated with the unconscious realm, because this would imply some notion of repression. People know how to go on with their daily activities, without needing to put that knowledge discursively. People's practical mastery draws upon *doxa*, or 'doxic experience', referring to a taken-for-granted world beyond reflection.[52] Bourdieu's notion of practical sense and *doxa* culminates in his highly acclaimed and widely misused concept of *habitus*. *Habitus* is a generative scheme of dispositions, tacitly acquired through early childhood and therefore durable. The dispositions generate people's practices, improvisations, attitudes or bodily movements. The *habitus* provides a 'feeling for the game' or 'practical sense', allowing people to develop an infinite number of strategies to cope with an infinite number of situations.[53] As the dispositions are adjusted to the constraints of the social surroundings in which they emerge, the *habitus* differs according to background. Manners of speaking or bodily gestures, concepts of beauty or self-identity – all these indeed differ according to class background. Notice that these differences in *habitus* often imply inequality in resources. For instance, compared with members of the working class, the middle class feels more confident with public speaking or with formal occasions, and this might be an important asset in the economic sphere. It is thus not surprising that Bourdieu's concept of *habitus* is central in his analysis of various forms of reproduction of social inequality.

Bourdieu uses the concept of 'field' to refer to those areas of social life in which, through strategies, struggles take place with respect to valuable goods or resources.[54] In the context of fields, Bourdieu relies rather heavily upon economic metaphors, and this has occasionally led to confusion amongst commentators. For example, he coins the term 'capital' to refer to the goods and resources which are at stake, but it would be mistaken to restrict fields only to struggles over economic capital. Fields might also deal with social capital (where the main issue is who you know, and how you are related to that person), cultural capital (dealing with education, culture and aligned skills) or symbolic capital (dealing with social prestige and distinction).[55] Neither does Bourdieu's use of 'strategy' mean that, as assumed in mainstream economics, people necessarily adopt a conscious calculative orientation towards the interests at stake. On the contrary, people's strategies should be seen as skilful achievements operating against the background of the pre-reflective *doxa*.[56]

Some of these ideas might appear less striking and innovative now than they used to be. I would say two things in favour of Bourdieu. First, he introduced most of these ideas in the 1960s and he brought them together as early as 1972 in his *Outline of a Theory of Practice*. By the time that *le tout Paris* celebrated the achievements of structuralism, Bourdieu had already become aware of its limitations and had tried to supersede these. He anticipated some important developments of social theory in the Anglo-Saxon world, especially key aspects of Giddens's structuration theory (see chapter 4) and Roy Bhaskar's transformational model of social action (see chapter 8). Amongst the similarities with Giddens and Bhaskar is, for example, his attempt to transcend the opposition between the individual and society (or, if you like, between subjectivism and objectivism), and his attempt to link structural notions to Wittgensteinian and phenomenological insights *vis-à-vis* shared, practical knowledge. Like Giddens and Bhaskar, Bourdieu notes that structures should not merely be seen as constraining; they are also enabling in that they allow for agency to be exercised.[57]

The second point in favour of Bourdieu is that his strength lies in the way in which his theory is interwoven with empirical research. Let me remind the reader that, for Bourdieu, theorizing should not be an isolated practice; it ought to emerge out of contact with empirical reality. Bourdieu's framework has shown itself to be very successful in elucidating empirical findings. First, consider the sociology of education and related fields, in which he has pointed out the subtle mechanisms through which 'symbolic power' or 'symbolic violence' operates. That is, with the help of various forms of 'pedagogic action', dominant groups of society are able to impose their culture onto others – to make it, in spite of the arbitrary nature of any culture, appear as legitimate or superior. Whether formal (for example, school) or informal (for example, the family or the peer group), pedagogic action may lead to cultural reproduction and eventually to the reproduction of underlying power relationships.[58] Second, there is Bourdieu's *Distinction* and related writings, in which the issue of reproduction is taken up again. Once members of the less privileged classes enter the struggle for status, the differences in *habitus* make for an unequal fight and hence for the reproduction of inequality. That inequality is both the medium and the outcome of their practices.[59] For example, for some people 'high culture' is intrinsic to their way of life, and dealing with culture appears 'natural'. For others culture can only be *achieved*, hence the slightly laboured, artificial manner in which this is done, or the lack of subtlety involved. In the battlefield over cultural or educational matters, members of the lower classes are bound to lose, entering an unfair game in which they are often forced to deny their own *habitus*. Every encounter implies that they can be 'found out', either because they inadvertently display a lack of knowledge, or because they display too much anxiety and lack of grace. More importantly, by attempting to emulate the higher strata and so uplift their status, the *petits bourgeois* implicitly acknowledge the legitimacy or superiority of the dominant culture.

Bourdieu's writings have sometimes been subject to pedantic criticisms. Some have argued that his conceptual scheme lacks analytical rigour; others that he reads too much into his empirical material. There is certainly some truth in these points, but they hardly hit the core of Bourdieu's writings. I would argue that his strengths reveal his weaknesses. His incisiveness lies in his account of stability, as becomes apparent in his notion of a skilful, unquestioned reproduction of structures or in the presupposition that the *habitus* tends to be adjusted to social constraints. One of the consequences of this is that Bourdieu pays less attention to the ability of individuals to distance themselves from the facticity of daily existence – the ability to turn tacit knowledge into theoretical knowledge. Bourdieu tends to focus on this only in so far as it is a result of social scientific intervention. He thereby fails to acknowledge fully that people may also exhibit the ability to distance themselves in the *absence* of scientific interference. If people's theoretical knowledge enters the public-collective realm, it might become an important source of change or deliberate maintenance of structures. Given Bourdieu's interest in reproduction of inequality, he could have been more sensitive to the extent to which people's theoretical, discursive knowledge about underlying structures is often constitutive of the maintenance of the very same structures. In *Learning to Labour*, for instance, Paul Willis shows how working-class children have clearly articulated conceptions about their limited opportunities.[60] Ironically, the very same conceptions are central to the fact that such adolescents drop out of school, and these conceptions therefore contribute to the reproduction of inequality. It is important, however, that this reproduction does not take place in the unquestioned world of Bourdieu's *doxa*.

On a related theme, Bourdieu has shown convincingly and repeatedly how the 'practical sense' of individuals makes for the unintended reproduction of social inequalities. He has shown the empirical validity of maintaining, for instance, that the *habitus* is relatively durable, that it takes different forms in different classes, and that it is adjusted to objective external constraints. Meanwhile, these assertions beg for explanation, rather than providing one. How is one to account for, say, the inflexibility of dispositions across the individual life-span, or for the adjustment of the *habitus* to objective structural conditions? Given Bourdieu's hostility to tight theoretical system-building, he would probably dismiss these questions as chimerical constructions to haunt solely the abstract theorist. But for those who expect theories to answer adequately 'why?' or 'how?' questions, that response would be found to be unsatisfactory.

Further reading

For an accessible introduction to structuralism and post-structuralism, Sturrock's *Structuralism and Since* or Harland's *Superstructuralism* can be recommended. Culler's *Ferdinand de Saussure* is an excellent introduction to the life and work of the Swiss linguist. The core of Saussure's ideas can be found in parts 1 and 2 of his *Course in General Linguistics*. Lukes's *Emile Durkheim; His Life and Work* remains by far the most comprehensive account of Durkheim's work. But this biography is long, and as a shorter introduction, Giddens's lucid *Durkheim* will do. For an overview of Lévi-Strauss's intellectual development, it is worth reading his own auto-biographical *Tristes Tropiques* or Pace's *Claude Lévi-Strauss: The Bearer of Ashes*. For a first approach to genetic structuralism, I suggest the excellent introduction to Bourdieu's work by Wacquant in Bourdieu and Wacquant's *An Invitation to Reflexive Sociology*. Both Bourdieu's *Outline of a Theory of Practice* and *The Logic of Practice* summarize the key notions of his theoretical viewpoint. The latter is more accessible.

References

Althusser, L. 1972. *For Marx*. New York: Pantheon (originally in French, 1965).

Althusser, L. and Balibar, E. 1970. *Reading Capital*. London: New Left Books (originally in French, 1968).

Barthes, R. 1972. *Mythologies*. London: Cape (originally in French, 1957).

Barthes, R. 1983. *The Fashion System*. New York: Hill and Wang (originally in French, 1967).

Bhaskar, R. 1989. *The Possibility of Naturalism*. Brighton: Harvester (2nd edition).

Bourdieu, P. 1969. Intellectual field and creative project. *Social Science Information* 8, 89–119 (originally in French, 1966).

Bourdieu, P. 1971. Champ du pouvoir, champ intellectuel et habitus de classe. *Scolies* 1, 7–26.

Bourdieu, P. 1973. Le marché des biens symboliques. *L'année sociologique* 22, 49–126.

Bourdieu, P. 1977. *Outline of a Theory of Practice*. Cambridge: Cambridge University Press (originally in French, 1972).

Bourdieu, P. 1984. *Distinction: A Social Critique of the Judgement of Taste*. London: Routledge and Kegan Paul (originally in French, 1979).

Bourdieu, P. 1990. *The Logic of Practice*. Cambridge: Polity Press (originally in French, 1980).

Bourdieu, P. 1993. *Sociology in Question*. London: Sage (originally in French, 1984).

Bourdieu, P., Chamboredon, J. -C. and Passeron, J. -C. 1991. *The Craft of Sociology: Epistemological Preliminaries*. New York: Walter de Gruyter (originally in French, 1968).

Bourdieu, P. and Passeron, J. -C. 1977. *Reproduction in Education, Society and Culture*. London: Sage (originally in French, 1970).

Bourdieu, P. and Wacquant, L. J. D. 1992a. *An Invitation to Reflexive Sociology.* Cambridge: Polity Press.

Bourdieu, P. and Wacquant, L. J. D. 1992b. The purpose of reflexive sociology. In: *An Invitation to Reflexive Sociology*, P. Bourdieu and L. J. D. Wacquant. Cambridge: Polity Press, 61–216.

Braudel, F. 1972. *The Mediterranean and the Mediterranean World in the Age of Phillip II, Volume 1.* Glasgow: William Collins (originally in French, 1966).

Braudel, F. 1980. *On History.* Chicago: University of Chicago Press (originally in French, 1969).

Burke, P. 1990. *The French Historical Revolution: The Annales School, 1929–89.* Cambridge: Polity Press; Stanford: Stanford University Press.

Cixous, H. 1981. The Laugh of the Medusa. In: *New French Feminisms*, eds E. Marks and I. de Courtivron. New York: Schocken, 245–64.

Culler, J. 1986. *Ferdinand de Saussure.* Ithaca: Cornell University Press (2nd edition).

Derrida, J. 1973. *Speech and Phenomena, and Other Essays on Husserl's Theory of Signs.* Evanston: Northwestern University Press (originally in French, 1967).

Derrida, J. 1976. *Of Grammatology.* Baltimore: John Hopkins University Press (originally in French, 1967).

Derrida, J. 1978. *Writing and Differences.* London: Routledge and Kegan Paul (originally in French, 1967; reprinted, 1993).

Durkheim, E. 1915. *The Elementary Forms of Religious Life.* London: Allen and Unwin (originally in French, 1912).

Durkheim, E. 1952. *Suicide; A Study in Sociology.* London: Routledge (originally in French, 1897; reprinted, 1992).

Durkheim, E. 1963. *Primitive Classification.* Chicago: University of Chicago Press (originally in French, 1903).

Durkheim, E. 1982. *The Rules of Sociological Method, and Selected Texts on Sociology and its Method.* London: Macmillan (originally in French, 1895; reprinted, 1992).

Durkheim, E. 1984. *The Division of Labour in Society.* London: Macmillan (originally in French, 1893; reprinted, 1993).

Foucault, M. 1977. *Language, Counter-memory, Practice.* Ithaca: Cornell University Press.

Foucault, M. 1980. *Power/Knowledge; Selected Interviews and Other Writings 1972–1977.* Hemel Hempstead: Harvester Wheatsheaf.

Giddens, A. 1978. *Durkheim.* London: Fontana (reprinted, 1990).

Giddens, A. 1984. *The Constitution of Society; Outline of the Theory of Structuration.* Cambridge: Polity Press.

Harland, R. 1988. *Superstructuralism; The Philosophy of Structuralism and Post-structuralism.* London: Routledge.

Irigaray, L. 1985. *The Sex which is not One.* Ithaca, NY: Cornell University Press.

Kristeva, J. 1982. *Desire in Language.* New York: Columbia University Press.

Lacan, J. 1989. *Écrits; A Selection.* London: Routledge (originally in French, 1966; reprinted, 1992).

Lane, M. (ed.) (1970) *Structuralism; A Reader.* London: Jonathan Cape.

Lévi-Strauss, C. 1973. *Tristes Tropiques.* New York: Cape (originally in French, 1955).

Lévi-Strauss, C. 1978. *The Origin of Table Manners; Introduction to a Science of Mythology 3.* London: Jonathan Cape (originally in French, 1968).

Lévi-Strauss, C. 1993. *Structural Anthropology, Part 1.* London: Penguin (originally in French, 1963).

Lévi-Strauss, C. 1994. *Structural Anthropology, Part 2.* London: Penguin (originally in French, 1973).

Lukes, S. 1973. *Emile Durkheim; His Life and Work: A Historical and Critical Study.* London: Penguin (reprinted, 1992).

Marks, E. and de Courtivron, I. (eds) 1981. *New French Feminisms.* New York: Schocken.

Pace, D. 1986. *Claude Lévi-Strauss; The Bearer of Ashes.* London: Routledge and Kegan Paul.

Poulantzas, N. 1968. *Political Power and Social Classes.* London: New Left Books (originally in French, 1968).

Saussure, F. 1960. *Course in General Linguistics.* London: Peter Owen (originally in French, 1916).

Sturrock, J. 1979. *Structuralism and Since; From Lévi-Strauss to Derrida.* Oxford: Oxford University Press (reprinted, 1992).

Wacquant, L. J. D. 1992. Toward a social praxeology: the structure and logic of Bourdieu's sociology. In: *An Invitation to Reflexive Sociology,* P. Bourdieu and L. J. D. Wacquant. Cambridge: Polity Press, 1–60.

Willis, P. 1993. *Learning to Labour; How Working Class Kids get Working Class Jobs.* Aldershot: Ashgate.

2
The Biological Metaphor
Functionalism and
Neo-functionalism

This chapter deals with the origins, rise and fall of functionalist theory. The functionalist label is used in many disciplines: for example, in linguistics, psychology and architecture. Although they share the same name, the frameworks which are used do not necessarily have much in common. I will in the following merely focus on functionalist theories of society.

'Functionalism' in sociology covers a wide variety of authors and schools which nevertheless tend to share a number of central tenets. First, they explain the persistence of social practices by referring to those (often unintended) effects which are beneficial for the equilibrium or integration of the social system in which these practices are embedded. Second, functionalism reconstructs the notion of rationality: it is assumed that certain practices which appear irrational can be made intelligible once their social functions are spelled out. Beneath the surface lies a deeper social rationality, which it is the task of the sociologist to uncover. Third, functionalism draws upon the notion of functional prerequisites. The argument is often that these prerequisites need to be fulfilled for a given society to survive, or alternatively that society operates such that these needs tend to be fulfilled.

During its emergence and rise in the 1940s and 1950s, functionalism fitted in well with the intellectual climate. First, it soon emerged that functionalist reasoning was not incompatible with some aspects of neo-positivist epistemology, the latter being one of the dominant strands in the philosophy of science at the time (see chapter 8). By paying attention to consequences of actions (instead of purposes or motives behind practices), functionalism fits, for instance, the positivist inclination to avoid reference to entities that are not immediately accessible to observation. Some philosophers of science attempted to merge the two doctrines by demonstrating that functionalist formats of explanation can be moulded within the straitjacket of the deductive-nomological method. Second, functionalism was even more compatible with the core features of structuralism – another important theoretical strand at the time (see chapter 1). Both support a holistic picture of society in which the interrelationship of sub-systems and practices is central. Both assume that the task of the social scientist is to unravel a deeper reality behind the conscious level of purposive action – for structuralists that hidden realm refers to unacknowledged structures, whereas functionalists search for latent functions. Both functionalism and structuralism minimize the role of agency, attributing importance to the broader social forces which transcend the individual. Finally, functionalist and structuralist frameworks strongly object to the interpretative claims of hermeneutics and phenomenology.

Although structuralism and functionalism have a different pedigree and are distinct from each other, they did coalesce on several occasions. The alliance is exemplified by both Alfred Reginald Radcliffe-Brown's and Talcott Parsons's structural-functionalism; I will pay special attention to the latter later in this chapter. Parsons's writings had a decisive impact on American sociology for several decades. Parsons was heavily influenced by German, French and Italian authors, but on the whole European sociology has been more resistant to the Parsonian challenge. For the American audience, however, the structuralist-functionalist paradigm was considered the ultimate successful attempt to bring together the sociological classics within one consistent theoretical frame of reference. The term 'paradigm' is not misplaced here. For a while it looked as if the new creed was so persuasive that a consensus might arise within the sociological community *vis-à-vis* its main assumptions. Although some expressed doubts at a remarkably early stage with respect to the validity of some of these structural-functional presuppositions, it was only in the late 1960s that a more coherent assault against structural-functionalism developed.

Early functionalism

Functionalism as a label and as a separate school only emerged in the course of the twentieth century, but functionalist reasoning in itself is much older. Many of the so-called founding fathers of sociology attempted to explain social phenomena by drawing upon analogies with the biological realm. Herbert Spencer and Émile Durkheim are especially important in this regard. First, these functionalists *avant la lettre* saw society as an organic whole, with the different sub-systems or practices functionally directed towards the persistence of the larger entity in which they are embedded. This notion of society as an organic entity became central to the functionalist argument in the twentieth century (see chapter 1). Second, many sociologists in the nineteenth century were fascinated with the application of evolutionary epistemology to the social sphere. Central to their analysis was the notion that, for social systems to survive, they needed somehow to adjust to their environment. Increasing complexity and system differentiation leads to forms of superior adjustment.

Likewise, twentieth-century functionalist theories reconstruct history in terms of intensifying complexity, compartmentalization and system differentiation. Third, these predecessors of the functionalist movement introduced the notion of societal needs. For social systems to be healthy or at least to survive, certain needs have to be fulfilled. The task of the sociologist is to identify these needs, and to help steer society such that its needs are fulfilled. The modern notion of 'functional prerequisites' denotes the same idea.

Given that Durkheim has inspired numerous sociologists and anthropologists in the twentieth century, I will briefly sketch the main functionalist tenets in his work. Durkheim himself does not need introduction, and has already been mentioned in chapter 1. The functionalist features are to be found in his *Rules of Sociological Method* and *Division of Labour*. In *Rules* Durkheim insisted that any adequate explanation combines both causal and functional analysis. Causal analysis explains the succession of social phenomena, whereas functional analysis accounts for the persistence of social practices in terms of the 'general needs of the social organism' in which these practices are embedded.[1] At several places Durkheim insisted that one should distinguish analytically between functions and intentions. After all, the functions of practices might be different from people's purposes in carrying out these practices.[2] Functional analysis is central to Durkheim's distinction between normal and pathological phenomena. Certain forms are normal in a given society, if they regularly occur in similar types of society, and if they fulfil essential functions in society. Phenomena are pathological if they do not fulfil these conditions. The distinction between normal and pathological forms is in its turn essential to Durkheim's attempts to prescribe what needs to be done. Normal forms are to be promoted, pathological forms to be eradicated. Social policy thus rests upon functional analysis.[3]

In *Division of Labour* Durkheim noticed that through time societies become more complex and differentiated. There is hardly any division of labour in earlier forms of society. Society is then kept together through what Durkheim called 'mechanical solidarity'; that is, a form of cohesion based on similarity of beliefs and sentiments.[4] Modern societies are characterized by an increasing division of labour. They can only be kept together through 'organic solidarity'; that is, cohesion based on interdependence and co-operation of its component parts.[5] The increasing division of labour needs to be explained by the increase in 'dynamic or moral density' which is itself to be explained by increasing population growth. The argument is basically Darwinian. Population growth amongst animals leads to functional specialization such that they can coexist. An analogous mechanism operates in the social realm where division of labour resolves the increased competition amongst human beings.[6]

But the transition towards a differentiated society has not run very smoothly. Durkheim diagnosed 'anomie' as one of the major social problems of his time. Anomie means literally 'normlessness'. In Durkheim's sociology, anomie refers to a significant lack of normative regulation in society. Durkheim believed that a healthy society is dependent on the institutionalization of central values and normative guidelines. Without these binding value patterns and norms, social and political life would be in disarray. The moral malaise of the Third Republic was indicative of the state of anomie in a differentiated society. But anomie is only a transitional phase. Sociology can contribute to the implementation of values and normative rules which fit modern society.[7]

The above summary suffices as an illustration of the functionalist tenets in Durkheim's reasoning. First, it shows that his sociological outlook relied upon the notion of societal needs: societies need solidarity and shared values. Second, it reveals the organicist tenets of Durkheim's thinking: social health depends on the extent to which different parts are functionally related to the whole. Third, it discloses Durkheim's preoccupation with analogies between social and biological evolution, and the central role of the notion of differentiation in his theory of evolution. It is thus not surprising that Durkheim had and still has an enormous impact on modern-day functionalists.

But functionalism as a separate school became dominant only after the First World War. It was first introduced by Bronislaw Malinowski (1884–1942) and Alfred Reginald Radcliffe-Brown (1881–1955). Both used the label 'functionalism' to refer to the theoretical frame of reference which they employed, although Radcliffe-Brown occasionally used 'structural functionalism' to distinguish his argument from Malinowski's.

Functionalists like Malinowski and Radcliffe-Brown rebelled against nineteenth-century anthropologists. There were basically two problems with the latter: they sometimes relied upon some kind of diffusionism, and they lacked direct empirical experience. According to diffusionism, social items or practices gradually spread themselves across societies due to migration and trade, so similar cultural artefacts or practices are explained by a common source. The problems with diffusionism are manifold. First, diffusionists ignored the extent to which the meaning of items or practices depends on the cultural context in which they are used. Second, even assuming that it is possible to conceive of two items or practices as identical, it is difficult to substantiate empirically that they have a single source. If some nineteenth-century anthropologists did not accept diffusionism, almost all lacked systematic exposure to non-western societies. Some had travelled abroad, but few had carried out extensive fieldwork, and of those who had even fewer used their findings to substantiate their theories. They tended to construct theories by relying upon secondary source material.

Malinowski, Radcliffe-Brown and other early functionalists developed their views partly in opposition to diffusionism and the 'armchair' anthropology of the nineteenth century. Functionalists became hostile towards diffusionist reasoning for two reasons. First, they realized that they were dealing with societies with extremely unreliable and incomplete historical records. Hence, any attempt to comprehend these societies within an all-embracing historical narrative would lead to 'pseudo-causal' explanations. Second, they thought that it was important to conceive of societies as wholes. The meaning of a social item depends on its relationship to other items currently in use in that society, and on its contribution to the society as a whole. Cultural artefacts, which are transmitted to a new society, become reappropriated and readjusted to the requirements of the new context. To trace back the origins of social items is not only an impossible task, it is to disregard the functional rationality of the items today. The unravelling of this synchronic-cum-holistic logic can only be made possible through a thorough understanding of the whole culture as it is in operation now. And this can only be accomplished through extensive fieldwork and rigorous research methods. It is ironic that the functionalist school, which subsequently developed into the highly abstract work of Talcott Parsons, Jeffrey Alexander and Niklas Luhmann, emerged out of concerns with the necessity of detailed ethnographic research.

There is a danger of regarding functionalist anthropologists as too homogeneous a group; there is indeed significant variation within early functionalism, notably between Malinowski and Radcliffe-Brown. I will deal with Malinowski first, as his influence predated Radcliffe-Brown's. Originally from Poland, Malinowski began to study natural sciences at the universities of Cracow and Leipzig, and then anthropology at the London School of Economics. This initial training in the natural sciences might account for the strong biological bias in his work. But even before he went to England he had developed a keen interest in the social sciences. At Cracow his attention was drawn to J. G. Frazer's *Golden Bough*, and at Leipzig he became a regular attender of Karl Bücher's and Wilhelm Wundt's lectures. In Malinowski's rejection of diffusionism, for instance, one finds the resonance of Wundt's insistence that social items cannot be studied in isolation from each other. At the LSE, Malinowski became acquainted with the art of ethnography, and he subsequently carried out fieldwork in New Guinea. This research led to several articles and monographs, amongst which *Argonauts of the Western Pacific* is especially well known. Malinowski taught mainly at the LSE, where he held the first chair in anthropology. With his overpowering personality he had a decisive impact on British anthropology between the wars. He taught briefly at Yale University until his death in 1942. His posthumous *Scientific Theory of Culture* summarizes very well his views on anthropological theory.[8]

I have already mentioned that functionalist anthropologists rebelled against some nineteenth-century frameworks. This is very much the case for Malinowski. First, he reacted strongly against Edward Burnett Tylor's and Frazer's notion that 'primitive man' does not possess the same rational faculties as 'modern man'. Malinowski tried to demonstrate that certain practices or thought processes, which are *prima facie* irrational, are reasonable after all, in that it can be shown that they serve certain needs, whether social or psychological.[9] Take the phenomena of magic and religion. Previous accounts failed to capture the 'pragmatic utilitarian performance' of religious practices and rituals. Malinowski suggested taking up the view 'that magic is as magic does'.[10] He noted that people try to know and control their environment in order to satisfy their biological needs. But the external environment is not entirely predictable, nor is it entirely controllable. This uncertainty leads to an accumulation of anxiety, which people have a need to relieve; magic and religion fulfil that function. Malinowski also stressed that people are sometimes faced with disruptions which undermine the unconscious flow of daily life. For example, when confronted with unexpected death, they resort to magic or religion to deal with these crises, as a result of which their anxiety and emotional unrest are reduced.

Second, nineteenth-century thinkers tended to believe that several contemporary cultural artefacts or practices are mere 'survivals' or 'borrowed traits' of the past. That is, current beliefs or practices might have fulfilled some purpose in the past, but as they become transmitted across generations they eventually lose their initial usefulness. They are like cultural fossils in that they are reminiscences of a distant past. Malinowski insisted that a closer look shows that many of these so-called 'survivals' are not mere 'deadweights' at all.[11] They might well have been transmitted from the past, but they are shown to fulfil vital functions in contemporary society. It is a mistake to conceive of cultural transmission as merely duplication. This would be the case only if people did not have the ability to learn from past experience and think ahead. But people do have that ability and often put it into practice. Hence, cultural items are, whenever necessary, readjusted to new contexts.

Third, many nineteenth-century social scientists attempted to establish laws or law-like generalizations which transcend the ability of individuals to interfere in the course of events. On the same theme, Comte, Durkheim and many others insisted that society is an entity *sui generis*. Of course, society consists of individuals with psychological and biological features. But it would be mistaken to attempt to explain society by attributing primal causality to either psychological or biological mechanisms. Malinowski's picture cannot be more different.[12] First and foremost, knowingly or unwittingly, people act in a self-interested fashion in that they ensure the satisfaction of their basic needs. These basic needs are biological. Cultural products are secondary in that they help people to satisfy the 'primary biological needs'. Furthermore, people are not mere passive recipients of external forces. Ever since the beginning of civilization human beings have developed technologies, aimed at controlling their future performance through systematic use of past experience.[13]

Fourth, as already mentioned, nineteenth-century anthropological theories lacked a solid empirical basis. It should now be clear why Malinowski felt so strongly about the need for detailed ethnographic research. Only through meticulous empirical research can the anthropologist learn about the rationale behind foreign practices, about the current functions of these practices, and about how the people involved constantly manipulate their environment. Many previous anthropological works conflated customs, actions and accounts. They assumed that people's reports about their customs provided reliable information about their actions. During his fieldwork, Malinowski became very much aware of the extent to which the natives said one thing and did another, and of the extent to which they were willing to break rules or conventions whenever it was in their interest to do so. And this finding in its turn suggested the necessity of extensive fieldwork.

Malinowski's theory of needs is essential to his functionalist framework, and it is thus worth developing here. His concept of need and his notion of function are very much interrelated: social practices fulfil a function if and only if they lead to the satisfaction of needs.[14] Malinowski basically distinguished between three types of needs. The first level refers to the 'primary biological needs' of individuals, such as the need for food or the need for sexual satisfaction, which are essential to their survival. The second refers to social needs, like the need for co-operation and solidarity. These social needs have to be fulfilled in order for primary needs to be satisfied. The third level refers to the integrative needs of society. These comprise institutions or traditions which allow for the transmission across generations of those behavioural patterns which make for the satisfaction of the societal needs.[15]

Malinowski observes some simple, but important, contrasts between humans and animals.[16] Animals lack culture, and they therefore cannot rely upon the satisfaction of the secondary needs in order to satisfy their primary needs. Neither do they have to do so, because their anatomical and physiological features allow them to satisfy primary needs anyway. Human beings have culture, and they can thus rely upon the fulfilment of the secondary needs in order to satisfy primary needs. But they are also dependent on culture for their survival because their anatomical and physiological characteristics do not allow them to satisfy primary needs without cultural assistance. For instance, human beings can (and must) rely upon social norms and conventions for the fulfilment of their needs for security. Given that these cultural artefacts are a *sine qua non* for the survival of the human species, it follows that humans are dependent on the continuation of culture across generations. If people had to reinvent culture with every generation, their survival capacity would indeed have been severely limited. Malinowski coined the term 'integrative imperatives' to refer to the necessity of the transmission of these norms and conventions across generations. Notice the contrast with animals again. Given that the latter are not dependent on culture, their survival is *a fortiori* independent of cultural transmission. But whereas animals might develop individual habit formations through instruction or trial and error, they are generally unable to transmit these skills to their offspring. In contrast, human beings have been rather ingenious in compensating for their inbuilt weakness: first, by invoking practices which make for the satisfaction of the secondary needs, and then, by preserving and transmitting these practices across time.

Radcliffe-Brown first studied psychology and philosophy at Cambridge, and then anthropology under W. H. R. Rivers. At Cambridge, he showed an interest in the theoretical aspects of the discipline, already developing some of his core ideas concerning anthropological theory. He had become acquainted with Durkheim's writings, which were to have a lasting influence on his thinking.

Compared to Malinowski, Radcliffe-Brown is not remembered for his fieldwork. Whilst holding a fellowship at Trinity College, Cambridge, he did carry out some empirical research, notably on the Andamans and the Australian aborigines. But he lacked Malinowski's meticulous research methods and language skills; nor did he share Malinowski's perseverance, or his genuine empathy with and passion for the people whom he studied. Instead, he became directly involved in the academic institutionalization of anthropology, contributing to the setting-up of departments in various parts of the world. He held posts and established departments at the universities of Cape Town, Sydney and Alexandria. After a short spell at the University of Chicago, he took up the first Chair of Anthropology at Oxford in 1937. After retiring from Oxford in 1946, he continued teaching at various places until he was too ill to continue. His influence on anthropology was strongest in the 1940s.

Radcliffe-Brown's contribution to anthropological theory differs from Malinowski's. Remember that Malinowski's theory rests upon the causal primacy of biological drives. Culture and the transmission of culture derive from the need to satisfy these biological drives, upon which depends the survival of the species. Radcliffe-Brown's functionalism is very different. Paraphrasing Durkheim, he argued that society has its own irreducible complexity; it cannot be explained by referring to mechanisms which operate at a lower level.[17] Society needs to be explained by social mechanisms, not psychological, and certainly not biological ones. Hence, he strongly distanced himself from Malinowski's functionalism.[18] Radcliffe-Brown's anthropology is deeply sociological, although he carefully avoided that label. The reason he provided for his reluctance to refer to his work as 'sociology' was that he did not wish to be associated with what he regarded as the impressionist and shallow work often carried out in the English-speaking world under that heading.[19]

Like Malinowski, Radcliffe-Brown was especially suspicious of diffusionist theories. Diffusionist explanations around the turn of the century often combined psychological theory and historical guesswork. The work of Rivers, Radcliffe-Brown's teacher at Cambridge, was an example *par excellence* of the supremacy of these psychologico-historical explanations. Radcliffe-Brown's approach differed substantially. First, against Rivers's heavy reliance upon psychology, Radcliffe-Brown denied that society can be understood as an aggregate of psychological phenomena.[20] Second, he thought it necessary to abandon the diffusionist search for origins; any such enterprise lacks the necessary empirical support.[21] Third, instead of Rivers's attempts at making historical conjectures, Radcliffe-Brown heralded comparative sociology, which allows the anthropologist to find universal laws about synchronic relations.[22] Fourth, whereas diffusionists relied upon secondary sources, Radcliffe-Brown regarded extensive fieldwork as essential to the scientific study of non-western cultures. After all, the meaning of cultural items depends on the social context, and only systematic observation will allow the anthropologist to uncover the local meanings.[23]

Radcliffe-Brown's lifelong involvement in the academic institutionalization of anthropology was interwoven with his commitment to the subject as a scientific discipline. He thought that hitherto anthropology had been too often in the hands of well-meaning dilettantes, who developed highly speculative theories based on unreliable source material. Anthropology had to become a science, aimed at developing general laws of society. This meant that anthropologists needed to draw systematically upon what he called the inductive and comparative method. But Radcliffe-Brown's position also implied that anthropology was in need of professionalization. The emphasis on scientific method called for a rigorous training in fieldwork methods,[24] and this instruction was to be provided at universities. Once anthropology was established as a science, it would be able to inform and guide colonial administration, educators and policy-makers.[25] Radcliffe-Brown's own prescriptions very much resemble Durkheim's. Society should aim at a state of *eunomia* as opposed to *dysnomia*. *Eunomia*, or social health, occurs when the different parts are in harmonious relation to each other. The thoroughly trained anthropologist helps colonial and local administration in the accomplishment of *eunomia*.[26]

Radcliffe-Brown introduced a number of concepts, central to his line of argument, which include social structure, structural form and social function. Commentators have often misunderstood Radcliffe-Brown because they failed to capture the exact meaning which he attributed to these key concepts of his framework. 'Structure', especially, was used rather distinctly from its ordinary use in sociology and anthropology (see chapter 1). Radcliffe-Brown insisted that his notion of structure is not as an abstraction or model used in order to approach reality. Instead, he regarded structure (and hence *social* structure) as an observable reality. The general concept of structure refers to an arrangement of interrelated parts, and structures can be observed in different realms. For example, the structure of a piece of music refers to an arrangement of sounds, and the structure of a molecule is an arrangement of atoms. Likewise, social structure is the entire set of actually existent relations which connect certain individuals at a given time. So the ultimate components of social structure are human beings. Their relations involve well-defined rights and duties for the individuals involved. The institutionalization of incentives and sanctions ensure people's compliance with these prescriptions.[27]

Some structures, such as that of a building, are relatively invariant. But many change. Like the structure of the human body, social structure is in constant flux; like the changing molecules of the human body, people come and go, or take up different positions and roles. Now, in the midst of any structural change, there is continuity. Radcliffe-Brown coined the term 'structural form' to refer to this observable structural continuity. For example, a human organism retains its structural form in spite of the changing molecules. Likewise, social structure exhibits an observable structural form: the usages or norms shared by the individuals are relatively invariant.[28] The relative stability of the forms is due to what Radcliffe-Brown coined 'functions' fulfilled by the different parts of the system. By a function, he meant the sum total of all relations that a component has to the entire system in which it is embedded. The notion of function is again applicable to many realms of reality: in the same way different parts of the human body fulfil vital functions, so do various components of social life.[29] The stability of structural form is dependent on the 'functional unity' of the whole; that is, the mutual adjustment of the different parts. Particularly central to the persistence of social forms is 'coaptation', referring to the standardization and mutual adjustment of the attitudes and behaviour of the members of that society.[30]

Malinowski and Radcliffe-Brown had an enormous impact on social anthropology. The reception of early functionalism by social theorists was not as unequivocally positive. This ambiguous response is to be explained partly by the subsequent rise of rival functionalist theories. By the end of the 1940s, Talcott Parsons had established himself as the main exponent of functionalist theory, and very soon after that Robert Merton made his reputation. But the mild reception of early functionalist theories was also a consequence of their own shortcomings.

For illustration, two pivotal weaknesses in the argument of early functionalists can be cited. The first is their tendency to describe *all* cultural items as functional. Malinowski, for instance, postulated this 'universal functionalism' when he described culture as 'a system of objects, activities, and attitudes in which *every* part exists as a means to an end'[31]. For him, '*every* cultural achievement that implies the use of artifacts and symbolism is an instrumental enhancement of human anatomy, and refers directly or indirectly to the satisfaction of a bodily need'.[32] Now, the assumption of universal functionalism can be understood in two ways; there is a strong and a weak version. On the one hand, it can be understood to mean literally that every social item fulfils a central function. This strong version would be an untenable position to hold. Evolutionary theory might imply that highly dysfunctional items are selected out. But from this it does not follow that the items which do persist fulfil central functions. On the other, a more charitable interpretation is that universal functionalism means that only those items which fulfil central functions count as socially relevant items. For methodological purposes, every item should be treated as if it fulfils a vital function; the empirical researcher needs to be sensitive to the fact that every observed item *might* serve central needs of society. Although more plausible, this weak version of universal functionalism is not without problems either. It is unclear which criteria ought to be employed in order to decide whether or not an item *is* functional, and if it is, which function it fulfils.

The second weakness of early functionalism is its tendency to assume that a certain amount of cohesion and cohesiveness is necessary for society to survive. Radcliffe-Brown, for instance, held to this assumption of functional unity when he wrote that 'all parts of the social system work together with a sufficient degree of harmony or internal consistency'.[33] The problems with this position are twofold. One, the notion of 'survival' might have a clear meaning in the biological realm, but it does not to the same extent in the social realm. It is unclear whether the survival of a society or culture refers to continuity at a political or cultural level, or to the absence of biological extinction of its members. Also, if social survival refers to political or cultural constancy, then it remains unclear how much of that continuity constitutes survival. Two, to say that a certain degree of cohesiveness or internal consistency is necessary is a vacuous claim to make. The question is not whether or not cohesiveness is essential, but *how much* is needed. None of the early functionalists even began to answer that question. In practice, they often portrayed societies as if they were in need of high levels of standardization of sentiments and beliefs. This is not surprising given that the societies which they investigated already exhibited such high levels. But some awareness of their own culture would have taught them that although modern western societies do not quite conform to that picture, they nevertheless manage quite well.

To avoid being too harsh on Malinowski and Radcliffe-Brown, one should not forget that they were, first and foremost, empirical anthropologists, not social theorists. Their merit lies in demonstrating that many nineteenth-century speculative theories lacked an empirical basis. They carried out detailed ethnographies, and showed their theoretical relevance. They established a tradition of rigorous empirical research. Given these achievements, it would be unfair to claim that the onus of developing a convincing and coherent functionalist framework was on them. It is ironic that this task was to be taken up by a man for whom Malinowski's lectures were one of his first exposures to the social sciences. That young American graduate student attending Malinowski's lectures in 1925 was Talcott Parsons. He was to change the face of social theory for ever.

Talcott Parsons

Talcott Parsons (1902–79) first studied philosophy and biology at Amherst College, and then social science in England and Germany. He studied under L. T. Hobhouse, Ginsberg and Malinowski at the LSE, and then embarked upon a doctoral dissertation at Heidelberg. During his stay in Europe Parsons became heavily influenced by European social theory. His doctoral dissertation dealt with the notion of capitalism in the work of Weber, Marx and Werner Sombart. Further lasting influences on Parsons's thought include Durkheim and Vilfredo Pareto. Throughout his life he would attempt to incorporate these various European thinkers into a unified theoretical framework. On his return to the United States, he soon took up a position at the University of Harvard where he would stay until his retirement in 1973. Besides being a prolific writer, Parsons also held many offices: for instance, he was founding editor of *The American Sociological Review*, and President of the Eastern Sociological Society, the American Sociological Association and the American Academy of Arts and Sciences. Parsons was the first ever sociologist to occupy this last position.

Parsons's abstract theorizing was initially at odds with the highly atheoretical climate of American sociology at the time. When his first book, *The Structure of Social Action*, came out in 1937, it only attracted interest amongst specialists in social theory.[34] But his writings gradually had more impact, and by the time *The Social System* was published in 1951, he had become one of the most influential social theorists of his time.[35] The impact was not limited to social theory; his work was now also regarded as useful for empirical purposes. However, even in Parsons's heyday in the 1950s, his work never ceased to be controversial, regarded as pure genius by some and disguised conservative ideology by others. His influence declined in the late 1960s and 1970s, and only recently has there been a revival of interest in his work; for instance, in the writings of Jeffrey Alexander and Richard Münch.

Parsons's functionalist theory differs substantially from the early functionalism of Malinowski and Radcliffe-Brown. Whereas most early functionalists were sympathetic towards a positivist conception of social science, Parsons was not. He insisted that positivist social science is erroneous because it fails to recognize the essentially purposeful nature of human action (see chapter 8). It is intrinsic to agency that it cannot be reduced to external conditions. What is needed is a theory which takes into account the fact that people are both goal-orientated and constrained. Neither the purposiveness of action nor its external constraints can be ignored; neither can be reduced to the other.

This attempt to transcend both extreme forms of positivism and idealism runs throughout the whole of Parsons's *oeuvre*.

This is revealed clearly in his early work. Central to *The Structure of Social Action* is Thomas Hobbes's problem of order: how can society persist given that each of its members pursues his or her own goal?[36] Idealist, positivist and utilitarian attempts to solve the problem of order are shown to be inadequate. Idealist views mistakenly ignore the extent to which human conduct is conditioned by external constraints.[37] Likewise, positivist perspectives erroneously ignore the relatively independent role of the symbolic realm, and utilitarian perspectives are mistaken in reducing value patterns to a mere cost-benefit analysis.[38] Instead, Parsons found inspiration for his sociological answer to Hobbes's problem of order partly in Weber's action theory, and partly in Durkheim's notions of *conscience collective* or *représentations collectives* (see chapter 1). Parsons's solution to the problem of order is basically a Durkheimian one, referring to the internalization of shared central values and norms of society within need-dispositions of the personality structure. People tend not to adopt an instrumental attitude towards internalized values. By pursuing their own goals, socialized individuals unwittingly contribute to fulfilling the central needs of society.[39]

In the course of the 1940s and 1950s, Parsons developed his 'general theory of action'. Given its central place in his work, I will pay special attention to it here. The aim of the theory was to provide a theoretical framework which united various disciplines in the social sciences: sociology, politics, psychology and economics. Parsons's attempt to develop this unifying framework fitted in with his position at that time at Harvard. After teaching in the economics and sociology departments, he became chairman of the newly founded Department of Social Relations in 1946. The new institute grouped together several disciplines. Amongst Parsons's colleagues at the department were the psychologists Gordon Allport, Henry Murray and Robert Bales, the sociologists George Homans and Samuel Stouffer, and the anthropologist Clyde Kluckhohn. Many of these collaborated with Parsons and influenced his thinking. Parsons's general theory of action was both the academic backbone and the output of his tenure in office.

Central to Parsons's general theory of action is the notion of a 'system'. System theory had become increasingly popular at the time, and Parsons was heavily influenced by it. For him, a 'system of action' refers to a durable organization of the interaction between what he called an 'actor' and a 'situation'. The actor might be an individual or a group. The situation might or might not incorporate other 'actors'. Parsons argued that there are three features to any system. First, a system is relatively structured. In the social realm, he maintained that value patterns and what he called the 'pattern variables' contribute to the structured nature of the system. Second, certain functions need to be fulfilled for a system to survive. Social systems thus have particular needs, and Parsons tried to list and classify these 'functional prerequisites'. Third, social systems change, and that change takes place in an ordered fashion. Parsons introduced the notion of cybernetic hierarchy in order to capture the phenomenon of ordered transformation in the social realm.

These three components require elaboration. Before discussing his notions of functional prerequisites and internal dynamics, I will first analyse at length Parsons's treatment of the structured nature of interaction. His starting point is that systems of action are structured by value patterns, which stipulate the ultimate objectives towards which people's action will be directed. Without those ordering principles, people would not have any guidelines regarding their conduct. But Parsons argued that the value patterns are structured as well, by what he termed 'pattern variables'. He considered these to be the ultimate principles through which systemic structure is achieved. They are universal dichotomies which represent basic choices underlying social interaction.[40]

Parsons's pattern variables can also be seen as an attempt to reconstruct in a sophisticated manner dichotomies which were introduced by earlier authors. In particular, Tönnies's distinction between the *Gesellschaft* and the *Gemeinschaft* springs to mind. Tönnies described earlier types of society as *gemeinschaftlich*, based on personal relations and affective bonds. Modern society is more *gesellschaftlich* in that impersonal interactions are more frequent. Parsons's view was that Tönnies's typology of relationships conflates several dichotomies, and is thus too crude to have any heuristic value. Several observed relationships are indeed *gesellschaftlich* in some respects, *gemeinschaftlich* in others. Parsons set out to distinguish analytically the underlying dichotomies or pattern variables. This enabled him to redefine Tönnies's question. Rather than attempting to establish whether a given relationship is *gesellschaftlich* or *gemeinschaftlich*, Parsons's pattern variables enable him to establish *in which sense* that relationship is one or the other.

The pattern variables apply to any system of action, and refer to choices faced by an actor in relation to an object. As mentioned earlier, the actor does not have to be an individual – it can be a collectivity or a group. Likewise, the object does not have to be an inanimate object – it can be an individual or a social group. The pattern variables are universalism versus particularism, performance versus quality, specific versus diffuse relations, and affective neutrality versus affectivity. The first of each pair is characteristic of Tönnies's *Gesellschaft*, the second of each pair ties in with the *Gemeinschaft*. Underlying Parsons's scheme is the observation that our society is moving in the direction of universalism, performance, specific relations and affective neutrality. Whereas the first two pairs refer to the meaning which the actor attributes to a particular object, the remaining pairs allude to the nature of the relationship between actor and object. In Parsons's terminology again, the first two are the pattern variables of the modality of the object, and the others are the pattern variables of orientation to the object.

As to the pattern variables of the modality of the object, the actor makes use of universalistic criteria if he attributes meaning to the object according to criteria applicable to many other objects, whereas he draws upon particularistic criteria if the object is defined and judged in terms which are unique to that object. A bureaucracy, for instance, draws upon universalistic criteria, whereas relationships within the nuclear family are particularistic. Whereas the actor can judge the object in terms of its performance or achievement, the actor may also treat it in terms of its intrinsic quality. Performance is more prominent in the occupational structure, whereas quality can be exemplified in friendships. With respect to the pattern variables of orientation, the actor might adopt an attitude of affective neutrality towards the object as opposed to a relationship of affectivity. For example, the relationship between a doctor and patient demonstrates affective neutrality, whereas affectivity characterizes the interaction within the family. Finally, the actor may be involved with an object in rather specific ways, or relate to the object in multiple ways. Again, the relationship between doctor and patient is typically specific, and relationships within a family typically diffuse.

The pattern variables refer to the more voluntaristic dimensions of Parsons's theory, for they summarize and classify choices on the part of the actor. In contrast, Parsons's notion of 'functional prerequisites' points out the extent to which these attitudes or meanings are embedded within and constrained by social sub-systems. Parsons's functionalist theory rests upon the notion that any system of action only exists in so far as four basic needs are at least in part fulfilled by four types of function.[41] The four needs and functional prerequisites of any system of action are, according to Parsons, adaptation (A), goal-attainment (G), integration (I) and latency or pattern-maintenance (L). Hence Parsons often refers to this aspect of his theory as the AGIL-scheme. 'Adaptation' refers to the fact that any system of action should be able to adapt to its external environment and make the environment adapt to its own needs. 'Goal-attainment' is the need of any system of action to define its goals and to mobilize resources in order to obtain them. 'Integration' refers to the need of any system of action to regulate and co-ordinate its parts for the sake of its stability and coherence. Finally, 'latency' or 'pattern-maintenance' means that a system must provide means for sustaining the motivational energy of its members.

Parsons noted that the four functions can be arrived at with the use of two dichotomies: external versus internal, and instrumental versus consummatory. Activities directed towards goal-attainment and integration are 'consummatory' in that they aim at the accomplishment of the ultimate goals of the system, whereas activities directed towards adaptation or latency are 'instrumental' in that they are directed towards the employment of means in order to achieve the ultimate goals. Likewise, Parsons noted that adaptation and goal-attainment refer to the interaction between the system and its external environment, whereas latency and integration refer to issues concerning the internal organization of the system. So the AGIL-scheme can be summarized by noting that any system of action needs to relate successfully to its environment and internally organize itself.

For every system of action four sub-systems can be identified, each specializing in fulfilling one of the four functions: the organism directed towards adaptation, the personality system related to goal-attainment, the social system directed towards integration, and the cultural system geared towards pattern-maintenance. The difference between the four sub-units can also be captured in terms of Parsons's 'cybernetic hierarchy'. From cybernetic theory Parsons derives the idea that a system of action, like any other system, circulates and exchanges information and energy. The units with high information tend to control the units with high energy, whereas the latter tend to condition the former. The sub-system directed towards pattern-maintenance tends to control the other sub-systems. Similarly, the sub-system geared towards adaptation conditions the other sub-systems.[42]

Parsons's theory of action is general. For each sub-system similar distinctions can be identified. It follows that his scheme is like a set of Russian dolls, each doll incorporating a smaller version of itself with an identical structure. For example, the social system itself can be divided up into four sub-systems. There is, first, the economy which deals with the adaptation of society towards its environment. Second, the polity of society deals primarily with goal-attainment. Third, the social community focuses upon integration and solidarity. Finally, the cultural sub-system provides values and normative regulations which make for appropriate socialization.

Parsons goes to great lengths to show the interrelationship between the AGIL-scheme and the pattern variables.[43] Systems with different functions imply different pattern variables. For instance, systems directed towards fulfilling the adaptive function are characterized by universalism, neutrality, specificity and performance, whereas systems fulfilling the integrative function emphasize particularism, affectivity, diffuseness and quality (see table 2.1).

Whereas Parsons's earlier work ignored issues related to long-term change, his later work drew upon analogies with biological evolution to develop a 'paradigm of evolutionary change'.[44] Four notions are crucial here: differentiation, adaptive upgrading, inclusion and value generalization. First, with time, a process of 'differentiation' occurs in that different functions are fulfilled by sub-systems within the social system. For instance, the economic and the family unit gradually become differentiated. Second, with differentiation goes the notion of 'adaptative upgrading'. This means that each differentiated subsystem has more adaptive capacity compared to the non-differentiated system out of which it emerged. Third, modern societies tend to rely upon a new system of integration. Process differentiation implies a more urgent need for special skills. This can only be accommodated by moving from a

Table 2.1 Relations between pattern variables and functional prerequisites of any system of action

	Universalism (O) Neutrality (M)	Affectivity (O) Particularism (M)	
Specificity (O) Performance (M)	ADAPTATION	GOAL-ATTAINMENT	Performance (O) Specificity (M)
Quality (O) Diffuseness (M)	PATTERN-MAINTENANCE	INTEGRATION	Diffuseness (O) Quality (M)
	Neutrality (O) Universalism (M)	Particularism (O) Affectivity (M)	

O = pattern variable of orientation to the object
M = pattern variable of object-modality

Source: Based on Parsons (1960, p. 470)

status based on 'ascription' to a status on the basis of 'achievement'. This implies the 'inclusion' of previously excluded groups. Fourth, a differentiated society needs to develop a value system that incorporates and regulates the different sub-systems. This is made possible through 'value generalization': the values are pitched at a higher level in order to direct activities and functions in various sub-systems.

Three basic weaknesses can be identified in Parsons's social theory. First, his general theory of action is a conceptual scheme, rather than an adequate theory. There is no doubt that, as such, the general theory is a remarkable achievement. It is, after all, analytically very tight and, because of its high level of generality, it allows us to categorize various aspects of the social realm. But equally beyond question is that the explanatory power of the theory is weak. It provides few testable propositions about social reality.[45] Second, intrinsic to Parsons's theoretical frame of reference is a neglect of conflict and disequilibrium. In his earlier work he developed a theoretical argument aimed at understanding how social order is brought about. Likewise, his system analysis was primarily aimed at explaining how the stability of a system is achieved – how it manages its boundary-maintenance and its internal integration. Parsons's frame of reference not only fails to account sufficiently for widespread dissensus and major political or industrial conflicts, but also occasionally seems to exclude the very possibility of their existence.[46] Third, some of the weaknesses of early functionalism reoccur in Parsons's work. He argued that there are four functional prerequisites to any social system. Underlying his theory is thus the assumption that these pivotal functions are essential to the maintenance and survival of the system. If these pivotal functions were not fulfilled adequately, the social system would disintegrate and eventually be selected out. However, like Malinowski and Radcliffe-Brown, Parsons remains ambiguous about what exactly constitutes survival and maintenance in the social realm. And as with early functionalists, it remains unclear *how much* goal-attainment, adaptation, latency and integration are needed for a system to maintain itself.

Robert Merton

Talcott Parsons trained several promising sociologists who later turned out to be influential scholars in their own right. His long list of Ph.D. students included, for example, Robert King Merton and Harold Garfinkel. Robert Merton (1910–) was one of Parsons's first doctoral students at Harvard. His dissertation dealt with science and economy in seventeenth-century England, and it already exhibited his functionalist viewpoint, albeit in an embryonic form. Other influences on Merton during his stay at Harvard included the sociologist P. A. Sorokin and the historian of science George Sarton. Amongst European scholars Émile Durkheim and Georg Simmel had a lasting impact on his work.

Merton spent most of his teaching career at the University of Columbia, which, with him, Paul Lazarsfeld and others, became a centre of excellence for sociology. There was a remarkable compatibility between Merton's 'middle-range' functionalism and Lazarsfeld's quantitative methodology. In comparison to Parsons's abstract theorizing, Merton's middle-range theory seemed more obviously suited to empirical research, for which Lazarsfeld's sophisticated use of statistics would provide the methodological backbone. Merton had a remarkable gift for demonstrating the validity of his theoretical constructions with the help of relevant empirical applications. He dealt with several substantive topics, ranging from American politics to science. With the publication of *Social Theory and Social Structure*, he became one of the leading proselytizers of the functionalist cause.[47]

Although once a pupil of Parsons, Merton's functionalist viewpoint differed substantially from that of his former mentor. Merton's writings were more cautious and defensive; underlying them is a constant awareness of the various criticisms levelled against previous functionalist frames of reference. A significant part of his work deals with these criticisms. Indeed, he regularly attempted to show that they were invalid, or pointed to errors which, although committed by some functionalists, were not intrinsic to the functionalist argument. Merton's proposal for a functionalist paradigm endeavoured to avoid these intellectual faults.

A similar prudence lies behind Merton's middle-range theories.[48] Contrary to Parsons's grand theory, a middle-range theory does not aim to encompass the whole of society. But neither is it a sequence of unrelated empirical hypotheses. 'Theories of the middle range . . . lie between the minor but necessary working hypotheses that evolve in abundance during day-to-day research and the all-inclusive systematic efforts to develop a unified theory that will explain all the observed uniformities of social behavior, social organization and social change.'[49] Merton believed the theory of reference groups (and relative deprivation) to be an example of a successful middle-range theory in sociology. This theory, to which Merton himself contributed, set out that individuals evaluate their own situation by comparing and contrasting it with that of a reference group. Merton thought that the theory was successful in that it counters common sense and has been validated empirically.[50]

Although Merton is considered to be one of the high priests of modern functionalism, he distanced himself from a significant number of writings under that banner. He tried to demonstrate that most early functionalists drew upon untenable presuppositions. The German word *hineinlesen* summarizes well what Merton found so problematic in early functionalism. *Hineinlesen* (not a term used by Merton himself) refers to the activity of reading too much into something. And that is exactly what, according to Merton, early functionalists did. They tended *ex post facto* to read too much functional rationality into social practices.

How did early functionalists attribute too much functional rationality onto social reality? Merton argued that they did so by adhering to three erroneous principles: the postulate of functional unity of society, the postulate of universal functionalism and the postulate of indispensability.[51] The first principle states that society is a functional whole, and all its parts are fully integrated and well balanced. The second principle asserts that all cultural items and social practices are functional. The third principle states that there are certain universal functional prerequisites to any society, and *only* specific cultural items or practices can fulfil these functions. Merton argued that the early functionalists were mistaken in postulating these principles in advance. They need to be shown empirically, and empirical research shows them to be incorrect. The first principle might be consistent with Malinowski's and Radcliffe-Brown's data on 'primitive' non-literate societies. But it would be a gross error to extend this principle to differentiated literate societies. The second principle fails to acknowledge the existence of social survivals: that is, items which might have fulfilled a function at some point in the past but which do so no longer. The third principle disregards the existence of 'functional alternatives' or 'functional equivalents'. The fact that a given item fulfils a particular function does not necessarily imply that the very same function cannot be fulfilled by alternative items.

Merton's proposal for a functionalist perspective was based on his criticisms of the above trinity of functional postulates. First, he abandoned the early functionalist view that we live in the best of all possible worlds. Many beliefs or practices persist in spite of the fact that they do not have notably beneficial effects for the individuals involved or for the wider society. They might have negative consequences, or they might have no socially significant effect. Merton argued that early functionalists have hitherto been biased towards exclusively focusing on the *positive* consequences of social items for the wider social system in which these items are situated. His paradigm for functional analysis, on the other hand, attributed equal status to what he coined 'functions' and 'dysfunctions'. He defined functions as those observed effects of social items which contribute to the adaptation or adjustment of a system under consideration. Dysfunctions are those observed consequences which lessen the adaptation or adjustment of a given system. Certain items might appear to be neither functional nor dysfunctional. They are 'nonfunctional' in that they are irrelevant for a given system. Merton believed that his attention to dysfunctions makes his functionalism well suited for analysing social transformation.[52]

Second, early functionalists tend to focus on so-called functions for 'the society'. But the notion of society as a totality is misleading, because the same item might be functional for some individuals, group(s) or system(s), whilst dysfunctional for others. Merton therefore distinguished between different units for which the item might have consequences. So rather than referring to observed effects *in general*, he chose to specify the nature of the units which are affected and how these units are affected. The unit might be the society, the cultural system, a group, the psychological unit, etc. Likewise, there are societal (dys)functions, cultural (dys)functions, group functions, psychological functions, and so forth.[53]

The phenomenon of war can be used to clarify Merton's distinction between functions and dysfunctions and his distinction between various units of analysis. Consider the following units: the society, the economic unit, the psychological level and the political realm. At the societal level, war is obviously dysfunctional in that it leads to the immediate breakup of families, and the likely injury and possible death of relatives. But war also tends to enhance the internal solidarity of a country. Confrontation with a visible external enemy tends to increase feelings of togetherness and belonging.[54] At the psychological level, some point out that the increased cohesiveness in its turn contributes to the well-being of the citizens – hence the observed decrease in suicide rates during periods of war. Notwithstanding this, going to war also has damaging psychological effects for the soldiers and their families, and for anybody who cares for peace and humanity. At the economic level, war efforts are beneficial for those sectors of the economy which are directly or indirectly involved in the production of arms. However, war also inevitably leads to the neglect of other sectors of the economy; it occasionally leads to economic sanctions from other countries, and it is almost always accompanied by decreasing trade and a decline in the standard of living. At a politico-strategic level, going to war might deflect attention from domestic problems, raise the popularity of those in power, and thus be crucial to their re-election. But strategic errors might also have the opposite effect.

Third, Merton noted that a common critique of functionalism was its conservative bias. He acknowledged that early functionalists tended to provide interpretations which legitimized the existing order, though he denied that this tendency was intrinsic to functionalism. Early functionalists came to such conservative conclusions precisely because their analysis was confined to the identification of positive effects for the society as a whole. Once functionalists include dysfunctions and once they specify various units or levels of analysis, they will be able to establish a 'net balance of an aggregate of consequences' for every item. By searching for which functional alternatives are possible in a given social structure, functionalism can help us to improve society.[55]

Fourth, some functionalist accounts conflated subjective states of individuals with objective consequences. Merton insisted that the function of a practice is an observable effect, and therefore to be distinguished from the motive underlying the practice. Some practices have, of course, functions which are both intended and recognized by the individuals who are involved in the practices. Merton called these 'manifest functions'. But other functions are neither intended nor recognized by the individuals involved. Merton called the latter 'latent functions'. Take the example of Christian church-going. One of its manifest functions is to commemorate Jesus and to be closer to God. One of its latent functions consists of reinforcing social integration. Functional analysis can be liberating in that it makes latent (dys)functions manifest.[56]

An example of Merton's middle-range, functionalist theory can be found in his seminal articles 'Social structure and anomie' and 'Continuities in the theory of social structure and anomie'.[57] Underlying this theory is the distinction between culture and social structure: whereas culture provides people with normative guidelines, social structure refers to the organized set of social relationships. Culture informs people about what is desirable and to be aimed at, whereas the very fact that they operate within a social structure implies various opportunities and constraints.

More specifically, Merton distinguished between the ultimate values which are central to a particular culture on the one hand, and the availability of legitimate means to achieve these goals on the other. Anomie is defined as a state of discrepancy between ultimate values and legitimate means. For example, whereas material and professional success are highly valued in western society, few people have the structurally induced opportunities to achieve these goals. Merton argued that people will be driven towards reducing the discrepancy, and that deviant behaviour can be seen as an attempt to restore the equilibrium.

Merton devoted much time to the construction of a classificatory scheme about different ways in which individuals can adjust to this state of anomie

Table 2.2 How people adapt to the state of anomie

Modes of adaptation	Culture goals	Institutionalized means
I. Conformity	+	+
II. Innovation	+	−
III. Ritualism	−	+
IV. Retreatism	−	−
V. Rebellion	+/−	+/−

Source: Based on Merton (1968, p. 194)

(see table 2.2). 'Innovation' occurs when people accept the ultimate goals but introduce illegitimate means to achieve them. Merton cited some forms of white-collar crime as examples of this particular phenomenon. 'Ritualism' is reserved for cases in which people have lowered their aims but in which they do accept the institutionalized ways of doing things. 'Retreatism' occurs when both goals and means are rejected, and when people retreat from involvement with society. Certain subcultures fall under that category. 'Rebellion' occurs when individuals seek to change the culturally prescribed goals of society and the legitimate means for achieving them. To complete the picture (although not a case of deviancy), Merton talked about 'conformity' when people accept both the ultimate goals and the institutionalized means.

Merton's accomplishment was to reflect critically upon and to elucidate pivotal concepts which were regularly in use at the time; for instance, the concept of function or the notion of functional equivalent. His framework was more sophisticated than that of early functionalists, and he carefully avoided some of their errors; for instance, he distanced himself success-fully from the once-widespread picture of society as an organic whole with nothing but functional and indispensable parts. But Merton's frame of refer-ence is not without weaknesses either. First, although he developed a frame of reference, which, he hoped, would avoid the errors committed by early functionalism, he ultimately failed to provide convincing explanations for people's actions. By rejecting the simple functionalism of his predecessors in favour of a more cautious approach, he unfortunately managed to throw the baby out with the bath-water. Compared to Malinowski's and Radcliffe-Brown's theories, Merton's framework has merely a descriptive and heuristic value; it might delineate and categorize social life, but that is all there is to it. Indeed, to point out existing or potential unintended effects of recurring prac-tices, as Merton does, is, in isolation, not an explanation of those patterns.

Second, commentators have rightly indicated that some of Merton's own contributions to middle-range research can hardly be called functionalist. He does not pay much attention to the unintended outcomes of people's practices, and certainly not in the way in which functionalists normally proceed. Most of his assertions in 'Social structure and anomie', for instance, allude to a causal, non-functionalist logic. It is, of course, not surprising that, in practice, Merton deviates from his functionalist framework. Its explanatory power is so weak that he has to resort to alternative modes of explanation in order to say anything significant at all.

Third, there are a number of imprecisions in Merton's framework. These are especially problematic given that, if there is any value to the framework, it should lie in its descriptive or heuristic qualities, and therefore analytical precision is central. One example of the lack of precision concerns his definition of manifest and latent functions. In this definition, he conflated knowing something will occur and intending it to take place. Neither latent nor manifest functions cover instances where individuals wittingly, though unintentionally, bring about particular functional effects.[58]

Once a promising research programme aimed at unifying the manifold branches of the social sciences, functionalism came under severe criticism from the late 1960s onwards. At least part of the upsurge of dissident voices can be explained by the changing political climate of the time. In a period of political radicalization, students and academics became increasingly dissatisfied with the alleged ideological bias in functionalism. It is ironic that whilst many regarded the functionalist emphasis on equilibrium and stability as conservative, if not reactionary, quite a few of the 'radical' alternatives in vogue at the time employed functionalist types of reasoning.[59] Notwithstanding this, functionalism as a school became equated with justifying the existing order and was therefore to be abandoned. Furthermore many critics argued that, because of its focus on 'social statics', functionalism is inherently ahistorical. Functionalist research became associated with synchronic types of analysis in which a snapshot of society is regarded as sufficient for grasping the mechanisms of stability. Against this ahistorical bias, it was argued that a diachronic analysis is needed even for the purposes of explaining social order (see chapter 4).[60] In addition, sociologists became dissatisfied with what they saw as the functionalist neglect of agency – the ability of people to intervene in the course of events. In functionalist reasoning, people's conduct was mistakenly conceived to be the mere product of system imperatives. Relatedly, it was argued that functionalism wrongly underplayed people's knowledgeability: the fact that they know a great deal about social life and that they actually employ that knowledge in their daily interaction (see chapters 3 and 4).[61]

These criticisms were often justified, but they unintentionally reinforced a stereotyped picture of what functionalism stands for. First, the political implications of functionalism are not as clear-cut as some critiques have made them out to be. It is true that functionalist reasoning *can* be used to legitimize existing patterns in society. Functionalists *have* done so in the past. However, from this does not follow that functionalism *ipso facto* justifies the status quo. Merton's writings demonstrate that it is possible to employ functionalist notions without falling victim to a conservative bias. Second, although it is true that early forms of functionalism tended to focus only on the present, this was often due to methodological considerations (for instance, the absence of reliable historical sources), not theoretical ones. Any type of functionalist reasoning necessitates some form of evolutionism, and thus a sensitivity to longer temporal spans. It is therefore not surprising that Parsons's later work dealt very much with long-term change, and that other functionalists were to follow him in this regard. Third, a similar argument applies to the alleged neglect of agency. Some functionalists, indeed, purposefully or unwittingly neglect people's active intervention in the course of events, but for others (like Parsons) agency remains a pivotal feature of their theory. But even in the case of the former, there is no need for a theory to take everything into account, and no theory *can* account for every feature. Neglecting agency is not problematic as long as the theoretical format has satisfactory explanatory power.

Neo-functionalism and Niklas Luhmann

As has been noted, from the mid-1960s onwards functionalism lost its wider appeal. Sociologists became dissatisfied with the alleged conservative bias in functionalist reasoning, and they soon became attracted to a number of alternative theoretical arguments; for instance, Norbert Elias's figuration sociology, Giddens's structuration theory and Bourdieu's generative structuralism (see chapters 1 and 4). But since the early 1980s there has been a revival of functionalist reasoning, at first mainly in Germany, and later in the United States. In Germany Niklas Luhmann's (1927–) 'functionalist structuralism' has been decisive for the re-emergence of functionalist reasoning. In the United States Jeffrey Alexander's and Paul Colomy's writings heralded the neo-functionalist movement. Both functionalist structuralism and neo-functionalism draw upon Parsons, but they are not uncritical inheritors of his legacy.

Whilst following the basic outlines of a Parsonian argument neo-functionalists aim at being less dogmatic than their predecessors, and they address a number of criticisms. They try to merge Parsons with other 'classics' in social theory (in particular Marx and Durkheim) and with other schools of thought (especially phenomenology, symbolic interactionism and exchange theory). Like functionalism, neo-functionalism pays attention to the interconnections between different components of a social system. But unlike most functionalist authors, neo-functionalists are particularly sensitive to the potential conflicts between the different sub-systems. Whereas some earlier functionalists were inclined to overestimate the impact of culture onto other parts of society, neo-functionalism explicitly rejects any reductionist or mono-causal argument. Whereas some functionalists dismiss the micro-dimension of social life as irrelevant for the purposes of social theory, neo-functionalists also pay attention to the extent to which order is continually produced in our daily interactions (see chapter 3). Whereas some earlier functionalists saw social integration as given, neo-functionalism recognizes its problematic nature within modern society. Whereas former functionalist accounts of social change conceive of societal development in terms of increasing and irreversible differentiation, neo-functionalists like Colomy acknowledge the possibility of de-differentiation and uneven differentiation. The concept of de-differentiation is self-explanatory: it refers to the process by which society moves towards a less differentiated state. That is, de-differentiation occurs when several functions which were previously fulfilled by various differentiated sub-systems are now fulfilled within one system. Uneven differentiation takes place when certain sectors of society are more (or less) differentiated than others.

Niklas Luhmann has probably been the most innovative German contributor to a functionalist theory of society. He relies upon a wide variety of sources ranging from general system theory, to Parsons's structural-functionalism, Gehlen's philosophical anthropology, and phenomenology. Luhmann also relies upon analogies between the social world and other realms, hence his interest in the theory of autopoiesis and self-organizing systems. Although he is a theorist at heart, he has also provided many examples and applications of his viewpoint, ranging from legal and administrative matters to the issue of romantic love. Luhmann's impact on European sociology has been very important, whilst Anglo-Saxon sociologists seem in general to be more reluctant to adopt his ideas.

Niklas Luhmann's starting point, one could say, is the system. In his view, the workings of a system can only be fully understood if the relationship between that system and its environment is taken into account.[62] Luhmann's main assertion is that systems in general reduce the complexity of the environment in which they are embedded. The complexity of an environment depends on the number of actual or possible events in that environment. Reduction of complexity refers to the process by which a system selects relevant events from the environment, and how it reduces the number of ways of dealing with that environment. The process of internal system differentiation is one of the mechanisms by which complexity becomes managed or filtered.[63] In Luhmann's abstract terminology, systems can range from, say, physiological systems to social systems.

Luhmann's interest is obviously in social systems; these are defined as organized patterns of behaviour. The term 'social system' can refer to societies at large, institutions within societies, or rule-governed forms of behaviour. Social systems are different from other systems in that the reduction of complexity takes place through communication of meaning (*Sinn*).[64] Here, Luhmann relies heavily upon Gehlen's philosophical anthropology and in particular his notion of *Entlastung*, referring to the way in which institutionalization allows human beings to compensate for their intrinsic indeterminacy and open-endedness. In contrast with animals, the innate adaptation of humans to their environment is far less developed, and this intrinsic lack of orientation leads to the necessity of regulative principles.

In Luhmann's parlance, the main regulative device is 'double contingency', referring to the process by which in interaction individuals have to take into account the orientation of others towards them. From double contingency, Luhmann argues, it follows that social systems are autopoietic systems. These are systems which, once faced with an environment which potentially endangers their autonomy, record and interpret that environment such that it contributes to their autonomy. Through double contingency, potential threats to the autonomy of the social system are processed such that they enhance that autonomy. Luhmann takes a lot of effort to explain the autopoietic nature of social systems (and hence their self-referentiality).[65] The main thrust of his argument is that there are three dimensions to self-referential systems: the 'code' of the system, its 'structure' (or programme), and its 'process'. Codes are binary procedures through which information is processed – binary oppositions such as 'true versus false', or 'significant versus insignificant'. The structure or programme involves the central values, norms and expectations held within that system, whereas the process is the ongoing interaction. For a system to reproduce itself, the code needs to remain identical, whilst the structure or process might be altered.

Double contingency is thus a universal ordering principle, but as modernity implies increasing contingency and complexity, more sophisticated mechanisms are needed which would allow for further reduction of complexity. Luhmann provides many examples of progressive reduction of complexity in high modernity, ranging from changes in the legal system to transformations in administration. With the advent of high modernity 'self-reflexive' procedures and social differentiation become especially important for diminishing complexity. Self-reflexive procedures are those that can be applied not only to other phenomena but also to themselves. Teaching others how to teach, or carrying out scientific investigation of scientific activities – these are examples of self-reflexive procedures. Self-referential procedures imply the possibility of readjustment and therefore become essential for the continuous adaptation of a social system to a rapidly changing and increasingly unpredictable environment.[66]

Modern social systems are not only self-reflexive; they are also differentiated. For instance, Luhmann observes that through time three levels of social systems become distinct from each other: the level of situational interactions, the realm of organizations, and the societal level. But Luhmann also talks about differentiation in a less trivial fashion. In a way reminiscent of Durkheim's distinction between mechanical and organic solidarity, Luhmann distinguishes between 'segmental' and 'non-segmental' differentiation: the former implies the splitting-up of systems into differentiated units which perform identical functions, whereas the latter involves parts which are functionally different. The non-segmental type of differentiation can be either 'hierarchical' or 'functional': the former implies a hierarchical structure and the latter does not. With respect to the ability to lessen complexity, functional differentiation is superior to hierarchical differentiation, and the latter is superior to segmental differentiation. Given that modernity is characterized by increasing complexity in the social environment, it is not surprising to find that the evolution of society follows these different types: segmental differentiation comes first, then hierarchical differentiation and finally functional differentiation. Luhmann's evolutionary view of history relies upon three central concepts: variation, reproduction and selection. Variation refers to the fact that the emergence of social systems is accidental. Their reproduction takes place, for instance through socialization, and in the long run they are selected on the basis of their ability to adjust to the environment.[67]

It is obvious from the above that Luhmann is highly critical of those theorists who conceive of compartmentalization and differentiation as sources of social conflict and disorder, or who see modern depersonalization in terms of alienation or 'mass culture'. For him, this is to conceive of modernity in terms of a pre-modern sociological logic: rather than a source of disorder, various forms of differentiation are central to the creation of order in modern society; rather than alienating, impersonal relations provide new forms of freedom previously unknown to mankind. Luhmann is also critical of Parsons's assertion that common values and norms are a prerequisite for social order. With the advent of modernity, social order is accomplished without central values or widespread normative integration.

There is a tension between Luhmann's philosophical anthropology on the one hand, and his evaluation of the cultural manifestations of modernity on the other. Influenced by Gehlen and coming close to Malinowksi, Luhmann's philosophical anthropology postulates that human beings have no significant inborn traits, and that they need effective institutions to counteract the lack of an internal structure. However, this position necessitates a more critical attitude towards modernity than Luhmann is willing to adopt. He tries to get around this problem by reducing modernity mainly to differentiation and related notions. But it is obvious that modernity also implies a decrease in the power of value patterns and institutions. Taking on board Gehlen's philosophical anthropology cannot be reconciled with an uncritical appraisal of contemporary society.

Further reading

A concise, but critical account of functionalism can be found in Giddens's 'Functionalism: après la lutte' (in his *Studies in Social and Political Theory*). An extended, and more sympathetic, overview of functionalist theories can be found in Abrahamson's *Functionalism*. Kuper's *Anthropologists and Anthropology* includes two excellent chapters on Malinowski and Radcliffe-Brown, elucidating the intellectual background at the time. Rocher's *Talcott Parsons and American Sociology* is a remarkably lucid introduction to Parsons's writings. For those who insist on reading the master himself, *The Structure of Social Action* is probably one of Parsons's more accessible texts; *The Social System* has undoubtedly been his most influential work. Sztompka's *Robert Merton: An Intellectual Profile* remains the best introduction to Merton's functionalist framework, although it is not very critical. I very much recommend Merton's seminal article 'Manifest and Latent Functions' (in the collection *Social Theory and Social Structure*). *The Differentiation of Society* is Luhmann's most accessible work in the English language.

References

Althusser, L. 1972. *For Marx*. New York: Pantheon (originally in French, 1965).

Althusser, L. and Balibar, E. 1970. *Reading Capital*. London: New Left Books (originally in French, 1968).

Abrahamson, M. 1978. *Functionalism*. Englewood Cliffs, NJ: Prentice Hall.

Cohen, P. 1968. *Modern Social Theory*. London: Heinemann.

Durkheim, E. 1982. *The Rules of Sociological Method, and Selected Texts on Sociology and its Method*. London: Macmillan (originally in French, 1895; reprinted, 1992).

Durkheim, E. 1984. *The Division of Labour in Society*. Basingstoke: Macmillan (originally in French, 1893; reprinted, 1993).

Elias, N. 1970. *Was ist Soziologie?* München: Juventa.

Giddens, A. 1977. *Studies in Social and Political Theory*. London: Hutchinson (reprinted, 1979).

Giddens, A. 1979. *Central Problems in Social Theory: Action, Structure and Contradiction in Social Analysis*. London: Macmillan.

Giddens, A. 1981. Agency, institution and time-space analysis. In: *Advances in Social Theory and Methodology: Towards an Integration of Micro- and Macro-Sociologies*, eds K. Knorr-Cetina and A. V. Cicourel. London: Routledge, 161–75.

Giddens, A. 1984. *The Constitution of Society; Outline of the Theory of Structuration*. Cambridge: Polity Press.

Homans, G. 1961. *Social Behavior: Its Elementary Forms*. New York: Brace and World.

Knorr-Cetina, K. and Cicourel, A. V. (eds) 1981. *Advances in Social Theory and Methodology: Towards an Integration of Micro- and Macro-Sociologies*. London: Routledge.

Kuper, A. (ed.) 1977. *The Social Anthropology of Radcliffe-Brown*. London: Routledge and Kegan Paul.

Kuper, A. 1978. *Anthropologists and Anthropology; The British School 1922–1972*. London: Penguin.

Luhmann, N. 1982. *The Differentiation of Society*. New York: Columbia University Press.

Luhmann, N. 1990. *Essays on Self-Reference*. New York: Columbia University Press.

Malinowski, B. 1944. *A Scientific Theory of Culture*. Chapel Hill, Carolina: University of North Carolina Press (reprinted, 1960).

Marcuse, H. 1968. *One-dimensional Man*. London: Verso.

Merton, R. K. 1968. *Social Theory and Social Structure*. New York: The Free Press (enlarged edition).

Parsons, T. 1937. *The Structure of Social Action; A Study in Social Theory with Special Reference to a Group of Recent European Writers*. New York: McGraw-Hill.

Parsons, T. 1951. *The Social System*. London: Routledge and Kegan Paul (reprinted, 1979).

Parsons, T. 1960. Pattern variables revisited: A response to Robert Dubin. *American Sociological Review* 25 (4), 467–83.

Parsons, T. 1966. *Societies: Evolutionary and Comparative Perspectives*. Englewood Cliffs, NJ: Prentice-Hall.

Parsons, T. 1977. *The Evolution of Societies*. Englewood Cliffs, NJ: Prentice-Hall.

Radcliffe-Brown, A. R. 1952. *Structure and Function in Primitive Society*. London: Cohen and West Limited (reprinted, 1971).

Radcliffe-Brown, A. R. 1958. *Method in Social Anthropology*. Chicago: University of Chicago Press.

Radcliffe-Brown, A. R. 1977. *The Social Anthropology of Radcliffe-Brown*, ed. A. Kuper. London: Routledge and Kegan Paul.

Rocher, G. 1974. *Talcott Parsons and American Sociology*. London: Thomas Nelson (originally in French, 1972).

Sztompka, P. 1986. *Robert Merton: An Intellectual Profile*. London: Macmillan.

3

The Enigma of Everyday Life
Symbolic Interactionism, the Dramaturgical Approach and Ethnomethodology

In the previous chapters I discussed two theoretical traditions which tend to focus upon macro-sociological issues, dealing with those societal entities which transcend the routines and contingencies of our daily life. In a sense, this picture dominated the sociological scene in the 1950s, and probably added to an increasing, though fragile, sense of self-assurance amongst sociologists. Whereas social psychology was thought to deal merely with the empirical study of interactions between individuals, to sociology was attributed the pivotal task of unmasking latent functions or hidden societal structures stretching over long periods of time. Back in the early nineteenth century, Auguste Comte, never missing an opportunity to express his feelings of grandeur, christened his own child, *la physique sociale* or *la sociologie*, as nothing less than the queen of sciences. During the heyday of structuralism and functionalism, and after having lost part of its dominance, sociology considered itself still to be the head of the social sciences. Soon, however, even that title had to go.

The pretension to supremacy disappeared once sociologists were forced to recognize the sociological importance of a number of studies which were traditionally considered only to be relevant to social psychology. Three schools are significant here, all distinctly American, but each conceptually very different from the other. The first school, often referred to as 'symbolic interactionism', goes back to pragmatism in philosophy and in particular to the work of the American philosopher G. H. Mead (1863–1931); other influences include Georg Simmel (1858–1918) and G. H. F. Hegel (1770–1831). The second school, the so-called 'dramaturgical approach', centres around Erving Goffman's (1922–82) writings. Mead, Simmel and Durkheim had a significant impact on Goffman's thought. The third school, headed by Harold Garfinkel (1926–), answers to the unfortunate name of 'ethnomethodology'.

It is philosophically rooted in, *inter alia*, Alfred Schutz's phenomenology and the later Wittgenstein.

If macro-sociology lost its monopoly in the 1960s, it did not happen all at once. Once the ideas of symbolic interactionism, the dramaturgical approach and ethnomethodology became widespread within the sociological community, they received mixed and extreme responses. For some the new creeds represented innovative and challenging alternatives to the hypothetico-deductive and structural-functionalist 'dogmas' of the day. But others saw the new approaches as trivial, as stating the obvious, or as new wine in old barrels. More extreme critics challenged their alleged subjectivist and individualistic biases as nothing less than heresy from a sociological point of view. At the time there was no decisive winner in this battle, but attitudes have since changed. Some of the concepts and methods introduced by these new approaches have gradually filtered through, and are now considered respectable alternatives, which, in their turn, lead to interesting new developments. This gradual acceptance is demonstrated by their usage in recent attempts to develop a grand theory of society. Jürgen Habermas's theory of communicative action makes use of symbolic interactionist notions, and Anthony Giddens's structuration theory relies heavily on Goffman's dramaturgical approach and ethnomethodology (see chapters 4 and 6).

Symbolic interactionism

As mentioned above, symbolic interactionists depended on Mead's work. Although some would argue that they use a particularly idiosyncratic reading of it, an exposition of Mead's social psychology acts as an important stepping-stone towards understanding the full scope of symbolic interactionism. Although the term itself was only coined by Herbert Blumer in 1937 and the movement was not in full swing until the 1960s, Mead was a contemporary of Durkheim and Weber.

Mead studied at Oberlin College, Harvard, Leipzig and Berlin, and taught most of his life alongside John Dewey in the philosophy department of the then newly founded University of Chicago. Mead and Dewey became close friends, regularly exchanging ideas; this explains, to some degree, the similarities of their respective philosophies. However, where Dewey's influence was prominent in philosophy and education, Mead's work was to be remembered especially for its contributions to core issues in social psychology and sociology. Whilst Dewey was very prolific and, at an early age, already the rising star of American philosophy, Mead, although an inspiring teacher, clearly suffered from writer's block. He never completed a book or monograph and only published his first fully developed article at the age of forty. He only gained wider renown posthumously through the publication of a number of books based on his lectures. Amongst these 'student notes', *Mind, Self and Society* has been particularly important for our understanding of the relationship between language, social interaction and reflectivity.[1] Less widely known, but still of some interest to sociologists, is the enigmatic and vast *The Philosophy of the Act*, which links insights from evolutionary theory with Mead's own 'social behaviourism'.[2] For those interested in the philosophical problem of time, there is the even more obscure *The Philosophy of the Present*, Mead's somewhat muddled attempt to integrate evolutionary biology, Bergsonian philosophy, the theory of relativity and his own social psychology.[3] Finally, there is his sketchy *Movements of Thought in the Nineteenth Century* which, amongst other things, attempts to show the growing importance of time in science and philosophy.[4] Of these four volumes, *Mind, Self and Society* is undoubtedly the most accessible, although there are the inevitable ambiguities to be expected from a book not directly written by the author.

Although partly borrowed from nineteenth-century German philosophy, Mead's views, as expressed in *Mind, Self and Society*, were very much ahead of their time. For instance, by elaborating upon the social nature of the self and meaning, he anticipated some of the pivotal ideas in Wittgenstein's *Philosophical Investigations*. Long before the adequacy of positivist epistemology became an issue for the social sciences; Mead expressed doubts on the validity of J. B. Watson's behaviourism for social psychology, and developed an alternative scenario in which the notion of reflective self-monitoring plays a central role.[5] It comes as no surprise that those contributors to social psychology, such as Rom Harré and Paul Secord, who attempted to create a counterweight to the imperium of positivist and quantitative methods, drew heavily, not only upon the widely acclaimed 'later' Wittgenstein, but also upon Mead.[6]

One of Mead's core concepts is the self. The self is a feature of human beings, and of human beings only. It implies the capacity to be an object to oneself from an outsider's perspective.[7] Whilst writing this paragraph, for instance, I take up the attitude of the imaginary reader and thereby look upon alternative ways of expressing myself before choosing one of them. Strongly opposing the Cartesian picture of a 'solitary' self, one of Mead's central claims is that the self cannot but be a *social* self, bound as it is with social interaction and language.[8] It is fair to say that there are two ways in which Mead's concept of the self is a *social* self, although the distinction is not one drawn by himself. Let me call them the 'symbolic' and the 'interactionist' dimensions of the social self, for reasons which will soon become clear.[9] The interactionist dimension is the more straightforward of the two. It refers to people's capacity to adopt the attitude of others. It is indeed by seeing myself from the perspective of the imaginary reader that I am able to reflect upon the meaning of alternative ways of expressing myself.

The self is social not only because of its interactionist dimension, but also because of its dependency on the sharing of symbols, in particular language, with other selves. Here, the symbolic dimension comes into play. To take up the above example again, it is precisely because the reader and I share knowledge of the English language that I am able to anticipate what the meaning of my writings would be for him or her. Whenever signs are shared, Mead uses the terms 'significant gestures' and 'significant communication'.[10] Interaction amongst animals is limited to non-significant communication. The barking of one dog to another might elicit the latter's reaction, but that reaction is never anticipated by the first dog. Although my examples hitherto have been limited to language, Mead's symbolic world also involves 'non-verbal gestures' and 'non-verbal communication'. Greeting somebody, nodding, table manners, winking at somebody or ignoring that person – all of these are examples of non-verbal communication. They are not dissimilar to verbal communication in that they also involve the self and its attendant reflectivity, and rely upon a background knowledge of shared meaning for a successful outcome.

Obviously, the self ties in with self-reflection and what are currently called self-control and self-monitoring. By self-reflection, a term occasionally employed by Mead himself but left undefined, social psychologists refer to the ability of individuals to reflect upon their own circumstances, on the meaning and effects of their own (imaginary, possible or real) actions, on their beliefs about themselves, and on their beliefs about their beliefs. Self-control or self-monitoring are terms of more recent origin, not explicitly used by Mead, but clearly implied in his writings on the self. As it is now commonly used, self-control refers to the ability of individuals to direct their own actions on the basis of self-reflection; self-monitoring is that form of self-reflection directed towards self-control.[11] To consider again the example of writing, self-monitoring implies that one reflects upon the meaning of alternative ways of expressing oneself and then chooses from amongst these alternatives. The picture thus provided is very different indeed from Watson's behaviourism – the dominant argument in American psychology at the beginning of this century. Watson's view was unsubtle, if not crude, even by behaviourist standards: human actions were to be seen as analogous to animal behaviour, to be explained and predicted through a stimulus-response mechanism. Watson excluded concepts that are not immediately observable, such as mind or self. Mead's social psychology is very much directed against this extreme form of external determinism. People are different from animals because they have selves. The fact that the self is not immediately accessible to observation is not sufficient for it to be banned from scientific analysis. The self and reflectivity go hand in hand, and reflectivity implies that people's actions cannot be explained, let alone predicted, by a simple stimulus-response mechanism.

It is not uncommon for authors to become well known to the public for some of their less penetrating or less well-developed notions, and Mead is not an exception to this unfortunate pattern. His distinction between the 'I' and the 'me' occupies a central role in the secondary literature, whilst it remains ill-defined throughout *Mind, Self and Society*.[12] The distinction is reminiscent of Henri Bergson's dynamic and static self, and it is not unlikely that in this context Mead was directly influenced by the French philosopher, since, as can be inferred from some of his articles and lecture notes, he was well acquainted with Bergson's work.[13] On one reading, the 'me' stands for the societal, conservative components of the self, and the 'I' refers to its idiosyncratic, innovating aspects. If the 'me' sets the limits of the game through rules about which moves are allowed and which are not, the 'I' refers to the unpredictable nature of any move. But on another reading the difference between the 'I' and the 'me' is that the latter is by definition an object to the former. The 'I' can never be observed. Whenever one tries to catch the 'I', whenever one attempts to observe it, it vanishes, for that which one observes cannot but be the 'me'. Whenever the 'I' acts, it instantly transforms into the 'me' and is thus inevitably lost in the past. One can recall it, but only as the 'me'.

The interactionist dimension of the self has so far been discussed in terms of an individual's ability to take up the attitude of *single* others. However, one of Mead's central assertions in *Mind, Self and Society* is that people, looking at themselves from the perspective of other individuals, often take up the attitude of the 'generalized other'.[14] This refers to a collective whole, which transcends the idiosyncratic features of its individual members. Whilst writing, I see myself from the perspective of an imaginary reader in so far as he is representative of a larger community of English language readers. By taking up the attitude of the generalized other, one takes into account rules and conventions which belong to a larger community, not merely to isolated individuals. The generalized other thus points at the societal nature of the 'me' component of the self. However, this should not compel us to believe that the generalized other is merely constraining the 'I'. It is not *in spite of*, but *because of* a set of commonly shared rules and conventions that a creative 'I' is able to come into being. If there were no language, the creative poet would have no resources. Change presupposes structure – there can be no creation *ex nihilo*.

Mead's writings are not free from criticism. Given that Blumer's symbolic interactionism very much relied upon Mead's social psychology, I will deal with Mead's relevance for sociology when I discuss Blumer. I will now assess the validity of some core philosophical argumentations which Mead presented. Mead's central philosophical position is the notion that the self is social, but Mead was unclear as to what this meant exactly. Going through his writings, it is possible to attribute two separate meanings to this notion.

First, he made the strong claim that society and shared symbols are a necessary (and maybe sufficient) condition for the emergence of the self. Second, he made the weaker claim that it is fruitful, for the purposes of social psychology, to conceive of the self in relation to society and shared symbols. Mead's writings have shown convincingly the validity of the weaker claim, but they fail to provide any substantial support for the stronger anti-Cartesian thesis. At times, he seemed to assume mistakenly that evidence in support of the weaker claim necessarily implies evidence in support of the stronger claim.

There are similar ambiguities in his philosophical critique of behaviourist psychology. First, he presented an internal criticism. He seemed to claim in particular that the importance of reflectivity in human conduct makes for the inherent unpredictability of human behaviour to the extent that behaviourism fails to make the accurate predictions which it sets out to make. Second, he presented an external critique. The argument here is that, by neglecting the self, behaviourism cuts out that which is essential to human interaction. Taking the self into account leads to an enriched understanding of human conduct. Mead backed his external critique rather well, though not his internal critique. He did show successfully that his notion of the self leads to a more sophisticated understanding of the interface between individual and society. But nowhere in his writings can be found conclusive evidence or argumentation to support the statement that, due to the self, behaviour is inherently unpredictable.

As mentioned earlier, Mead's notion of a creative social self was directed against the dominant views of the day. It was Watson's determinism which had to be defeated, not by regressing into an introspective subjectivism, but by going beyond a Cartesian dualism of mind and body, and beyond an opposition between society and the individual. If behaviourism was always at the back of his mind, a similar mainstream argument was, half a century later, the target of the new school of symbolic interactionism. Symbolic interactionism emerged as a reaction against the dominant sociological practices of the day – against the alleged obsession with quantitative methods and structural-functionalist explanations (see chapters 1 and 2). Durkheim's heritage, and particularly his positivist methodology, was now considered too burdensome for the social sciences, whose subject area, because of its very nature, resists a positivist strait-jacket (see chapter 8).

Herbert Blumer (1900–87) was one of the instigators of the rebellion and, incidentally, also responsible for coining the term 'symbolic interactionism'.[15] He had been a student at Chicago, taught there for a while, and then moved to Columbia where he became a central counterpart to and critic of Merton's functionalism and Lazarsfeld's quantitative sociology. Blumer had been a student of Mead's, and was of the opinion that the sociological community had much to learn from him. Then followed a long journey of rediscovery

– not only of Mead, but also of Dewey and the origins of American pragmatism. As so often with rediscoveries, however, it was a somewhat coloured one, directed towards Blumer's ambitions for a new paradigm of sociology and inevitably reflecting his own ideas as well as those of Mead. Although it is an endearing feature of Blumer that he attributed so many of his own ideas to his mentor, and was sometimes justified in doing so, it has nevertheless unintentionally led to a slightly distorted reading of Mead.

Blumer's research programme is best approached through *Symbolic Interactionism*, a collection of essays in which he spelled out the core propositions of his theoretical argument. Four ideas are central to his version of symbolic interactionism. First, he followed Mead in stressing that individuals have selves and therefore have a capacity for 'self-interaction'.[16] Self-interaction comes into play whenever people make indications to themselves – whenever they address themselves and respond to the address before acting in public. Self-interaction enables them to evaluate and analyse things in order to plan ahead. So the individual's behaviour is not to be seen as a mere response to the environment; neither is it the outcome of need-dispositions, attitudes, unconscious motives or social values. Through interacting with themselves, people are able to anticipate the effects of alternative lines of conduct and thus to choose amongst them.

Second, Blumer deviated from Mead's social behaviourism in adding a sociological dimension, alluding, like Parsons, to Hobbes's problem of order. Parsons's answer to Hobbes's dilemma is essentially a Durkheimian one, referring as it does to the internalization of central social values; for Blumer, the persistence of established social patterns is contingent upon people's recurrent use of identical forms of interpretation.[17] One's interpretative scheme is, in its turn, dependent on confirmation by consistent interpretative schemes by others. By thus opening the path for a cognitive account of social order, Blumer anticipated Garfinkel's ethnomethodology. He went further than that, however. Compared to Garfinkel, he is more wary of portraying social life as nothing but social order, insisting that people regularly redefine each other's acts, possibly leading to new objects, new interactions or new types of behaviour.

Third, people act towards their environment on the basis of the meaning they attribute to it. For Blumer, meaning is not intrinsic to objects, neither is it a mere expression of the individual's mind.[18] Following the American pragmatic tradition, Blumer argued that the meaning of an object for an individual emanates from the individual's tendency to act towards it. Thus, a person's readiness to use a pencil as something to write with gives the object the meaning of what we call 'a pencil'. It follows that each object can have various meanings – potentially an infinite number of them. Grouse are not the same to a grouse-shooter, as to an animal rights campaigner. Again, they are different objects for a discerning gourmet who chooses them for his or her main course, a bird-watcher or a scholarly ornithologist. This tendency to act in a particular way is in its turn constituted, maintained and modified by the ways in which others refer to that object or act towards it. Within the household, for instance, numerous expectations by husband and children obviously reinforce a particular meaning of womanhood.

Fourth, Blumer used the term 'joint action' to refer to a 'societal organization of conduct of different acts of diverse participants'.[19] Examples of joint actions are a marriage, a lecture, a tennis match or a church service. Like Durkheim's concept of social fact which should not be seen as the mere outcome of psychological phenomena, Blumer's 'joint action', although made up of the component acts, is different from each of them, and from their aggregate. In other respects, however, Blumer's symbolic interactionism differs substantially from the view spelled out in Durkheim's *Rules of Sociological Method*, or it at least contrasts with a number of views that have traditionally been attributed to Durkheim. Durkheim's notion of social facts as *external* led to a picture of repetitive and pre-established forms of social life that are independent of an interpretative process. Blumer, instead, insisted that joint actions, however stable, are formed out of the component acts, and hence dependent on the attribution of meaning. So even in the most repetitive of joint actions 'each instance of such joint action has to be formed anew. The participants still have to build up their lines of action and fit them to one another through the dual process of designation and interpretation.'[20] Despite this, Blumer came closer to Durkheim's claim about the externality of social facts when he argues that people, whilst attributing meaning, draw upon pre-existing frames of interpretation. This Durkheimian notion allowed Blumer to allude to the historical dimension of joint actions. Each form of joint action, whether old or new, grows out of previous joint actions. As for Mead, there is no *tabula rasa* possible in Blumer's portrait of the social world.

Sociologists and social theorists have remained critical of Mead's social behaviourism and Blumer's symbolic interactionism. Underlying their scepticism is often the assumption that any substantial theoretical contribution to the study of society ought to take account of two core insights. First, there is the Durkheimian view that sociology should focus on the way in which people's conduct is constrained by social structure. Second, there is the Weberian position that sociologists should be sensitive to the unintended effects of purposive action. The critique of Mead and Blumer has often been that they do not account for either social structure or unintended effects, and thus that, however fruitful their work might be as a contribution to social psychology, they fail as a social theory. My view is that the critique is partly justified, and I will explain why.

Let me first consider the Durkheimian notion, and assess Mead's and Blumer's work in this light. There is no ambiguity in the case of Blumer: he deliberately avoided reference to structure. However, things are more complicated in the case of Mead. Contrary to the accepted view, I believe that Mead's writings do *not necessarily* neglect social structure; it simply depends on how one wishes to define structure. If one decides to follow the more recent trend in social theory to conceive of structures as rules and resources,[21] Mead's notion of the self and its attendant concept of the generalized other indeed imply the concept of structure. After all, to adopt the arguments of others implies the internalization of the community's implicit shared rules. Notwithstanding this fact, in so far as Mead's writings do recognize structure, they exhibit a one-sided, if not an impoverished, understanding of it. In Mead's work, the generalized other appears mostly as a medium which allows for (rather than precludes) agency, and as enabling (rather than constraining). Remember that, from a Meadian perspective, it is precisely because of the 'me' components of the self that the creative 'I' comes into being. There is no hint of the Durkheimian insight that structures, as unacknowledged conditions, constrain and determine people's actions.[22] From a Durkheimian view, language or mental frameworks can limit people's capacities to imagine what are possible forms of life or possible life choices. Moreover, even if certain choices are thought of as theoretically possible, the internalized generalized other is constraining in that it links particular imaginary choices with particular effects (see chapter 1).

Mead and Blumer have also been criticized for neglecting the concept of unintended consequences. Here again, critiques are partly justified. Mead and Blumer did occasionally mention that individuals are regularly faced with novel or unanticipated events, which lead to the emergence of reflectivity.[23] Moreover, in his writings on pragmatic philosophy, Mead also referred to the phenomenon of trial and error of scientific activities in which scientists learn from their mistakes.[24] Nevertheless, nowhere in Mead's or Blumer's work can be found a systematic attempt to see some of these unanticipated events or 'mistakes' as unintended or unforeseen effects of previous actions. Again, from the point of view of sociology, though not social psychology, this is a serious lacuna.

There are other ambiguities in Mead's and Blumer's work, which make it less useful for sociological purposes. Take, for instance, the notion of reflectivity, one of the key notions in symbolic interactionism. Mead and Blumer used this concept in at least two different ways. One is what might be called 'reflectivity of the first order', which involves tacit knowledge and self-reflective monitoring. Here, people reflect upon their actions, imaginary or real. When I speak, for instance, I reflect upon imaginary ways of expressing myself. This reflectivity of the first order is obviously prominent in *Mind, Self and Society* and *Symbolic Interactionism*, but occasionally both Mead and Blumer seemed to suggest a very different type of reflectivity, alluding to people's capacity to reflect not just upon their actions, but upon the underlying structural conditions of these actions. This 'reflectivity of the second order' ties in with explicit and discursive knowledge.[25] In Mead's and Blumer's work, both types of reflectivity blur into one. For sociological purposes, however, the distinction is indispensable. Reflectivity of the first order is central to our daily interactions, embedded as they are in routine practices and interwoven with the unintentional reproduction of structures.[26] Reflectivity of the second order is characteristic of 'high modernity' and, if developed by more than the single individual and part of a public-collective discussion, becomes a potential source for deliberate maintenance or deliberate change.[27]

How, from a sociological point of view, does Blumer compare to Mead? First, it is ironic that, whereas Blumer tried to demonstrate the sociological significance of Mead, he failed to take on board some of the latter's crucial sociological insights. Mead recognized the central role of the generalized other in reflectivity. It is due to shared meaning that people are able to anticipate the effects of alternative lines of conduct. The generalized other is absent in Blumer's picture, and that is a major weakness. Second, compared to Blumer, Mead's work erroneously presents a view of society that is too consensual, which may be reminiscent of more traditional orders, but surely inadequate for grasping more advanced societies. Blumer avoided presenting this picture, and rightly so. Some shared meaning might be necessary for any society to operate smoothly, but society today is characterized by the mutual co-existence of distinct cultural forms. There is certainly not just one set of implicit rules and procedures. Third, compared to Mead's purely philosophical enterprise, Blumer's strength lay in the way in which he was able to link his theory with issues of research methodology, as can be inferred from his criticisms of survey research and from his writings on the role of qualitative research methodology within a symbolic interactionist frame of reference. Loyal to the dynamic features of Mead's theory of the self and society, Blumer stressed the dynamic nature of social life – the continuous readaptation to an ever-changing environment – a feature that a number of contemporary methods failed to capture.

Erving Goffman's dramaturgical approach

Goffman's decision to study sociology was not a straightforward one. Goffman initially specialized in the natural sciences, then dropped out of university, toyed with the idea of going into films, and only later decided to take up postgraduate work in sociology and anthropology at the University of Chicago. Chicago had built up a considerable tradition of empirical social research; Everett Hughes and Blumer were amongst the inspiring teachers there. After graduating and publishing the widely acclaimed *The Presentation of Self in*

Everyday Life,[28] Goffman taught for ten years at the University of Berkeley, where he collaborated closely with Gregory Bateson. Bateson and his group studied, amongst other things, the phenomenon of mental illness, and there are, undoubtedly, similarities between their approach and Goffman's account of the mentally ill. Goffman subsequently moved to the University of Pennsylvania, where he developed a keen interest in the work of a group of sociolinguists. Again, this interest led to intense collaboration, and Goffman's writings increasingly dealt with the sociological dimensions of speech and conversation. His last book, *Forms of Talk*, is a compilation of essays dealing with this topic,[29] and conversational analysis often draws on Goffman's later work.

Goffman's work is sometimes referred to within the context of symbolic interactionism, and there are obvious reasons for linking the two. Both made a conscious attempt to avoid explaining human conduct in terms of system imperatives. Both saw as their object of study the interaction patterns between individuals. Both emphasized that these individuals have the ability to reflect upon their actions, and thus to manipulate their environment. However, there are also clear differences. Compared with Blumer's ambitious claims, for instance, Goffman consciously avoided the development of a consistent theoretical frame of reference (something he has often been criticized for). Also, in some respects, Goffman's work is even closer to Garfinkel than to Blumer, in particular when he referred to the way in which social order and predictability are skilful accomplishments of the individuals involved. Goffman's work, idiosyncratic and innovative as it was, cannot be written off as a mere appendix to symbolic interactionism, and it is worth elaborating upon its major themes.

Goffman has always been rather critical of the tendency to categorize or classify an author's work. This might explain why he hardly ever acknowledged major intellectual influences on his own work. Two influences are, however, beyond doubt: Simmel and Mead. Let me first deal with the German sociologist Simmel. His attention to the 'unnamed or unknown tissues' of social life struck a chord with Goffman. First, like Simmel, Goffman portrayed daily life as a highly complex enterprise in which human beings employ tacit and practical knowledge as they go along. Analogously to Simmel and anticipating some of Garfinkel's central assertions (see pp. 82–9), Goffman referred to the seen-but-unnoticed character of most of our mundane activities.[30] Second, Simmel's analysis of modern culture demonstrated the extent to which the anonymous character of modern life, rather than leading to an ethos of cynical manipulation, made for the emergence of interactions which are heavily dependent on complex mechanisms of secrecy and mutual trust. Simmel's starting point is that for interaction between modern, urban individuals to be possible they need a minimum of information about each other. However, even as each individual attempts to obtain information about others, so must the information which others receive from him or her be controlled.[31] Goffman presented a similar view. People are constantly monitoring themselves, masking bits of their selves and accentuating other aspects. The way we dress, the way we speak, our gestures – all these are meant both to convey and conceal who we are.

This brings me to Mead's influence. Mead and Goffman both portray a dynamic self, actively intervening in the world. Like Mead, Goffman accentuated the extent to which people are reflective beings, able to monitor their actions, and thus to manipulate their surroundings. Remember that Mead acknowledged that people share meaning, and are thus able to anticipate the effects of alternative imaginary courses of action. Goffman's portrait of social life assumes this Meadian framework. The existence of what Mead called a generalized other is indeed a *sine qua non* for the successful masking and presenting of the self. Without shared meaning, the subtle mechanisms of concealment and revelation would break down.

Goffman's interest was in 'encounters'; that is, face-to-face interactions where people are constantly in the physical presence of others. Encounters can involve 'unfocused' or 'focused' interaction, the distinction being mainly a matter of absence versus existence of mutual awareness amongst the participants involved.[32] Reminiscent of Mead's account of the self and role-taking, Goffman argued that, in interaction, human beings are continuously attending to their actions whilst adopting other people's views. A brief account of his *The Presentation of Self in Everyday Life* will demonstrate how his analysis of encounters works.

Goffman analysed encounters by drawing upon metaphors from and analogies with the theatre, hence the reference to his work as dramaturgical. He was, of course, not the only one to do this. Shakespeare is renowned for portraying social life by means of role-playing. Ralf Dahrendorf's concept of *'homo sociologicus'* draws upon a similar picture. However, analogies with acting and the stage have often led to a picture of social life as somehow predetermined. This is surely not the case in Goffman's dramaturgical approach. In his view, it is fair to say, people do not merely follow a script, and in so far as they do, they are also the author of that very same script. Hence 'performances', Goffman's main topic of research, are defined by him as all activities by individuals which serve to *influence* the 'audience' within the encounter.[33] In his view, these performances are rule-governed, in that rules refer to tacit, practical codes with respect to appropriate behaviour.

The 'front' is that aspect of the performance which, in a 'general and fixed fashion', helps the audience to define the situation.[34] There are two important aspects to a front: the setting and the personal front. The setting, 'the scenic parts of expressive equipment', refers to background items which provide the scene and 'stage props' for the action to take place; for instance, *décor*. Whereas the setting is usually linked to a particular place, the 'personal front' refers to those items which are intimately linked to the performer and which therefore are likely to follow him or her around; for instance, body language or speech patterns. Personal front can be divided into 'appearance' and 'manner'. Appearance refers primarily to the social status of a performer, but it also indicates his or her 'temporary ritual state'; for instance, whether he or she is involved in work or in leisure, or how busy he or she is. Manner indicates which role the performer intends to play in the forthcoming inter-action; for instance, an aloof manner might indicate a reduced commitment on the part of the performer. Normally, people expect some consistency between setting, appearance and manner, but sometimes this is not the case, which can lead to quite humorous situations – for instance, where somebody puts on a manner out of synch with his or her social status. It is characteristic of social fronts that they are abstract and general, applicable to different situations. In this context, Goffman gives the example of white lab-coats commonly used in many professions, creating an aura of 'professionalism' and reliability.[35]

In general, whilst interacting, people have to dramatize their activities in order to give the impression that they are performing well and that they have things under control. Sometimes the two are not compatible. A student who focuses on conveying to a teacher that he or she is listening might exert so much time and energy doing so that little of the teaching is absorbed. Part of this dramatization is that people, during their performances, tend to give expression to the 'officially accredited values of society', a habit obvious from examples of those who aspire to the lifestyle of their social or eco-nomic superiors (or at least what they believe that lifestyle to be). Some-times people downplay their qualities, such as in the case of teenagers who, in the company of members of the opposite sex, may play at being rather naïve and silly. In both these scenarios, people often have to conceal those actions or signs that are inconsistent with the yearned for standards.

Whereas the above might appear highly individualistic, Goffman intro-duces the concept of 'team' to refer to a group of people who co-operate to maintain a particular definition of a situation. Teams have certain character-istics in common.[36] They imply loyalty and competence by each of the individuals involved, since a failure by one of them might be threatening for all. Goffman also introduces space into the analysis, the concept of region referring to any place which indicates the barrier between what is visible to the audience and what is not.[37] Whereas performances take place in the front region, the back regions involve supporting or preparatory activities for the front region. The back region provides the means for an emotional outlet for the front region, an obvious example being the waiter who politely takes orders, but once in the kitchen expresses his contemptuous feelings for the customer. Goffman introduces the concept of 'impression management' to summarize the above mechanisms.[38] Individuals tend to control the way in which they are perceived by others through a number of devices. There are, first of all, the 'defensive attributes and practices', including, for instance, 'dramaturgical loyalty', which means that team members have to be able to trust each other and to keep secrets. Second, there are the 'protective practices'. Here, through tact, it is the audience itself that helps the performers save their show. An example of this counter-intuitive claim is the case where the audience voluntarily stays away from back regions, or where people display tactful inattention once confronted with embarrassing situations. A third type of device refers to the fact that performers have to be sensitive to any hints provided by the audience so that they can alter their behaviour accordingly.

In other works, Goffman elaborated upon the rule-governed nature of the social world, drawing a number of central distinctions: between symmetrical and asymmetrical rules, between regulative and constitutive rules and, above all, between substantive and ceremonial rules.[39] Compared to asymmetrical rules, symmetrical ones imply reciprocal expectations. Whereas regulative rules provide people with behavioural guidelines in particular circumstances, constitutive rules provide the context in which regulative rules might apply. Whereas substantive rules direct behaviour with respect to those areas of life which seem to have significance in their own right, Goffman's interest was directed towards those rules which he coined 'ceremonial' and which are directed towards conduct in matters which have, at most, secondary significance by themselves. These rules, however trivial at first blush, are central to sustaining feelings of psychological security and trust. Goffman distinguished between two components of such ceremonial rules: demeanour and deference.[40] The latter refers to the way in which people present themselves as reliable and able to be counted upon. The former refers to the way in which people sustain ontological security and trust by expressing appreciation through 'avoidance rituals' and 'presentational rituals'. Avoidance rituals keep intact the ideal spheres (Simmel's terminology) surrounding the individuals: silencing embarrassing episodes are one of them. Presentational rituals are positive tools for honouring individuals through, for example, salutations, invitations and compliments.

A central notion in Goffman's work is that of 'situational propriety', referring to the way in which the meaning of actions or concepts is dependent on the context in which they emerge.[41] This notion ties in with a previous point in that, as human beings, we gradually learn practical and tacit knowledge which enables us to understand the meaning of actions within a particular context. Many manifestations of mental illness demonstrate situationally inappropriate behaviour in that the very same conduct might have been acceptable were the context a different one. The notion of practical and tacit knowledge also ties in with Goffman's concept of 'involvement', referring to the way in which people are able to give or withhold attention to others in a given situation. Involvement ties in with two other notions: accessibility and civil inattention. The former refers to our tacit knowledge with respect to the degrees of availability towards strangers and acquaintances, whereas the latter refers to our ability to acknowledge the presence of strangers whilst avoiding prolonged attention through a sign of deference. Civil inattention is one of the ways in which strangers mutually reinforce feelings of trust and of relative predictability. This becomes especially obvious whenever civil inattention is not obeyed, often a sign of outright hostility on the part of the person who breaks the rule, and which results in the other party feeling uneasy and distraught.

For a long time, social theorists have neglected Goffman's work for three reasons. First, some stated that, although he introduced a wide range of new concepts, his work lacks a consistent theoretical frame of reference. His work is descriptive. At best, the theory is implicit in it; at worst, the theory is absent. Second, some critics have stated that Goffman expressed nothing new. There are two sides to this critique. On the one hand, it is argued that a significant number of Goffman's insights had already been made by social scientists and novelists who preceded him. On the other hand, some objected to the fact Goffman's work states the obvious: it articulates what every socially accomplished person already practically knows. Third, it has been argued that Goffman's concept of the self is not a universal one. His framework is indicative of modern western culture, 'other-directed' as it is, in which people cynically stage things, constantly calculating and manipulating their environment, and in which other individuals are treated as mere objects.

These criticisms are only partly justified. With regard to the first, it is worth mentioning that Goffman did not intend to be a social theorist, and that he was actually rather hostile to the enterprise of grand theory. He would probably have been sympathetic towards Nietzsche's dictum that 'any system is a lack of honesty', but it does not follow from this that his work is altogether irrelevant for the purposes of social theory. Any study of social life rests upon some theory, and this applies particularly to perceptive analyses like Goffman's. More recently, social theorists such as Giddens have tried to reveal the core theoretical propositions which underlie Goffman's argument. Giddens's view is that Goffman shows that social order is contingent upon the constant implementation of a vast array of complex rules and assumptions which people draw upon without being immediately aware of them. The implementation of these rules tends to interlink with people's need for a feeling of ontological security. I will deal with this interpretation in the next chapter. Some people would insist that this is Giddens's view, not Goffman's. Be that as it may, Giddens's reading is certainly not incompatible with Goffman's analysis. Hence, although Goffman does not wish to present a theory, and although there is a debate as to what his theory might be, his writings are nevertheless relevant to social theory. They can inspire and have inspired those who wish to develop a grand theory.

With regard to the second criticism, it is not within the scope of this book to deal with the question of how much others adumbrated Goffman's ideas. An intellectually more challenging question is whether Goffman stated the obvious or not, and whether this affects the relevance of his work. In some respects, he did express that which is already 'seen-but-unnoticed'. Many of his observations are articulations of those trivial aspects of daily life which remain unnoticed by the individuals involved, but this does not make them insignificant for the purposes of social theory. Goffman has provided insights into the complex interrelationship between self-presentation, trust and tact, and there is a growing recognition amongst social theorists, such as Giddens and Randall Collins, that these notions are central to the production of social order and predictability in daily social interaction. Giddens and Collins over-state the case for Goffman by adopting a vague notion of social order. There are basically two meanings to order. One is politico-strategic order, referring to a relative absence of dissensus and disagreement concerning the distribu-tion of scarce goods or power. The other is symbolic order, referring to a kind of agreement concerning the meaning of objects and actions, and, relatedly, to the co-ordination of everyday interaction. Goffman's work might be relevant for the explanation of symbolic order, though not for dealing with politico-strategic order, and it goes without saying that the latter does not follow from the former. So to say that Goffman's work provides insights into the production of order *in toto* is wrong. However, his writings certainly help to explain symbolic order and are thus relevant to social theory.

With regard to the last criticism, I wish to make three points. First, it is probably true that Goffman's view is deeply ingrained in modern western culture. But *any* conceptual framework or analysis about society shares some presuppositions with the culture in which it arises. So this argument in isolation cannot be held against Goffman. Second, without question Goffman's examples are specific to the cultural settings which he was describing, but this does not imply *ipso facto* that his work is ethnocentric. As a matter of fact, a significant number of *concepts* which he employed can be and have been applied to understand other cultural settings as well. Third, it is not true that Goffman relied upon the notion of an atomistic, calculating self. For instance, the individuals portrayed have a strong emotional commitment towards their presentation of the self. Through tact, they help others with *their* presentation of the self – and they trust others to do the same. These individuals are far removed from cynical, manipulative individuals.

Let me summarize the above. For a long time, Goffman was considered a maverick, the *enfant terrible* of American sociology. He was seen as a novelist or impressionist. Only more recently has he been presented as a reluctant theorist. Isaiah Berlin famously described Tolstoy as somebody who 'was by nature a fox, but believed in being a hedgehog'[42] – that is, while Tolstoy aimed to present a single organizing principle, his thought was actually extremely scattered and diffuse. Some have presented Goffman in opposite terms. They argue that while he conceived of himself as fascinated by the minutiae of daily existence, he could not help presenting a bigger picture. I am sympathetic towards this reading. But it should also be remembered that, unlike Blumer, Goffman himself did not wish to address core questions of social theory, and that there is no systematic attempt at theory-building in his work. This leaves his writings open to various interpretations.

Ethnomethodology

The name 'ethnomethodology' was coined by Harold Garfinkel, who founded a new sociological school under that banner. Although some recent ethnomethodologists deviate slightly from Garfinkel's initial party line, his work remains very much associated with the school. Garfinkel originally carried out doctoral work at Harvard under the supervision of Talcott Parsons. Garfinkel had already developed some ideas in his doctoral dissertation which were to become prominent in his later work.[43] He subsequently joined the department of sociology at UCLA, where he inspired many postgraduates and built up a thriving research centre. The publication of his *Studies in Ethnomethodology* in 1967 led to a worldwide interest in the newly founded school.[44] Other scholars were to follow the new creed: well-known ethnomethodologists include Deirdre Boden, John Heritage, Michael Lynch, Harvey Sacks and Don Zimmerman.

Symbolic interactionism and ethnomethodology share much in common. Both analyse patterns of daily interaction rather than broader social structures; both neglect longer historical spans; both emphasize the extent to which social order is a negotiated and skilful accomplishment of the individuals involved; both strongly oppose the Durkheimian notion that social facts have to be treated as things, analogous to physical objects; and both symbolic interactionism and ethnomethodology direct their attention instead to the sense-making practices in which people are involved – the way in which meaning is attributed to the social world.

However, symbolic interactionism and ethnomethodology arise out of different philosophical traditions. Remember that symbolic interactionism was very much indebted to Mead's reflections upon the interaction between self and society. The intellectual influences on Garfinkel and his followers are more varied. There is, first of all, the influence of Parsons, especially his account of Hobbes's problem of order. Second, there is the influence of Alfred Schutz's phenomenology, in particular his concept of *epoché* of the natural attitude. There is, third, Mead's influence on Garfinkel and other members of the school. Mead had an impact on ethnomethodologists, both direct and indirect (via Schutz). Finally, there is the influence of the later Wittgenstein, in particular his discussion regarding the relationship between meaning and shared rules. Within the limited scope of this book, I will only concentrate on Garfinkel's contributions to ethnomethodology. He was especially influenced by Parsons and Schutz, and less so by Mead and Wittgenstein. I will therefore concentrate on the formers' impact.

Garfinkel and ethnomethodology are often seen in opposition to mainstream sociology, in particular to Parsons's frame of reference. It is undoubtedly true that Garfinkel rebelled against some aspects of Parsons's work, but the two also share a number of features. Their similarities and differences are closely bound together. First, Parsons's voluntarist theory strongly opposed those positivist accounts which saw people's action as biologically determined or as passive recipients to their environments.[45] In his action frame of reference, people attribute meaning to their surroundings, they have goals, they also have information about how to achieve these goals and they act accordingly (see chapter 2). Garfinkel likewise developed a view which conceived of individuals as exercising agency – not as mere products of social or biological factors. But Garfinkel presented a more 'cognitive' or 'reflective' account. He was interested in the tacit knowledge which people employ in order to make sense of reality, and, as such, affect reality. Whereas Parsons's action frame of reference played down the knowledgeability of people, Garfinkel attributed an important role to how people understand and reason.[46] From this follows Garfinkel and H. Sacks's notion of 'ethnomethodological indifference': whilst studying how people account for and produce reality, ethnomethodologists need to refrain from making judgements regarding the validity of people's sense-making practices.[47]

Second, one of the recurrent questions in Parsons's writings is how social order is brought about. This question was first raised by Hobbes, and Parsons considered it to be one of the core questions of any substantial theory of society. He thought that utilitarian frameworks could not answer Hobbes's 'problem of order'. The solution, so he argued, needs to be found mainly in Durkheim's work and to some extent in Freud's.[48] For Parsons, Durkheim has shown convincingly that the problem of order is resolved through the internalization of the central values and norms in the personality structure of the individuals involved. Values, which are internalized through socialization, have a lasting effect on both the ends of action and the means to achieve them. In general, people will not be able to adopt an instrumental orientation towards the values and norms which they have internalized. The internalization explains need-dispositions which cause people to act (see chapter 2). Garfinkel dealt with exactly the same question: how does social order come about? He found Parsons's answer unsatisfactory, however, and instead paid attention to the shared common-sense procedures by which people constantly interpret their surroundings. After all, 'ethnomethodology' literally alludes to the methods or procedures by which ordinary members of society make sense of and act upon their everyday lives.[49] From this angle, it became possible to see social order as contingent upon continuous interpretative acts by the individuals involved.

There is one obvious way in which Garfinkel differed from Parsons. Unlike most of current American sociology which was empirical and rather compartmentalized, Parsons was an incurable grand theorist, who occasionally carried out empirical research, but whose prime aim was to develop an overarching theory which would embrace a multitude of disciplines in the social sciences. Garfinkel, on the other hand, dealt with only a few questions, and he and his team carried out numerous empirical researches in order to answer those questions. Garfinkel and other ethnomethodologists recognized the empirical bent as central to their work. Examples of Garfinkel's researches are the well-known breaching experiments, his work on the 'accomplishment of gender', and his analysis of the 'documentary method of interpretation'.[50] All of these play a fundamental role in Garfinkel's intellectual development.

Besides Parsons, Garfinkel found most of his theoretical inspiration in the work of the banker-cum-philosopher Alfred Schutz (1899–1959). Schutz opposed the neo-positivist tendency to postulate a unity of method between the social and the natural sciences, arguing that the former deal with an already 'pre-interpreted' world which begs for an interpretative methodology.[51] Schutz's attempt was to merge Edmund Husserl's phenomenology with sociological concerns, trying to grasp the way in which individuals understand and make sense of the surrounding social world. Schutz followed Husserl's phenomenology in attributing importance to the 'natural attitude' and its attendant common-sense knowledge. A number of features are characteristic of the sense-making practices of people in daily life activities, and these become prominent once juxtaposed with the scientific way of making sense of the world.[52] For instance, contrary to scientific rationality in which one's own biography is reduced to a minimum, common-sense rationality is perceived from a particular individual perspective, specific to time and space. Whereas scientific rationality always doubts the facticity of the social world, common-sense rationality rests mainly upon the *epoché* of the natural attitude, which implies that the social world should be taken for granted unless disruptions or new events occur. A suspension of doubt is deeply ingrained in our daily life. Through the medium of a 'stock of knowledge at hand', predominantly social in origin, people approach the social world in terms of 'familiarity and pre-acquaintanceship'. Whilst interacting with each other, people assume 'the general thesis of reciprocity of perspectives'. Schutz went on to argue that, rather than remaining at the level of scientific rationality and imposing this onto the social world, sociologists should attempt to register the common-sense, practical rationality by which individuals make sense of and account for their surroundings. This idea was taken up by ethnomethodologists and acted as one of their pivotal methodological devices. Schutz's work and his distinction between different forms of rationality was, likewise, very prominent in Garfinkel's breaching experiments. These demonstrate the extent to which scientific rationality, once applied to ordinary daily situations, erodes the implicit presupposition of reciprocity of perspectives and eventually leads to disorganization, disruption and anomie.

For Garfinkel, what is crucial to Schutz's view is that, unlike scientists, people involved in everyday situations assume an undoubted correspondence between the world as it appears to them and the world as it is.[53] Furthermore, each individual expects other individuals to assume this correspondence and to act accordingly. In their daily lives, people draw upon an unquestioned 'stock of knowledge at hand' or 'common-sense understandings' through which they and their actions are typified. Typification ties in with the capacity of an individual to anticipate another's responses to his or her actions – a truly Meadian notion. Similar to Mead's notion of a 'world taken for granted', a person's stock of knowledge is taken to be 'self-evident' until 'further notice', until disruptions occur. Implicit in most daily interactions is also the 'et cetera' assumption – the assumption that we can reasonably expect things in the future to be as they were in the past. Garfinkel added the importance of Schutz's thesis of reciprocity of perspectives, alluding to both the 'assumption or idealization of interchangeability of standpoints' and the 'assumption or idealization of the congruency of relevances'. The former refers to the way in which any person takes for granted that others would see events in the same typical way if that person's here-and-now became theirs, and to the fact that others assume this as well. The latter refers to the fact that individuals assume that, in spite of their differences, they select and interpret the surrounding objects in an empirically identical manner. It also includes the fact that people implicitly assume that other people act in accordance with the same assumption.[54] This notion of intersubjectivity was to become one of the leitmotivs of ethnomethodology as it was thought to be crucial for understanding the reproduction of social order. It is people's mutual expectations which make for the unintended reproduction of society.

Ethnomethodologists study the routines of daily life. Ethnomethods refers to the way in which, in daily life, ordinary citizens draw upon a complex network of interpretative procedures, assumptions and expectations through which they make sense of and act upon their surroundings.[55] Garfinkel introduced the notion of 'reflectivity of accounts'. By this, he meant that people constantly make sense of their surroundings, and these sense-making practices are constitutive of that which they are describing.[56] Ethnomethods is achieved through tacit and practical knowledge, rather than discursive or theoretical knowledge. That is to say, ordinary citizens do not have to know the rules or procedures explicitly. They *know* the rules only in the sense that they are skilful in acting in accordance with them, but this differs from knowing the rules theoretically in the sense of being able to state them discursively. The 'seen-but-unnoticed' character of our knowledge in daily interactions is exemplified in Garfinkel's famous analysis of 'Agnes', who was born as a male, but in adolescence purposefully designed an idiosyncratic endocrinological configuration, and at the age of nineteen decided to have a sex-change operation. After biologically 'becoming' female, Agnes still had a long way to go. She had to learn a complex set of new rules and procedures about how to behave and speak as a woman. Whereas girls would gradually 'learn' this through practice, Agnes developed a more discursive knowledge about 'how to go on' as a female, similar to somebody who is learning a foreign language. Agnes is a fascinating study of the construction of gender.[57]

Indexicality is central here. The term 'indexical sign' was originally introduced by Charles Peirce and later developed by Y. Bar-Hillel, referring to the fact that the context in which a token is used provides meaning to that token. Analogously, Garfinkel used 'indexicality' and 'indexical expressions' to allude to the extent to which the meaning of objects, social practices and concepts depends on the context in which they arise.[58] It follows that his notion of indexicality demonstrates striking similarities with Goffman's concept of situational propriety. Part of people's tacit knowledge is indeed a capacity to grasp the meaning of objects or practices within a particular context, and, moreover, to infer meaning by 'creating' or 'attributing' a context. However, the creation of meaning is not a one-sided process. Indeed, in a manner reminiscent of the notion of the hermeneutic circle, people draw upon the context or situation to attribute meaning to practices, but the latter also enable people to create or sustain their sense of the context. This 'mutual elaboration of action and context' is central to Garfinkel's documentary method of interpretation, which I will discuss shortly.

Garfinkel is especially known for his empirical research, in particular his breaching experiments and the so-called documentary method of interpretation. Garfinkel's breaching experiments were designed to explore the consequences of disrupting the routines of daily life.[59] For example, students were asked to act as if they were lodgers at home. So the parents were confronted with children who acted according to rules and procedures which differed radically from what the parents used to expect from them. They were very formal with their parents, only spoke when spoken to, etc. The parents, who were unaware of the experiment, reacted with anger, discomfort and bewilderment. Garfinkel and his colleagues inferred two conclusions from these experiments. First, that people have a strong emotional allegiance towards the implicit rules and procedures upon which they continually draw. Second, they demonstrated the way in which the interpretative procedures are 'doubly constitutive' of the activities which they organize: the rules, expectations and assumptions not only make for the visibility of normal conduct in daily interaction, but also for the visibility of conduct which deviates from it. Once the rules are broken, people do not necessarily adjust their interpretative procedures, but instead tend morally to condemn the 'deviant'.[60]

Equally important is Garfinkel's concept of the documentary method of interpretation – a term borrowed from Karl Mannheim – and the related empirical research.[61] Analogously to the notion of the hermeneutic circle, Garfinkel's documentary method of interpretation alludes to a recursive mechanism in which people draw upon interpretative procedures to construct 'documentary evidences', which are, in their turn, employed to infer the interpretative procedures.[62] Whilst people draw upon interpretative procedures which make sense of reality, the very same framework remains intact and is reproduced, even in cases where the reality concerned is potentially threatening for that framework. For instance, students were asked to attend a counselling session: in spite of the fact that the counsellors gave random answers to their queries, the students said afterwards that they had had a great time and that they learned a lot about themselves. Obviously, they did not realize that this was a 'false' setting. The reason is that they drew upon an interpretative framework with background expectations about the social situation to be encountered; this framework helped them make sense of the situation and in such a way that those expectations remained intact in spite of the fact that the situation was an 'obvious' potential threat to the very same expectations.

For a long time Garfinkel and ethnomethodologists were regarded as irrelevant for the purposes of social theory. The study of mundane activities was seen as relevant for the purposes of social psychology, not for social theory. Many social theorists today conceive of Garfinkel's ethnomethodology differently. They recognize that its strength lies in its ability to account for social order as a skilful accomplishment of knowledgeable people. There is a growing consensus that the minutiae of everyday interaction may be central to the explanation of social co-ordination and cohesiveness (see chapter 4) – there is certainly some truth in that defence. Garfinkel has indeed shown that individuals have a remarkably strong emotional commitment to their interpretative procedures and expectations, and that they are reluctant to reassess their validity when confronted with disruptions. Furthermore, whereas mainstream sociology has treated common-sense knowledge as an epiphenomenon, Garfinkel has illustrated how it needs to be seen instead as a worthwhile topic of investigation.

There are, nevertheless, weaknesses to Garfinkel's ethnomethodology. First, he claimed to have answered more adequately than Parsons the age-old question of how social order is brought about. However, as with Goffman, whether he is successful in doing so depends entirely on the meaning of 'social order'. Like Goffman, Garfinkel's strength lies in accounting for the production and reinforcement of shared meaning. Like Goffman, however, Garfinkel's frame-work cannot explain a relative lack of dissensus regarding allocation of scarce goods and power. Whether Garfinkel's view is superior to that of Parsons depends on which aspect of order is focused upon. However successful Garfinkel might be in accounting for symbolic order, Parsons's scheme seems more appropriate for explaining politico-strategic order.

Second, partly because Garfinkel focused on people's 'natural attitude of everyday life', he failed to account for transformations in the underlying social structure. His empirical analyses have shown that most daily life activities involve the continuous application of shared commonsensical knowledge, and that, once confronted with potentially disruptive experiences, people tend to design complex mechanisms which enable them to restore order. Despite this observation, Garfinkel seemed to ignore the potential that people had, once confronted with novel experiences, to reflect upon the underlying interpretative procedures, rules and expectations previously drawn upon. In *The Structure of Scientific Revolutions* Thomas Kuhn demonstrated how scientists, faced with the accumulation of anomalous results, have a public-collective reflection upon the underlying rules and assumptions of their paradigm, leading to substitution by a new set of rules and assumptions.[63] All this is relevant for the main project of ethnomethodology. Ethnomethodologists set out to explain social order, whilst conceiving of the latter solely as an *unintended* accomplishment. However, the reproduction of structures can also be accomplished intentionally. Indeed, people's reflection upon the structures underlying their actions can lead to the *deliberate* maintenance of the very same structures.

Third, equally problematic is the absence of a substantial explanatory format in Garfinkel's work. He did not address the question *why* people become upset or outraged when rules or procedures are broken, or *why* they attempt to reinstate order when confronted with potential disruptions. In this sense, his ethnomethodological research is descriptive – begging for explanations, rather than providing them. This does not make Garfinkel's work insignificant for the purposes of social theory. However, it does imply that, if his work is to be of any use at all to social theory, it needs additional social-psychological back-up.

Fourth, Garfinkel's tendency to neglect problems of power, prestige and asymmetrical relations is another problem, as they are likely to be constitutive of some of the mechanisms that he investigated. Take, for instance, the documentary method of interpretation and, in particular, the case of the students and the counselling session. The general aura, authority and prestige which surround the practices of the professionals are likely to be constitutive of the disposition of students somehow to suspend disbelief once they enter the counselling session, and they are also constitutive of the tendency of the students to sustain this suspension even if the advice provided is less than satisfactory. It is, therefore, indicative that in Hans Christian Andersen's tale 'The emperor's new clothes', it takes an innocent child, not properly socialized yet, to reveal that the emperor is naked. The adults in the story, obviously more susceptible to the asymmetry in social relations, are apparently more inclined to suspend disbelief in the face of authority.

Further reading

As far as the social sciences are concerned, Mead's major ideas appear in his *Mind, Self and Society*. From a social-psychological point of view, the articles 'A Behaviorist Account of the Significant Symbol' and 'The Genesis of the Self and Social Control' are important, and they are both available in Mead's *Selected Writings*. For a brief, but adequate introduction to Mead's work, see chapter 3 in Schellenberg's *Masters of Social Psychology; Freud, Mead, Lewin, and Skinner*. Blumer's reading of Mead is spelled out in a number of articles in his *Symbolic Interactionism; Perspective and Method*. For a challenging overview of symbolic interactionism, there is Rock's *The Making of Symbolic Interactionism*. For a more detailed in-depth account of the debates surrounding symbolic interactionism, an interesting collection of articles can be found in *Symbolic Interactionism*, two volumes edited by Plummer. Schutz's *magnum opus* is undoubtedly *The Phenomenology of the Social World*, but for those who want a less philosophical introduction to a phenomenologically inspired sociology, there is also, by Schutz in collaboration with Luckmann, *The Structures of the Life World*. Garfinkel's style of writing is rather inaccessible and jargonistic, and therefore Heritage's *Garfinkel and Ethnomethodology* might be a *sine qua non* for understanding Garfinkel's *Studies in Ethnomethodology*. Leiter's *A Primer on Ethnomethodology* reads well, and is an excellent introduction to various concepts and themes in ethnomethodology; so too is Benson and Hughes's *The Perspective of Ethnomethodology*. With respect to Goffman, it is worth starting with his *The Presentation of Self in Everyday Life*, and then moving on to his *Asylums, Encounters, Stigma* and finally his *Strategic Interaction*. Philip Manning's *Erving Goffman* is a good introduction, linking Goffman to broader issues in social theory, though rather close to Giddens's interpretation. A more advanced secondary source on Goffman is *Erving Goffman; Exploring the Interaction Order*, edited by Drew and Wootton.

References

Baert, P. 1992. *Time, Self and Social Being; Outline of a Temporalised Sociology*. Aldershot: Ashgate.

Benseler, F., Hejl, P. M. and Köck, W. K. (eds) 1980. *Autopoiesis, Communication and Society: The Theory of Autopoietic Systems in the Social Sciences*. Frankfurt: Campus Verlage.

Benson, D. and Hughes, J. A. 1983. *The Perspective of Ethnomethodology*. London: Longman.

Berlin, I. 1967. *The Hedgehog and the Fox; An Essay on Tolstoy's View of History*. London: Weidenfeld and Nicholson.

Blumer, H. 1969. *Symbolic Interactionism; Perspective and Method*. New York: Prentice Hall.

Coss, H. (ed.) 1929. *Essays in Honor of John Dewey*. New York: Henry Colt.

Drew, P. and Wootton, A. (eds) 1988. *Erving Goffman; Exploring the Interaction Order*. Cambridge: Polity Press.

Durkheim, E. 1982. *The Rules of Sociological Method, and Selected Texts on Sociology and its Method*. London: Macmillan (originally in French, 1895; reprinted, 1992).

Garfinkel, H. 1952. The Perception of the Other: a Study in Social Order. Unpublished Ph.D. dissertation. Harvard University.

Garfinkel, H. 1963. A conception of, and experiments with 'trust' as a condition of stable concerted actions. In: *Motivation and Social Interaction* ed. O. J. Harvey. New York: Ronald Press, 187–238.

Garfinkel, H. 1967. *Studies in Ethnomethodology*. Englewood Cliffs, NJ: Prentice-Hall.

Garfinkel, H. 1974. On the origins of the term 'ethnomethodology'. In: *Ethnomethodology*, ed. R. Turner. Harmondsworth: Penguin, 15–18.

Garfinkel, H. and Sacks, H. 1970. On formal structures of practical actions. In: *Theoretical Sociology*, eds J. C. McKinney and E. A. Tiryakin. New York: Appleton-Century-Crofts, 338–66.

Giddens, A. 1984. *The Constitution of Society; Outline of the Theory of Structuration*. Cambridge: Polity Press.

Giddens, A. and Turner, J. (eds) 1987. *Social Theory Today*. Cambridge: Polity Press.

Giddens, A. 1989. *The Consequences of Modernity*. Cambridge: Polity Press.

Giddens, A. 1992. *Modernity and Self-identity; Self and Society in the Late Modern Age*. Cambridge: Polity Press.

Giddens, A. 1993. *New Rules of Sociological Method*. Cambridge: Polity Press (2nd edition).

Goffman, E. 1961. *Asylums*. Harmondsworth: Penguin.

Goffman, E. 1963. *Behavior in Public Places; Notes on the Social Organization of Gatherings*. New York: Free Press.

Goffman, E. 1964. *Stigma*. Englewood Cliffs, NJ: Prentice-Hall.

Goffman, E. 1969. *The Presentation of Self in Everyday Life*. Harmondsworth: Penguin (reprinted, 1980).

Goffman, E. 1970. *Strategic Interaction*. Oxford: Basil Blackwell.

Goffman, E. 1972a. *Encounters; Two Studies in the Sociology of Interaction*. London: Penguin.

Goffman, E. 1972b. *Interaction Ritual: Essays on Face-to-face Behavior*. Harmondsworth: Penguin.

Goffman, E. 1981. *Forms of Talk*. Oxford: Basil Blackwell.

Harré, R. and Secord, P. 1972. *The Explanation of Social Behaviour*. Oxford: Basil Blackwell.

Harvey, O. J. (ed.) 1963. *Motivation and Social Interaction*. New York: Ronald Press.

Heritage, J. 1984. *Garfinkel and Ethnomethodology*. Cambridge: Polity Press.

Heritage, J. 1987. Ethnomethodology. In: *Social Theory Today*, eds A. Giddens and J. Turner. Cambridge: Polity Press, 224–72 (reprinted, 1990).

Kuhn, T. 1970. *The Structure of Scientific Revolutions*. Chicago: University of Chicago Press (2nd edition).

Leiter, K. 1980. *A Primer on Ethnomethodology*. Oxford: Oxford University Press.

Maines, D. R., Sugrue, N. M. and Katovich, M. A. 1983. The sociological import of G. H. Mead's theory of the past. *American Sociological Review* 48 (2), 161–73.

Mannheim, K. 1952. *Essays on the Sociology of Knowledge*. London: Routledge and Kegan Paul.

Manning, P. 1992. *Erving Goffman and Modern Sociology*. Cambridge: Polity Press.

Maturana, H. R. 1980. Man and Society. In: *Autopoiesis, Communication and Society: The Theory of Autopoietic Systems in the Social Sciences*, eds F. Benseler, P. M. Hejl and W. K. Köck. Frankfurt: Campus Verlag, 11–32.

McKinney, J. C. and Tiryakin, E. A. (eds) 1970. *Theoretical Sociology*. New York: Appleton-Century-Crofts.

Mead, G. H. 1907. Review of Henri Bergson's *L'Évolution créatrice*. *Psychological Bulletin* 4, 379–84.

Mead, G. H. 1929. The nature of the past. In: *Essays in Honor of John Dewey*, ed. J. Coss. New York: Henry Colt, 235–42.

Mead, G. H. 1934. *Mind, Self and Society. From the Standpoint of a Social Behaviorist*. Chicago: University of Chicago Press (reprinted, 1970).

Mead, G. H. 1936. *Movements of Thought in the Nineteenth Century*. Chicago: University of Chicago Press (reprinted, 1972).

Mead, G. H. 1938. *The Philosophy of the Act*. Chicago: University of Chicago Press (reprinted, 1972).

Mead, G. H. 1959. *The Philosophy of the Present*. Chicago: University of Chicago Press.

Mead, G. H. 1964. *Selected Writings*. New York: The Bobbs Merill Company.

Mischel, T. (ed.) 1977. *The Self: Psychological and Philosophical Issues*. Oxford: Basil Blackwell.

Mischel, W. and Mischel, H. N. 1977. Self-control and the self. In: *The Self: Psychological and Philosophical Issues*, ed. T. Mischel. Oxford: Blackwell, 31–64.

Plummer, K. (ed.) 1991. *Symbolic Interactionism* (volumes I and II). Aldershot: Edward Elgar.

Parsons, T. 1937. *The Structure of Social Action*. New York: McGraw-Hill.

Rock, P. 1979. *The Making of Symbolic Interactionism*. London: Macmillan.

Schellenberg, J. A. 1978. *Masters of Social Psychology; Freud, Mead, Lewin, and Skinner*. Oxford: Oxford University Press.

Schutz, A. 1962. *Collected Papers, Volume 1*. The Hague: Martinus Nijhoff.

Schutz, A. 1967. *The Phenomenology of the Social World*. Evanston, Ill.: Northwestern University Press (originally in German, 1932).

Schutz, A. and Luckmann, T. 1974. *The Structures of the Life-World*. London: Heinemann.

Simmel, G. 1950. *The Sociology of Georg Simmel*. Glencoe, Ill.: Free Press.

Turner, R. (ed.) 1974. *Ethnomethodology*. Harmondsworth: Penguin.

4
The Skilful Accomplishment of Social Order
Giddens's Structuration Theory

Although Anthony Giddens (1938–) has been one of the main contributors to Anglo-Saxon social theory since the early 1970s, he was initially trained as a psychologist. He subsequently switched to sociology for his postgraduate work, but in some respects he remained loyal to his initial interest in psychology. Whereas most social theorists before Giddens would 'snub' Goffman or Garfinkel for dealing with 'trivial' matters of day-to-day life, one of Giddens's recurring themes has been that grand theory can learn a great deal from the empirical study of these routine practices (see chapter 3). Furthermore, his structuration theory is heavily supported by an in-depth reading of Sigmund Freud's work, and of E. H. Erikson's and E. V. Sullivan's ego-psychology. R. D. Laing's notion of ontological security occupies an important role in structuration theory, and Giddens's more recent works on modernity deal explicitly with a number of psychological issues such as intensified forms of reflectivity.

Giddens transferred to sociology for his Master's at the London School of Economics. The LSE was one of the main centres for sociology in England at the time – Oxford and Cambridge were still reluctant to accept the social sciences as a full academic discipline. Sociology was in the ascendant, though, especially in the newer universities such as Leicester, where Giddens joined the Sociology Department as a lecturer in 1961, initially teaching mainly social psychology. Leicester was a lively, cosmopolitan department, and Giddens's senior colleagues included Norbert Elias, Ilya Neustadt and Percy Cohen. At a remarkably late age, with the appearance of *What is Sociology?*, Elias was to become one of the forerunners of a theoretical assault on the empire of Parsonian functionalism – a position which Giddens was to inherit soon after.[1] During that period in Leicester, Giddens wrote a number of articles with substantial bearing on empirical research. In general, the 'earlier' Giddens seemed less preoccupied with grand social theoretical issues, although his articles on suicide and his edited book *The Sociology of Suicide* were not devoid of conceptual considerations.[2]

Another (though less clear-cut) example of this earlier phase is his *Class Structure of the Advanced Societies* which deals with substantive issues that are related to the problem of class and class formation in modern society.[3] However, in many respects this work already belongs to what might be called a later stage in Giddens's intellectual development. It involves a critical commentary on theoretical issues in the work of the classics of the social sciences, and it aims (although tentatively) at developing his own social theory. Giddens introduces the now well-known concept of 'structuration' in this book, linking it with a discussion of the extent to which classes are produced and reproduced through social practices.

The beginning of Giddens's second phase more or less coincides with his move from Leicester to Cambridge University, where he started as a University Lecturer in 1969 and fifteen years later became Professor of Sociology, whilst holding a fellowship at King's College. From around 1970 onwards, Giddens's writings demonstrate an increasing interest in grand theory, focusing upon a few classical social theorists, mainly Marx, Durkheim and Weber. His first book is a critical analysis of the work of these authors.[4] He also wrote introductory books on Max Weber and Emile Durkheim.[5] Although these works do not lack originality, especially in their critical evaluation of the authors discussed, their aim is to elucidate sociological classics, rather than to elaborate a new systematic frame of reference for understanding social life.

This changed with the appearance of *New Rules of Sociological Method.*[6] The reference in the title to Durkheim's *Rules of Sociological Method* is, of course, not accidental. Giddens's aim is nothing less than to develop a non-positivist conceptual framework and methodology for the social sciences, through the analysis of hermeneutic authors such as H.-G. Gadamer, Schutz and Wittgenstein. *New Rules of Sociological Method* is indicative of the third phase in Giddens's writings. Although he still rigorously discusses other authors, exegesis has now become secondary, and his principal aim is to establish the contours of his own contribution to social theory.[7] Through his discussions of a wide variety of different intellectual traditions (from functionalism to Habermas), Giddens gradually introduces his structuration theory. Although the two volumes of *A Contemporary Critique of Historical Materialism* deal with aspects of Marx's theory of history, they are also mainly directed towards the development of his own theory.[8] This third phase came to a close with *The Constitution of Society*, which is, as its subtitle suggests, considered to be Giddens's *magnum opus* in grand social theory.[9]

Giddens's fourth phase is marked by a radical break from his previous works. Whereas his earlier books focus on general social theory, Giddens now deals with the sociology of culture and in particular with problems related to modernity and detraditionalization. This new phase was initiated by lectures given at the Californian Universities at Stanford and Riverside in the late 1980s, and led to the publication of *The Consequences of Modernity*, in which Giddens explores the pivotal features of high modernity and their relationship with the so-called post-modern condition.[10] He went on to develop similar themes, focusing on concurrent changes at the level of the personality structure.[11]

The publication of *Beyond Left and Right* presumably heralds a fifth phase.[12] This work deals with the possibility of a new social democratic political agenda, taking into account recent societal changes such as detraditionalization and globalization. Giddens has always shown a keen interest in politics, but since the early 1990s he has become increasingly active in the British Labour Party. Some of the ideas in *Beyond Left and Right* inspired the British Prime Minister, Tony Blair, and influenced his policies. In general, Giddens's interest has moved beyond purely academic activities towards more practical issues. In 1997 he became the Director of the London School of Economics, a position that entails a broad involvement with educational policy matters in Britain and abroad.

In what follows I will focus on Giddens's third phase. That is, I will especially deal with his particular contribution to sociological theory – the so-called 'structuration theory'. Structuration theory is a general theory aiming to explore the interaction between social structure and human agency. It emerged in the late 1970s and early 1980s as a theoretical alternative to both structural-functionalist and interactionist perspectives (see chapters 1, 2 and 3). Although it is only associated with the work of Giddens, it would be mistaken to conceive of the theory as an isolated intellectual product. Indeed, some of the central notions of structuration theory were simultaneously developed by other authors. For instance, Giddens's argument shows striking similarities with Bourdieu's theory (see chapter 1).

Influences

Giddens's project is ambitious. He attempts to overcome a number of dualisms in social theory, for instance: the dualism between actor-orientated approaches and structure-orientated approaches, or between subjective and objective orientations. He integrates a wide diversity of very different disciplines: Martin Heidegger's existentialism, H. G. Gadamer's hermeneutics, Alfred Schutz's phenomenology, Harold Garfinkel's ethnomethodology and Michel Foucault's and Jacques Derrida's post-structuralism, to name only a few. Furthermore, his approach is aimed at replacing what he calls the 'orthodox consensus' which dominated sociology in the post-war period and which is characterized by its adherence to functionalist theory and positivist epistemology. But however wide-ranging Giddens's proposals are, it is important to remember that they did not arise out of an intellectual vacuum. Giddens's overall project was closely related to a number of other intellectual developments and a general dissatisfaction with some of the dominant views at the time. I will therefore indicate the extent to which his work should be considered within a broader movement in the social sciences (away from a previous consensus), and only deal later with the idiosyncratic features of Giddens's contributions.

Giddens's project follows a general trend away from positivist epistemology in the social sciences, and it is thus no surprise that positivism is often targeted in his work (see chapter 8). His concerns in this respect are not so much with general issues in philosophy of science, although he is aware, for instance, of Quine's critique of the alleged distinction between theoretical and observation statements, the problems with the verification theory of meaning, and so on. His interest is more with the distorted view of human conduct of what he calls the 'orthodox consensus' in the social sciences – a particular research programme, not necessarily explicitly articulated, which became dominant in the course of the twentieth century. Apart from the functionalist dimension, of which more in due course, the orthodox consensus courts the doctrine of naturalism which postulates a methodological unity between the natural and the social sciences. However unobtainable or unsatisfactory in practice, the way in which natural scientists operate remains the norm to be emulated by social scientists.

As will become clear later, Giddens believes a number of phenomenological insights have to be taken seriously, and that doing this jeopardizes the ambitions of the positivist tradition. People's conduct is simply not to be explained by referring to external societal factors acting upon them, as if these factors were not dissimilar from causes in the natural sciences. Giddens agrees with Harré and others who believe that lessons from the linguistic turn in philosophy led to a Copernican revolution in the social sciences: human conduct is no longer to be seen as pushed by external forces, but instead can only be understood in terms of reflective self-monitoring and tacit knowledge. Structures do not act upon people. Instead, people draw upon structures for the initiation of their actions.

Giddens rejects functionalism as vigorously as positivism (see chapter 2). Basically, he cites five arguments against functionalist explanations. First, functionalism somehow fails to conceive of social life as 'actively constituted' through people's actions, erroneously portraying individuals as 'cultural dopes'. Human agency is mistakenly subordinated to the process by which values are internalized in the personality structure of the individuals. Second, functionalism mistakenly attributes needs or 'functional exigencies' to social systems. Counterfactual arguments are the only ones in which it is defensible to talk about 'system needs', but close scrutiny shows that, in spite of *prima facie* similarities, their logical format differs from a functionalist type of argument. Third, whether in Parsons's work or in Merton's, the concept of power is secondary compared to the overriding role of norms and values. This lacuna is incompatible with Giddens's view; power plays a central role in his structuration theory. Fourth, functionalism fails to take into account the 'negotiated' character of norms and values. That is, value patterns and normative regulations can be (and often are) interpreted differently by various groups. Opposing interpretations are often due to conflicting interests in society.[13]

Finally, Giddens and functionalists differ particularly in the way in which they conceive of the relationship between time and social order. At least in its archetypal form, functionalist frames of reference tend to, implicitly or explicitly, conceive of social order by taking a snapshot of society. It is held that social order is revealed by analysing how different parts of a social system are (functionally) interrelated or related to a larger whole, and such an analysis does not involve the lapse of time. For understanding social change, a diachronic analysis ought to be adopted, but for understanding social order a snapshot will do. For Giddens, this view of the interrelationship between order and synchronic analysis is untenable. Functionalism disregards the insight that social order is produced and reproduced *through* time by knowledgeable agents. It erroneously equates time with social change, whereas time also implies the skilful production of order, and this production is due to tacit knowledgeability and practical consciousness on the part of the individuals involved.

Evolutionist theory in the social sciences is another of Giddens's *bêtes noires*. In his view, evolution, in order to be a distinctive explanatory frame of reference, should refer to a number of features. The first is the notion that there is an analogy or 'conceptual continuity' between social and biological evolution, and that there is a sequence of stages throughout history applicable to all societies. The second is the notion that there is a mechanism which explains the transition from one stage of society to another, often utilizing the concept of 'adaptation'. Giddens's main target for critique is this concept of adaptation, which, he argues, is either diffuse or vague.

Giddens's criticisms of evolutionism go, however, further than that. He asserts that any evolutionist perspective is in danger of drawing upon one of the following mistaken conceptions: 'unilinear compression', 'homological compression', 'normative illusion' or 'temporal distortion'. Unilinear compression is the erroneous belief that a statement about development in all societies can be inferred from the observation of sequences of stages in a particular society (or a limited number of societies). Giddens's objection is the standard argument against any inductivist reasoning: it is impossible to infer general laws from a finite number of observations (see chapter 8). Homological compression refers to the search for homology or structural identity between individual and societal development. Homological compression implies, amongst other things, that the earlier stages of societal development mirror the lack of complexity in early psychological development (see chapter 6). Giddens sees Freud, Marcuse and Elias as exponents of this view, and he argues against them on empirical grounds. For instance, he thinks that there is not enough evidence to support their argument that the 'psychic' organization between oral cultures and 'civilizations' differs significantly. Normative illusion is the erroneous tendency to understand economic or 'adaptive' power in terms of moral superiority. Many evolutionist theories implicitly or explicitly presume that more control (and more employment) of one's environment is a worthwhile aim. It might be true that contemporary societies have greater capacity to adjust to, or make use of, their environment, but this should not be seen as an unequivocally positive feature. Finally, temporal distortion refers to the inability to distinguish between 'history' and 'historicity', and therefore the mistaken tendency to reduce the lapse of time to change. One of the recurring ideas in structuration theory is that time also implies the production of order.[14]

Amongst the positive influences on Giddens's structuration theory are interpretative approaches to the social realm, in particular Schutz's phenomenology, Peter Winch's Wittgensteinian-inspired philosophy of the social sciences and Garfinkel's ethnomethodology (see chapter 3). Giddens argues that, because of its Durkheimian heritage and its naturalistic inclinations, the orthodox consensus disregarded the interpretative approaches as being outside the realm of a scientifically adequate explanation of the social. From a critical reading of these interpretative schools, a number of ideas and concepts are taken up by Giddens, and further incorporated within his broader framework. First, for him, sociology differs from the natural sciences in that it does not deal with a 'pre-given' universe of objects. People attribute meaning to their surrounding social world and act accordingly. It follows that sociology is characterized by a 'double hermeneutic': that is, sociology interprets its subject-matter, which is itself pregnant with meaning. Second, Giddens employs the notion of reflexivity. That is, he sees individuals as constantly attending to their actions, and regularly reflecting upon the conditions of these actions. He insists that people often incorporate this knowledge as they go along. Third, Giddens takes up the notion of tacit, mutual knowledge, and he links this with the concept of reflexivity. Individuals of the same culture share knowledge of their local social rules. This knowledge is not necessarily discursive or theoretical. It refers instead to skilled performances: to procedures of 'how to go on' in social life. Fourth, Giddens learns from these interpretative schools that structures should not be seen as merely constraining, but also enabling. Rather than conceiving them as an impediment to action, structures ought to be seen as a *sine qua non* for the emergence of agency.[15]

A second important influence is Goffman (see chapter 3). Giddens's argument is that Goffman's work has been misunderstood in a number of ways.

First, Goffman has been erroneously portrayed simply as a brilliant narrator, highly observant about the minutiae of social life, but whose work lacks intellectual unity. Against this view, Giddens argues that recurrent theoretical themes and preoccupations can be detected throughout Goffman's work. Second, Giddens opposes the view that Goffman's work is limited in scope, reflecting merely white American middle-class lifestyles. Giddens thinks that a number of Goffman's theoretical insights have more universal value than is often recognized. Third, it has sometimes been argued that Goffman portrays people as mere 'performers', cynically manipulating their social environment – a reflection, some would say, of the very amoral American middle class to which Goffman's analysis is restricted. Giddens argues that, rather than portraying social life as amoral, Goffman's analysis suggests the importance of trust and tact as crucial features of social interaction. In Goffman's work, Giddens finds a consistent attempt to draw our attention to the way in which people routinely 'repair' the moral basis of their interactions, through the use of tact, through 'remedial practices', through helping others to save face, and so on. It is this theme, in particular, that Giddens borrows for his structuration theory.[16]

A third source of influence is psychoanalysis and, in particular, Erikson's ego-psychology. Giddens is particularly interested in the early phases of Erikson's stage-theory of psychological development, seeing the first phase as one in which feelings of 'ontological security' are gradually instilled through warmth and affection. The unconscious is linked to people's avoidance of anxiety and their preservation of self-esteem. From an early stage onwards, trust is instilled within the personality structure of the child. By trust, Giddens understands here the psychological 'binding' of time and space in that the child learns that absence (of the mother) does not imply desertion. Later defences are constructed against other anxiety-provoking mechanisms such as shame, doubt and guilt. This form of generalized trust is the foundation for a stable personality, and, Giddens continues, it explains the close relationship between routines, rule-following and ontological security. This can also be used to explain the extent to which Garfinkel's experiments with trust upset the people who were subject to them.[17]

The sociological relevance of existentialism is relatively unexplored, and Giddens is a notable exception in this regard. For instance, his concept of agency as transformative capacity shows striking affinities with existentialist accounts of freedom, but it is especially with regard to the problem of time that he inherits existentialist notions. The German philosopher Heidegger has been a specific influence on Giddens in this respect. Giddens borrows Heidegger's distinction between ontology and epistemology, and, relatedly, between 'ontic' time and time at an existential level. Rather than conceiving of time as a measurable unit or 'framework' of objects or activities, time is constitutive of being. Rather than a 'contentless form' in which objects exist,

time and space have to be defined in terms of 'presencing'. That is, time–
space intervals are not instants, but '*structured differences* which give form
to content, whether this be hours on a clock, notes in a musical rhythm, or
centimeters on a ruler'.[18] From Heidegger, Giddens also recalls that, as contrasted with animals, human beings are aware of the finitude of their existence (*Sein zum Tode*). Furthermore, compared with animals, human beings,
through language, are able to transcend presence – to go beyond the immediacy of sensory experience. The interpenetration of presence and absence is
indeed a central feature of the time-related components of Giddens's theory
of structuration; it also appears in his use of time-geography.[19]

Giddens's interest in time-related topics is reflected in his discussions of
time-geography, especially Torsten Hägerstrand's, Allan Pred's and Tommy
Carlstein's. Whereas time and space have been traditionally conceived of as
mere environments of action, time-geography demonstrates how social systems are constituted across time and space. Time-geography pays attention
to the constraints of people's routine movements, in circumstances of co-
presence, through time and space. Amongst these constraints are 'corporeality'
(for instance, the mere fact that the human body is one and cannot be divided),
the finitude of the life span (relatedly, the fact that time is a scarce resource),
people's limited ability to do many things at once, the fact that movement in
space implies movement in time, and the limited 'packing capacity' of time
and space (the fact that only a limited amount of objects can be accommodated within a particular zone of time and space). Hägerstrand's time–space
maps draw patterns of movement of individuals within the above constraints.
However, Giddens deplores the fact that, whilst time-geography tends to
conceive of individuals as purposive beings, little attention is actually given
to the nature and origins of these intentions or goals. Furthermore, time-
geographers tend to take 'stations' or 'domains' as 'given'. They overemphasize the constraining features of social structure, and neglect its enabling
characteristics. Also, time-geography has an underdeveloped conception of
power.[20]

Structuralism and post-structuralism had an important effect on Giddens's
intellectual development, although he was not uncritical of these ideas (see
chapter 1). Saussure's distinction between speech and language is central to
Giddens's own distinction between system and structure, and he also draws
upon the distinction between the syntagmatic and the paradigmatic. Although
he does not accept the structuralist tendency to ignore the relation between
meaning and practice, overall he is sympathetic to its holistic theory of
meaning. Related to Giddens's rejection of the phenomenalist features of
positivist epistemology, is an apparent acceptance of the structuralist commitment to realism (see chapter 8). Structuralism, as a social theory, teaches
Giddens the importance of unacknowledged conditions of purposive conduct. What structuralist (and post-structuralist) authors lack, for Giddens, is

a theoretical account of agency and praxis, and their relationship to social reproduction. On the same point, whilst fully exploiting the Durkheimian notion of structural constraint, 'structural sociology' tends to ignore the fact that social structure also empowers the individual. Again and again, Giddens insists that far from structure precluding agency, it is the precondition for its emergence. Furthermore, some structuralists, such as Lévi-Strauss, tend to confuse discursive and practical consciousness, mistakenly assuming that if something is not discursively available then it must be unconscious. In contrast, Giddens's structuration theory acknowledges the central role of practical consciousness in everyday interaction.[21]

Structuration theory

Giddens attempts to link different temporal levels of analysis. At one end of the spectrum there is Schutz's *durée* of day-to-day experience, referring to the repetitive and routine nature of our daily activities. At the other end of the spectrum is Braudel's *longue durée* of institutional time, referring to the relatively invariant structures which stretch over long periods of time. In between these two spans of what Lévi-Strauss would call reversible time is the life span of the individual. Its irreversibility is captured by Heidegger's *Dasein* and its attendant notion of the finitude of people's existence – its *Sein zum Tode*. Giddens's work aims at linking these different temporal spans and thus demonstrates how, for instance, reproduction at the level of Schutz's *durée* contributes to reproduction at the level of Braudel's *longue durée*. One of the upshots of this is that Giddens's structuration theory aims at transcending the traditional micro–macro divide within sociology. In social life these three temporal spans intersect, and this has to be accounted for.[22]

A second opposition which Giddens attempts to overcome is that between what he calls 'institutional analysis' and the 'analysis of strategic conduct'. Both types of analysis are arrived at through 'methodological bracketing'. Institutional analysis is achieved by bracketing strategic action. It investigates the recursive model of reproduction of structures, and it does not treat people as knowledgeable or purposive individuals. The study of strategic action, on the other hand, is achieved through placing the institutional realm under an *epoché*. It studies how people draw upon rules and resources for the continuation of their activities. Here, people are treated as active agents who know a great deal about social life. Whereas social theory has been divided between strategic and institutional analyses, Giddens's structuration theory aims at attributing equal status to both types of analysis. Neither is more important than the other; both are necessary for a full understanding of the workings of society.[23]

Within this broader context, Giddens's structuration theory becomes understandable. One of his key notions refers to the so-called duality of structure, which postulates a particular relationship between social structure and human agency. The duality of structure, of which more in due course, allows Giddens to bind the different temporal levels, and to attribute equal status to strategic and institutional analysis. Before elaborating on this, I first need to clarify Giddens's conceptualization of human agency and, relatedly, his notion of power. I will then move on to his account of social structure and related terms.

Giddens relies upon Heidegger when he insists that action or agency does not refer to a 'series of discrete acts', but to a 'continuous flow of conduct'. Giddens indeed defines action as 'a stream of actual or contemplated causal interventions of corporeal beings in the ongoing process of events-in-the-world'.[24] Note that this definition uncouples agency from intentionality: 'agency refers not to the intentions people have in doing things but to their capability of doing those things in the first place'.[25] It follows that action ought to be seen as 'purposive' – not 'purposeful'. That is, people might lack clear intentions in everyday life, but they nevertheless regularly attend to their actions and to the actions of others. To say that people are agents is to acknowledge that they are always able to act otherwise: in any situation, people could either intervene or refrain from doing so. In short, Giddens's notion of agency implies that people are able to transform things, and that *a fortiori* the future is not pre-given.[26] In Giddensian parlance, this 'transformative capacity' is power.

It is worth briefly elaborating upon Giddens's concept of power, and to contrast it with alternative notions of power. Power is sometimes conceived of as the ability of an individual to achieve his or her will, often (though not necessarily) against others. It is occasionally seen as the property of a collectivity, as linked with interest, or as inherently oppressive. For Giddens, none of these conceptualizations will do. Power is intrinsic to agency: it refers to the individual's capability to intervene causally in a series of events. Two important points follow from this definition. First, power is not to be seen any longer as simply an impediment to freedom or emancipation. Instead, it becomes the very medium through which freedom is to be achieved.[27] Second, all relationships of dependence provide resources which allow the subordinated to influence the superiors. However unequal the relationships are, there is always a 'dialectic of control'.[28]

Giddens's account of structure is different from that of functionalist or structuralist-functionalist authors. Whereas they tend to conflate structure and system, Giddens goes out of his way to distinguish one from the other (see chapters 1 and 2). The latter refers to the patterning of social relationships across time and space, whilst the former refers to a set of social rules and resources which are recursively implicated in interaction. Similar to Saussure's distinction between language and speech, structure, marked by the 'absence of the subject', is located outside space and time, existing only in a virtual way as memory traces, to be implemented in spatially and temporally located interaction. Giddens draws heavily upon Wittgenstein's discussion of rules, defining them as implicit techniques or 'generalizable procedures' that are implemented in the enactment or reproduction of social practices.[29] Giddens distinguishes two types of rule and two types of resource. Rules either constitute the meaning of things, or they relate to the sanctioning of conduct. Resources can be either authoritative or allocative. Allocative resources refer to control over objects, and are traditionally focused upon by Marxist authors who tend to reduce domination to ownership or control of property.[30] Authoritative resources allude to types of transformative capacity, generating command over people. Authoritative resources are discussed by scholars like Foucault, and they refer to the organization of time and space, the body and life-chances (see chapter 5).[31]

Giddens is very careful in distinguishing various aspects of 'structure', and his terminology becomes rather complex. An exhaustive account of all his 'structure-related' concepts is impossible to provide here. Nor is such an account necessary for grasping the main line of his argument. So I will introduce only those terms that are really central to his view of institutional analysis. 'Structure' in the singular is to be distinguished from 'institutions', and from 'structural properties' of social systems. In Giddens's terminology, institutions are not organizations. Institutions refer to regularized practices stretching over long periods of time and across space: for instance, marriage. Structural properties are precisely the institutionalized features of social systems, providing their 'solidity' across time and space. Division of labour is an example of a structural property in a capitalist society.[32] Structural principles are the most deeply embedded structural properties implicated in the reproduction of societal totalities: they indicate, for instance, the extent to which the state and the economy are separated, or the degree of time–space distantiation. The study of structural principles is the most abstract level of social analysis, and it enables Giddens to distinguish between different types of society: tribal, class-divided and class societies. Whereas in tribal societies time–space distantiation is low, kinship networks and tradition are important, in class-divided societies the city becomes a 'storage container' of military and political power. In class societies, power is concentrated in the nation-state, and time and space become commodified.[33]

Structures, as rules and resources, are understood by analytically distinguishing between three 'modalities'; that is, 'lines of mediation' between social interaction and social structure. These modalities are communication of meaning, application of sanctions and use of power (see table 4.1). The analysis of strategic conduct conceives of people as knowledgeable individuals who draw upon these modalities in order to proceed in their daily interaction. First, in so far as social interaction deals with 'communication' of meaning, individuals draw upon 'interpretative schemes' which, at the level of social

Table 4.1   The dimension of the duality of structure

Interaction (modality) Structure	Communication Interpretative scheme Signification	Sanction Norm Legitimation	Power Facility Domination

Source: Based on Giddens (1979, p. 82; 1984, p. 29)

Table 4.2   Institutions and structural properties

Signification	Institutional Order
S-D-L	Symbolic orders / modes of discourse
D (auth)-S-L	Political institutions
D (alloc)-S-L	Economic institutions
L-D-S	Law / modes of sanction

Source: Based on Giddens (1979, p. 107; 1984, p. 33)

structure, can be treated as 'semantic rules'. Second, the application of sanctions in interaction implies that people draw upon 'norms' which, at the level of social structure, can be analysed as 'moral rules'. The third modality ties in with people's transformative capacity. The use of power in interaction implies that people draw upon 'facilities' which, at the structural level, can be analysed as 'resources' involving structures of domination. Although analytically separate, in reality these modalities or lines of mediation intersect.[34]

I can place an *epoché* upon reflexively monitored social conduct, and thus embark upon institutional analysis. Analogous to the distinction between different modalities, various institutions and structural properties can be distinguished: S stands for signification, D for domination and L for legitimation (see table 4.2). In reality, all three tend to play some role. For instance, whilst legitimation is undoubtedly central to the working of legal institutions, signification and domination are not entirely negligible either. Analogously, whilst domination is vital to the functioning of political and economic institutions, the latter also rely upon signification and legitimation.

It is now possible to specify more precisely what Giddens means by duality of structure, and to situate this notion within the intellectual field at the time. For those readers who are familiar with biology, there is a homology or structural identity between his notion of duality of structure on the one hand, and Maturana's and Varela's theory of autopoiesis and self-reproducing systems on the other. Although Giddens's and Maturana's terminologies are different, the similarity between the two theories is striking, and Giddens himself acknowledges the influence of these developments in biology on his work. Both his and Maturana's theories draw attention to the mechanisms by which systems or structures ensure their own reproduction.[35] Giddens's notion of duality of structure is basically that structures, as rules and resources, are both the precondition and the unintended outcome of people's agency. What does this mean precisely? I have already mentioned that, in Giddens's view, people draw upon structures in order to proceed in their daily interaction. Now, Giddens adds that, whilst drawing upon the structures, people cannot help but reproduce the very same structures. So structure allows for agency, which in its turn makes for the unintended reproduction of the very same structures. In other words, structures are recursively implicated in the process of social reproduction. It follows from the notion of duality of structure that there is a close relationship between the different temporal levels of social life. The 'reversible time' of institutions is, after all, both medium and effect of the social practices embedded in the 'continuity of daily life'.[36] It also follows from the duality of structure that a *tabula rasa* does not exist within the social realm. Any transformation, however radical, can only take place by drawing upon (and reproducing) the structural properties which are available. This explains why Giddens discards G. Gurvitch's notion of 'de-structuration'. Like Sartre, Gurvitch mistakenly opposes structure and freedom, and therefore attributes sociological significance to the notion of de-structuration. Any change, Giddens insists, goes hand in hand with structuration.[37]

Giddens's duality of structure is easily exemplified by analogy with the use of language. As they speak, people necessarily draw upon the syntactical rules of the English language, but their utterances help to reproduce the very same structural properties. This example also demonstrates the extent to which Giddens's recursive model conceives of the reproduction of structures as an *unintended* outcome of social practices. For instance, individuals do not speak with the intention of reproducing the English language, but their speaking does contribute unintentionally to the reproduction of that language. The same applies to other forms of rule-governed behaviour: for instance, as they interact, individuals draw upon local rules of politeness and appropriateness, and in doing so they unintentionally reproduce them. Structures are unintended consequences of our practices, and they feed back into our practices as unacknowledged conditions of further acts. But contrary to functionalism and its attendant notion of societal needs, these unintended consequences should not be conceived as explanations for the persistence of practices.[38]

Let me contrast this view on structure with a Durkheimian one (see chapter 1). There is the *locus classicus* in *Rules of Sociological Method*, where Durkheim defines social facts as general, external and constraining. Social facts are general because they apply to all people within a community: for example, the rules of English vocabulary and grammar are shared by all English speakers. Social facts are external in that they antedate people's existence: for instance, people necessarily draw upon a language which existed before they were born. Social facts are also constraining: for instance, our language puts limits on our thought. The concept of social facts was integral to Durkheim's attempt to demonstrate the extent to which society is an entity *sui generis*, and, *mutatis mutandis*, the extent to which sociology should be seen as independent, not to be reduced to other disciplines. In general, Durkheim, drawing upon a naturalist philosophy of the social sciences, adheres to a dualism between structure and agency in which the former somehow 'acts' upon the latter. Giddens demonstrates the paradox involved in this view with respect to the relationship between action and structure:

> the more that structural constraint is associated with a natural sciences model, paradoxically, the freer the agent appears – within whatever scope for individual action is left by the operation of constraint. The structural properties of social systems, in other words, are like the walls of a room from which an individual cannot escape but inside which he or she is able to move around at whim.[39]

Giddens attempts to overcome this Durkheimian dualism between structures and actions. First, he sees structures as memory traces which are constantly instantiated in social practices, and structures are as such *internal* to our actions.[40] The persistence of structures is dependent on these regular instantiations. If we were to cease speaking English, then that language would somehow cease to exist. Second, Giddens sees structures as not merely constraining, but also enabling.[41] In this sense, his approach demonstrates affinities with a Meadian or symbolic interactionist argument (see chapter 3). For instance, it is not *in spite of* language that we are able to think or intervene, but it is precisely *because of* the existence of language that we are able to do so. 'Structure thus is not to be conceptualized as a barrier to action, but as essentially involved in its production.'[42]

Giddens's concept of the duality of structure rests upon the notion of knowledgeability, tacit knowledge and practical consciousness. One of his basic assertions is that people are 'knowledgeable agents' who know a great deal about social life, albeit not necessarily in an explicit way. Take the example of language again. We know how to speak our language in the sense that we know practically how to speak in accordance with the rules of grammar. This does not mean that we have to know our native language in any explicit manner in order to speak properly. On the contrary, our native language use tends to rest upon tacit, implicit forms of knowledge. We know how to do it, how to go on. We do not necessarily know which rules we draw upon. The same applies to other forms of rule-governed conduct. We know how to behave in public, without having to explain discursively the rules that we draw upon. What Schutz calls the 'stocks of knowledge' or what Giddens calls 'mutual knowledge' is not immediately accessible to the consciousness of the people involved. Replacing the traditional psychoana-lytic distinction between the ego, super-ego and id, Giddens argues for his 'stratification model of action', according to which practical consciousness is to be distinguished from discursive consciousness or the unconscious. The distinction between the two levels of consciousness is not an impermeable one (one easily leads into another), whereas their separation with the level of unconscious motives or cognition is. In this context, people's knowledgeability is not only bounded by the unconscious, but also by the unacknowledged conditions and unintended consequences of their actions.

For Giddens, practical consciousness ties in with routines and with the reversible time of our daily activities, and it is here that he draws upon ethnomethodology and Goffman (see chapter 3). There are also similarities with, for instance, Garfinkel's work. In Garfinkel's breaching experiments, people draw upon cognitive frameworks which allow them to interpret real-ity such that the cognitive frameworks remain intact, even in cases where reality is potentially disruptive to the very same cognitive frameworks. Here we encounter a recursive model analogous to the duality of structure. But there is more to Giddens's interpretation of Garfinkel. Giddens sees evidence in Garfinkel's experiments with trust that many of our social rules are deeply intertwined with a sense of ontological security. We learn from these experi-ments that disruptions in the routine character of our daily activities lead to extreme forms of anxiety or anger. Giddens links this with a particular read-ing of Freud. Routines minimize unconscious sources of anxiety and thus sustain a sense of ontological security. It is thus not surprising that disruptions to our routines lead to the effects described by ethnomethodologists.

Giddens's duality of structure is central to his account of the problem of integration. Integration, so he argues, is in need of a radically new approach. In general, it involves 'reciprocity of practices (of autonomy and dependence) between actors or collectivities'.[43] However, previous theories fail to distin-guish between 'social integration' and 'system integration'. Social integration refers to the reciprocity between individuals in contexts of co-presence. Sys-tem integration, on the other hand, deals with the reciprocity between groups or collectivities across extended time–space intervals. System integration implies that structures 'bind' time and space, in that people's tacit knowledge enables society to proceed across longer temporal spans and across space. It follows from the duality of structure that social integration is essential to system integration. Indeed, any face-to-face interaction unintentionally leads to the reproduction of structures, and eventually contributes to the binding of time and space.

This is not to say that all system integration can be reduced to social integration. There are other types of unintended consequence, not accounted for in the duality of structure, which are essential to system integration. Giddens distinguishes here between 'homeostatic causal loops', 'self-regulation through

feed-back' or 'reflexive self-regulation'. All are crucial to system integration. Homeostasis refers to the operation of 'causal loops' whereby a series
of variables affect each other, and the first variable in the series is affected
by the last one such that the former is restored to its initial state. This is
exemplified by the poverty cycle of material deprivation, in which the latter
leads to poor education, which leads to low-level employment, which then
leads to continued material deprivation. Functionalism tends to limit system
integration to homeostasis, and it tends to disregard self-regulation through
feedback and reflexive self-regulation. Self-regulation through feedback differs from homeostatic systems in that directional change takes place. For
example, better education for the poor might lead to improved employment
prospects, so that the poverty cycle is broken. Reflexive self-regulation refers
to processes where people's knowledge about the social world is incorporated in their actions. For example, politicians might acquire knowledge about
the intricacies of the poverty cycle and act upon that knowledge.[44]

It should be clear from the discussion of social and system integration
that time–space intersections are crucial to social life. However, the spatio-
temporal characteristics of 'modern' societies are radically different from
those of 'traditional' societies. First, in modern societies time and space
become independent, abstract, standard yardsticks against which things are
measured. This particular notion of space and time is often treated as if it
were universal, but it certainly is not. For example, time-reckoning in most
traditional societies took place exclusively with reference to other 'socio-
spatial markers' or regular natural events.[45] Second, modernization is characterized by 'time–space distantiation', that is, the extension of social systems
across time and space. This phenomenon is due to, for example, centraliza-
tion, intensified forms of surveillance, and efficient communication systems.
Indicative of time–space distantiation is the increasing 'disembedding' of
social interactions. Disembedding mechanisms remove social relations from
the immediacy of a local context. Giddens distinguishes two types of disembedding mechanisms: 'symbolic tokens' and 'expert systems'. Symbolic
tokens are 'media of interchange' which transcend time and space. There
are various types of symbolic tokens, but money is an obvious example.
Expert systems are systems of specialized knowledge and professional expertise which make possible the adequate functioning of our daily life. There
are, for example, several expert systems which make for relatively safe
flying. Sophisticated technical competence and expertise are involved in the
making of the plane, the construction of the airport, the air traffic control,
and so on. Note that trust is central to both symbolic tokens and expert
systems. People tend to have 'faith' in money without a cognitive appreciation of its workings. Likewise, they generally trust expert systems without
really understanding the knowledge involved. Trust is thus a central feature
of modernity.[46]

Evaluation

Ever since the publication of *New Rules of Sociological Method* and especially since *The Constitution of Society*, structuration theory has been the subject of fierce debate and criticism. Five recurrent types of criticism are worth mentioning here. A first category objects to Giddens's definition of structure in terms of rules and resources. Some commentators indeed argue, amongst other things, that Giddens violates the concept of structure itself by defining it in this way, and that he fails to provide an accurate definition of what rules are.[47] Second, there are numerous assaults on the very essence of the duality of structure. For instance, those social theorists who adhere to morphogenesis argue for sequential analysis and 'analytical dualism': interactions exercise effects, which lead to different structural conditions, and so forth.[48] Third, several theorists object to Giddens's reading of other authors. Marxist-inspired authors, for example, object to his account of historical materialism, arguing that by seeing it as a particular type of evolutionism and functionalism, he simply misreads Marx's writings.[49] Fourth, some people question the relationship established by Giddens between theory and praxis. In particular, it has been argued that, in terms of its critical dimension, Giddens's theory of structuration is unsatisfactory, especially when compared with, for instance, the Frankfurt School (see chapter 6). Giddens flirts with the idea that the social sciences are potentially emancipatory, but fails to redeem his own promises.[50] Fifth, some people object to the alleged eclecticism of the theory of structuration, relying as it does upon a mosaic of intellectual influences, some of which are not really compatible. Giddens, so they argue, seems to specialize in reconciling the irreconcilable; Heidegger would turn in his grave if he knew that Garfinkel and Goffman were amongst his associates.

I will not elaborate upon the validity of these criticisms here. Instead, I will discuss what I consider to be the more problematic areas in structuration theory. In a sense, Giddens's strengths also reveal his weaknesses. It is in fact difficult to find logical gaps or contradictions in his theory of structuration. Whenever pressed on a particular aspect of social life, he appears able to point out successfully the extent to which this issue can be accommodated within the parameters of the theory. However, he is able to avoid criticisms and to 'absorb' reality within his work precisely because of the nature of the theoretical construction provided. Core parts of Giddens's theory of structuration constitute a mode of theorizing about which we have been warned ever since the appearance of Karl Popper's *Logic of Scientific Discovery* (see chapter 8). In contrast to other grand theorists, Giddens on the whole abstains from providing bold conjectures – quite a few of the basic statements actually verge on the tautological. It is difficult to argue against his notion that people's knowledgeability is always bounded by unacknowledged conditions and unforeseen consequences – how could it be otherwise? Many aspects of Giddens's carefully worked-out theory are simply immune to refutation, being as self-evident as logical formulae. Furthermore, even when he deals with more substantive issues such as long-term change, he remains rather cautious, referring to the relatively uncontroversial notion of time–space distantiation.

Giddens's avoidance of risk goes hand in hand with his tendency to set up straw men, only to destroy them. In contrast to his own cautious nature, Giddens's straw men live dangerously in so far as they cannot but be proven wrong. His portrait of functionalism, for instance, is a stereotypical and out-dated one, failing to tackle more sophisticated versions, such as Alexander's neo-functionalism, Luhmann's system theory or Cohen's consequence laws (see chapter 2). The main target throughout his critical analysis of function-alism is Merton, especially the latter's unfortunate discussion of latent and manifest functions. Even when explicitly asked to comment in a debate sur-rounding contemporary interpretations of Marx (focusing on the differences between Jon Elster's rational choice perspective and Cohen's interpretation in terms of consequence laws), Giddens does not really tackle the functionalist arguments involved, but takes the opportunity to reiterate his own position within social theory.[51] Similarly, Giddens's criticisms of evolutionism fail to take into account recent, more sophisticated developments in the area of analogies between biological and social evolution.[52] Ironically, Wright points out that once a less stereotypical definition of evolutionism is adopted, Giddens's own theory of history in terms of space–time distantiation falls within that category.[53]

More problematic than this, however, is that structuration theory, at least in its archetypal version, takes time into account only in so far as it reveals the production of social order. It rightly rejects the 'common-sense' (and functionalist) conflation of time with change (and order with synchronic analysis), but it tends to move towards the other extreme, subscribing to a conservative and recursive model of society.[54] Although structuration theory provides a different answer from the 'normative integration model' of Durkheim and Parsons, it tends to focus on the same question of how social order (as opposed to change) comes about. This ties in with a tendency on the part of structuration theory to overemphasize what Mouzelis calls the 'natural/performative' relationship drawing upon 'first-order' concepts.[55] By emphasizing the accomplished reproduction of society through tacit know-ledge and practical consciousness, structuration theory is especially appropri-ate for understanding the routines of daily life. What tends to be neglected, however, is the possibility of the emergence of explicit or discursive know-ledge, and its role in the process of deliberate change and maintenance of social structures. Once confronted with novel experiences which do not fit in with their taken-for-granted world, people might adopt a more distanced, theoretical attitude towards the structures which were hitherto taken for granted, and they might act in accordance with that knowledge. Even those who wish solely to explain the reproduction of structures cannot ignore the importance of people's ability to develop discursive, theoretical knowledge of previously tacit rules and assumptions. As I already pointed out in my discussion of Bourdieu (see chapter 1), it is misleading to conceive of the reproduction of structures as merely an unintended accomplishment via tacit knowledge and practical consciousness. It regularly happens that people's articulations and discursive awareness are constitutive of reproduction.

Giddens's neglect of second-order knowledge is linked to the choice of theories he draws upon whilst dealing with the erosion of routines. First, he uses Freud's mass psychology to tackle the social and psychological signific- ance of crises and the breakdown of routines, referring to people's attempts to regain lost 'ontological security' through regression into previous stages of development or through identification with a strong personality. Second, he employs an ethnomethodological perspective, drawing attention to the way in which people continuously recreate social order, even whilst con- fronted with potential disruption to that social order. None of these theories takes into account the extent to which people, confronted with novel or unanticipated experiences, are able to reflect upon their circumstances and structures, go through a learning process and act accordingly.

The problems with structuration theory become even more obvious once modernity is made the focus of attention. Giddens himself sees modernity as the breaking with routines, as the capacity of people to reflect upon their con- ditions and as their ability to bring this knowledge to bear on future actions. However, these are features which are hardly compatible with structuration theory, since the latter emphasizes the production of social order through the mechanisms of practical consciousness and tacit knowledge. It is therefore no surprise that in Giddens's texts on modernity the core of his structuration theory is absent. The concepts which he introduces (such as 'institutional reflexivity') are independent of structuration theory, and are not derived from it. The reason for this is precisely that structuration theory is not well placed to grasp modernity and that modernity in itself makes the inadequacies of structuration theory apparent.

But these criticisms should not detract from the obvious strengths of Giddens's contribution to social theory. First, he has demonstrated success- fully that various theoretical or philosophical arguments, which were previ- ously considered to be unrelated, have affinities after all. In particular, Winch's interpretation of Wittgenstein, Schutz's social phenomenology, Garfinkel's ethnomethodology and Goffman's dramaturgical approach are shown to have much in common: they all help with unravelling the intricate relationship between self-monitoring, shared meaning, tacit rules and practical knowledge.

Second, by linking these various arguments, Giddens has been able to identify the emerging post-empiricist view of social theory, and has helped to articulate it. It was probably not until he wrote *New Rules of Sociological Method* that this hermeneutically inspired argument began to take shape, and it would be unfair to underestimate that accomplishment. Third, Giddens's structuration theory has enormous breadth, and so is relevant to many facets of social life. For example, one of his remarkable achievements has been to show the suitability of the in-depth study of minutiae of daily life for the understanding of how shared meaning is brought about.

Further reading

For a brief introduction to structuration theory, I recommend the concluding chapter of Giddens's *New Rules of Sociological Method*, chapter 2 of his *Central Problems in Social Theory*, the introduction to his *The Constitution of Society*, and Cohen's chapter in Giddens and Turner's *Social Theory Today*. For an introduction to Giddens's views on modernity, I would suggest the opening chapter of his *Modernity and Self-Identity*. Interesting collections of essays on Giddens can be found in Held and Thompson's *Social Theory of Modern Societies*, Bryant and Jary's *Giddens' Theory of Structuration*, and Clark, Modgil and Modgil's *Anthony Giddens: Consensus and Controversy*. A very solid, although uncritical, introduction to Giddens's structuration theory can be found in Cohen's *Structuration Theory; Anthony Giddens and the Constitution of Social Life*. In *Anthony Giddens* Craib sets out clearly Giddens's view, but his criticisms are rather vague.

References

Archer, M. 1982. Morphogenesis versus structuration: on combining structure and action. *British Journal of Sociology*, 33(4), 455–83.

Archer, M. 1988. *Culture and Agency: The Place of Culture in Social Theory.* Cambridge: Cambridge University Press.

Archer, M. 1990. Human agency and social structure: a critique of Giddens. In: *Anthony Giddens; Consensus and Controversy*, eds J. Clark, C. Modgil and S. Modgil. London: The Falmer Press, 73–84.

Bernstein, R. J. 1989. Social theory as critique. In: *Social Theory of Modern Societies; Anthony Giddens and his Critics*, eds D. Held and J. Thompson. Cambridge: Cambridge University Press.

Bhaskar, R. 1981. The consequences of socio-evolutionary concepts for naturalism in sociology: commentaries on Harré and Toulmin. In: *The Philosophy of Evolution*, eds U. J. Jensen and R. Harré. Brighton: Harvester Press, 196–209.

Bryant, G. A. and Jary, D. (eds) 1991. *Giddens' Theory of Structuration*. London: Routledge.

Callinicos, A. 1985. Anthony Giddens – a contemporary critique. *Theory and Society* 14, 133–66.

Clark, J., Modgil, C. and Modgil S. (eds) 1990. *Anthony Giddens; Consensus and Controversy.* London: The Falmer Press.

Cohen, I. 1987. Structuration theory and social *praxis.* In: *Social Theory Today,* eds A. Giddens and J. Turner. Cambridge: Polity Press, 273–308.

Cohen, I. 1989. *Structuration Theory: Anthony Giddens and the Constitution of Social Life.* Basingstoke: Macmillan.

Craib, I. 1992. *Anthony Giddens.* London: Routledge.

Elias, N. 1978. *What is Sociology?* New York: Columbia University Press (originally in German, 1970).

Giddens, A. (ed.) 1971a. *The Sociology of Suicide.* London: Cass.

Giddens, A. 1971b. *Capitalism and Modern Social Theory: An Analysis of the Writings of Marx, Durkheim and Max Weber.* Cambridge: Cambridge University Press.

Giddens, A. 1972. *Politics and Sociology in the Thought of Max Weber.* London: Macmillan.

Giddens, A. 1977. *Studies in Social and Political Theory.* London: Hutchinson (reprinted, 1979).

Giddens, A. 1978. *Durkheim.* London: Fontana.

Giddens, A. 1979. *Central Problems in Social Theory: Action, Structure and Contradiction in Social Analysis.* London: Macmillan (reprinted, 1993).

Giddens, A. 1981a. *The Class Structure of the Advanced Societies.* London: Hutchinson (2nd edn).

Giddens, A. 1981b. *A Contemporary Critique of Historical Materialism: Volume 1; Power, Property and the State.* London: Macmillan.

Giddens, A. 1982. Commentary on the debate. *Theory and Society* 11, 527–39.

Giddens, A. 1984. *The Constitution of Society; Outline of the Theory of Structuration.* Cambridge: Polity Press (reprinted, 1993).

Giddens, A. 1985. *A Contemporary Critique of Historical Materialism: Volume 2; The Nation-State and Violence.* Cambridge: Polity Press (reprinted, 1992).

Giddens, A. 1987. *Social Theory and Modern Sociology.* Cambridge: Polity Press.

Giddens, A. 1989. Structuration theory: past, present and future. In: *Giddens' Theory of Structuration,* eds P. Bryant and D. Jary. London: Routledge, 201–21.

Giddens, A. 1990. *The Consequences of Modernity.* Cambridge: Polity Press (reprinted, 1994).

Giddens, A. 1991. *Modernity and Self-Identity; Self and Society in the Late Modern Age.* Cambridge: Polity Press.

Giddens, A. 1992. *The Transformation of Intimacy; Sexuality, Love and Eroticism in Modern Societies.* Cambridge: Polity Press (reprinted, 1993).

Giddens, A. 1993. *New Rules of Sociological Method.* Cambridge: Polity Press (2nd edition).

Giddens, A. 1994. *Beyond Left and Right: The Future of Radical Politics.* Cambridge: Polity Press.

Giddens, A. and Turner, J. (eds) 1987. *Social Theory Today.* Cambridge: Polity Press.

Harré, R. 1981. The evolutionary analogy in social explanation. In: *The Philosophy of Evolution*, eds U. J. Jensen and R. Harré. Brighton: Harvester Press, 161–75.

Held, D. and Thompson, J. (eds) 1989. *Social Theory of Modern Societies; Anthony Giddens and his Critics*. Cambridge: Cambridge University Press (reprinted, 1991).

Jensen, U. J. and R. Harré (eds) 1981. *The Philosophy of Evolution*. Brighton: Harvester Press.

Mouzelis, N. 1989. Restructuring structuration theory. *Sociological Review 37*, 613–35.

Thompson, J. B. 1989. The theory of structuration. In: *Social Theory of Modern Societies; Anthony Giddens and his Critics*, eds D. Held and J. Thompson. Cambridge: Cambridge University Press, 56–76.

Wright, E. O. 1989. Models of historical trajectory: an assessment of Giddens' critique of Marxism. In: *Social Theory of Modern Societies; Anthony Giddens and his Critics*, eds D. Held and J. Thompson. Cambridge: Cambridge University Press, 77–103.

5
The History of the Present
Foucault's Archaeology
and Genealogy

The initial setting is reminiscent of *Madame Bovary*: a quiet provincial town in France, a pious Catholic family, the father a medical practitioner. Michel Foucault (1926–84) was expected to follow in his father's footsteps, but like the heroine of the novel whose dreams and fantasies swept her away from the shelter and securities of provincial family life, his fascination was towards the arts, philosophy and literature, rather than towards the safe haven of a medical career. Foucault went to the Lycée Henri IV (one of the preparatory schools for the École Normale Supérieure) and the École Normale, and amongst his teachers were the Hegelian philosopher Jean Hyppolite, the philosophers of science Georges Canguilhem and Georges Dumézil, and the structuralist Marxist Louis Althusser. Marxism, existentialism and, later, structuralism were the dominant strands of thought during Foucault's formative years at the École Normale, and his work can be seen as very much in opposition to Sartrean Marxism. Like that of his friend Gilles Deleuze, Foucault's *oeuvre* was significantly marked by Nietzsche's influence; like Deleuze, Foucault strongly opposed the humanistic tenets of existentialist Marxism, the adherence of the latter to a Cartesian concept of the self, its penchant for constructing a grand narrative and the pivotal role it attributes to praxis.[1]

After the École Normale, Foucault taught at the University of Uppsala in Sweden, followed by a short spell as Director of the French Institutes of Warsaw and Hamburg, after which he returned to France. Meanwhile, he had published *Maladie mentale et personnalité*, a scholarly work about mental disorder, remarkably non-Foucauldian in style and spirit.[2] In 1961 he published his doctoral dissertation, *Madness and Civilization* (*Folie et déraison: histoire de la folie à l'âge classique*) – the now well-known study of the history of the relationship between madness and reason from the Middle Ages, focusing on the way in which reason and unreason become differentiated with the advent of modernity and the extent to which this differentiation was accompanied by the medicalization of madness.[3] Although *Madness and Civilization* was well received in academic circles, and its literary and allegorical style applauded, it did not reach a wider audience. The book did, however, provide Foucault with sufficient academic renown to be offered a chair in Philosophy at the University of Clermont-Ferrand.

The Birth of the Clinic (*La Naissance de la clinique*) followed in 1963.[4] In a similar vein to *Madness and Civilization*, but influenced more explicitly by structuralism, this book is an 'archaeological' study of medical perception, dealing with the relationship between medical knowledge and the emergence of the human sciences. I will expand on the method of archaeology later in this chapter; it suffices here to say that it aims at uncovering underlying assumptions that are dominant over a long period of time. The birth of the 'science of man' (*sciences de l'homme*) was also a central theme in *The Order of Things* (*Les Mots et les choses*).[5] Heavily influenced by the structuralist vogue, this is an archaeological history of the rules of organization and formation which structure the modes of intellectual frameworks. Its publication led at once to Foucault's spectacular breakthrough onto the French intellectual scene. Shortly afterwards, however, Foucault left France to teach at the University of Tunis, thus missing the events of May 1968. He returned one year after these upheavals to the newly founded University of Vincennes, and published at the same time *The Archaeology of Knowledge* (*L'Archéologie du savoir*).[6] This work can be seen as a methodological commentary on his previous books, his equivalent of Durkheim's *Règles de la méthode sociologique*, with the author elaborating upon, *inter alia*, his intellectual position and locating himself with regard to structuralism and other intellectual developments.

In 1971, Foucault left the turmoil of Vincennes to take up the chair of the History of Systems of Thought at the Collège de France. The contrast could not have been sharper. At the time, Vincennes was in a state of perpetual chaos, whereas the Collège de France was, and still is, the French equivalent of All Souls College, Oxford: with no students and hardly any teaching obligations, it is the archetype of an academic ivory tower. Interestingly enough, it was during this period that Foucault again became actively involved in politics, consistent with his concept of local struggle and its attendant role for the intellectual. In 1975 he published *Discipline and Punish* (*Surveiller et punir*), a history of punishment and imprisonment, probably his most influential work abroad, though less well received in France.[7] Although drawing upon Nietzschean genealogical rather than his own earlier archaeological methods, *Discipline and Punish* brings together a number of themes in Foucault's earlier work, in particular the role of the emerging social sciences in the formation of new disciplinary techniques.

A similar genealogical analysis and an analogous critique of psychoanalysis is central in the three volumes of *The History of Sexuality* (*L'Histoire de la sexualité*).[8] One of his main targets here is psychoanalytic discourse and its attendant 'repression hypothesis'. Rather than a liberating force, psychoanalysis is indicative of, and grew out of, the confessional procedures which are so central to modern society. More volumes on the history of sexuality were planned, but Foucault died suddenly in 1984. By then, he had acquired the reputation of the *enfant terrible* of French academia. He had secured a committed string of followers who admired his literary style and his new approach to history, and an equally committed consortium of enemies who maintained that he was nothing but a charlatan, shallow but shrewd in playing up to the media and into the latest Parisian fashion.

Some of these criticisms rely upon a superficial reading of Foucault's writings. As a matter of fact, many secondary sources fail to do justice to his work, and even the more sympathetic readings tend not to acknowledge the radical nature of his intellectual project. They evaluate his work by using traditional standards. Many commentators on Foucault are even unaware of the extent to which their criticisms are external ones. That is, they fail to recognize that Foucault has a different agenda from traditional social theory and history. In this chapter, I will focus on the distinctiveness of Foucault's project, and evaluate his work in that light.

A new conception of knowledge acquisition

The best starting point to elucidate Foucault is to contrast him with a mainstream view in sociology and social theory. Since the birth of the social sciences, there has been a consensus within social scientific and philosophical circles regarding the nature of social scientific knowledge. First, it is assumed that one's social scientific knowledge aims at depicting, explaining or understanding a 'world out there'. This world is different from and exists independently of one's theoretical presuppositions. Second, the type of knowledge involved is *ipso facto* not self-referential. That is, it is not the aim of social scientific knowledge to reveal or understand the presuppositions that are the medium through which that knowledge is arrived at. Third, this type of knowledge should aim at explaining unfamiliar phenomena by drawing upon analogies with phenomena that are familiar. To put it more bluntly, this type of knowledge attempts to eradicate the unfamiliar by turning it into the familiar (see chapter 8).

Much has, of course, been said about the differences between various philosophies of the social sciences. I do not wish to question the many dissimilarities between, for instance, positivism, realism or falsificationism, regarding the demarcation between science and non-science, the nature of explanation, or the notion of causality (see chapter 8). Despite these dissimilarities, the three characteristics mentioned above are shared by a significant number of philosophies of social science. Some philosophies might be more *explicit* in promoting one or more of these assumptions (for instance, the first and the third assumption are among the *idées maîtresses* of realism), but most subscribe at least *implicitly* to all three positions. More importantly, most empirical researchers in the social sciences carry out their studies in line with the three assumptions. It is therefore appropriate to talk about a 'traditional consensus' in sociology.

Now, I argue that Foucault presents an alternative to the traditional consensus. He presents a form of knowledge about the social world which is first and foremost 'self-referential'. That is, it is not primarily (and certainly not merely) directed towards reconstructing a world out there, but rather ultimately directed at revealing our own previously held assumptions. A related fact is that his principal target is the familiar, not the unfamiliar. More precisely, rather than drawing upon analogies with the familiar to explain the unfamiliar, his writings aim at creating distance, revealing and threatening what was hitherto taken for granted. In what follows, I will demonstrate that this type of knowledge acquisition runs throughout Foucault's work, and, given that he is a historian, I will reveal the consequences of that conception of knowledge when applied to the discipline of history. I hope thereby to point out some misreadings of Foucault, and to defend him against misguided criticisms.

Scholars familiar with Foucault might object to the way in which I identify one methodological theme running through his work. It has indeed often been pointed out that an 'epistemological break' or discontinuity distinguishes Foucault's earlier archaeology from his later genealogy.[9] Just as it is commonplace to talk about an early and a mature Marx, or about an early and a later Wittgenstein, so scholars similarly refer to archaeology and genealogy in Foucault. There are undoubtedly convincing arguments for seeing the two periods as radically different. The philosophical views which influenced them are, after all, clearly distinct: archaeological methods are very much embedded in French structuralist thought, whereas genealogy is heavily indebted to Nietzsche's writings. Hence Foucault, as an archaeologist, shares the scientific and objectivist pretensions of fellow-structuralists, whereas Foucault as a genealogist leads the way to post-structuralist thought. My position is, however, that by dividing Foucault's work into archaeology and genealogy his critics fail to recognize the methodological continuity throughout his work. If commentators acknowledge continuity, then this tends to be merely thematic. For instance, some argue that although Foucault fails to discuss *explicitly* the concept of power in his earlier work, it is nevertheless a continuous theme (a view expressed by Foucault himself). I wish to show instead that the types of knowledge acquisition involved in the early and the later Foucault are not as radically different as is sometimes suggested, and thus more methodological continuity can be attributed to his work than is customarily assumed. First, I will discuss his archaeological work, then I will elaborate upon his genealogical writings. Finally, I summarize the similarities with regard to the issue of knowledge acquisition.

First, however, I need to add one more qualification. It is well known that Foucault made several attempts to distance himself from particular labels such as 'structuralism' (see chapter 1).[10] Surely, given the Parisian cultural 'field', in which claims to originality are crucial to one's reputation, it is understandable that Foucault, like other French prima donnas, did not wish to be too closely associated with other intellectual trends. It would be a mistake, however, to think of Foucault as a mere *enfant terrible* working outside any intellectual setting. Despite his attempts to argue that archaeological methods are developed without resort to structural analysis, it is my conviction that the latter is indispensable for making sense of the former. This is not simply to say that Foucault's archaeological methods *in toto* are structuralist. For instance, his notion of language as an event or act is indeed far removed from, if not in contradiction to, the structuralist notion of *langue* as structure. What I wish to say, rather, is that the two perspectives do share a significant number of assumptions, and that pointing out their differences does not add significantly to the understanding of archaeology. Even if it is true that Foucault does not *consciously* use structuralism in his archaeology, it is perfectly legitimate (and, ironically enough, entirely in line with Foucault's own archaeological methods) to call archaeology structuralist because, first, structuralist analysis is a *sine qua non* for making sense of archaeology; second, structuralism became prominent during Foucault's formative years; and third, several of Foucault's teachers were well acquainted and sympathetic towards the new structuralist movement. Foucault's originality does not rely upon his ability to create ideas and concepts *de novo*. Rather, it lies in his ability to combine successfully different intellectual strands, and, of course, in his capacity to direct them towards a self-referential type of knowledge acquisition.

Archaeology

In general, Foucault's earlier historical writings rely upon what he calls archaeological methods. These underlie most of his publications in the 1960s, amongst which his *Madness and Civilization* and *The Order of Things* are best known.[11] In *The Archaeology of Knowledge*, Foucault sets out to elucidate his methodology and to situate it within the recent intellectual developments in France.[12] His archaeology is influenced by a wide variety of intellectual traditions, two of which are worth recalling. First, there is the (already mentioned) influence of the French structuralist movement in general and French structuralist history (the Annales School) in particular (see chapter 1). Second, there is the impact of French philosophy of science on Foucault's archaeology.[13]

Let me first start with structuralism and the structuralist historical research of the Annales School. For the sake of clarity, it is necessary to distinguish between two strands in structuralist social science (see chapter 1). One strand attempts to account for social systems by drawing on analogies with linguistic systems. This 'linguistic' strand often relies upon Saussure's (or Jakobson's) insights about meaning and its relation to *langue*. Social life is seen as an amalgam of signs; the meaning of each sign is arbitrary, and depends on each sign being different from other signs currently in use. This linguistic strand is represented in, for example, Barthes's *The Fashion System*.[14] The early Foucault also draws upon this type of structuralism, but the Annales School does not, and as I wish first to deal with its influence on Foucault, I will, *ad interim*, omit the linguistic strand.

This leads me to the second form of structuralism, which attempts to demonstrate the extent to which people's thoughts and actions are moulded and constrained by underlying structures. This strand necessarily relies upon a realist philosophy of science; it assumes a 'stratified' conception of reality which attributes reality status, not only to observed phenomena, but also to underlying structures which generate or cause the phenomena (see chapter 8).[15] This strand goes back to some of Durkheim's writings, and it is this kind of Durkheimian structuralism which has been taken up by members of the Annales School. They oppose what Braudel calls the '*courte durée*' or '*histoire événementielle*', the latter referring to the history of events or the history of great men or women who have shaped our past.[16] Against this narrative approach to history which is so typical of the *histoire Sorbonniste*, Braudel and others argue for the importance of structuralist types of historical enquiry. Reacting against the positivist tendencies of French historiography, structuralist historical research aims to uncover the '*longue durée*'; that is, the relatively stable, unacknowledged, constraining structures which stretch over long periods of time. Beyond the level of events, individual choices and other vicissitudes lie deeper more stable layers of underlying structures. Some of these structures are physical, for instance geographical or climatological constraints. Some scholars are more interested in mental constraints, focusing, for example, on the extent to which particular epistemological frameworks have dominated particular epochs.

Foucault's archaeological work is very much indebted to French structuralist history, as he also attempts to unravel the latent structures which have stretched over long periods of time.[17] When he mentions the 'archaeological' level of analysis, he is in fact referring to the rules of formation which stipulate the conditions of possibility of what can be said within a particular discourse during a relatively long timespan. For instance, he brings to light particular discourses about madness and sanity which were common for centuries, and similarly he detects 'epistemes' which dominated science and philosophy. Both discourses and epistemes refer to the implicit and shared rules which operate 'behind the backs' of individuals and which are a *sine qua non* for the formation of statements. These rules specify which statements can be made and which are true or false.[18]

As acknowledged by Foucault in *The Archaeology of Knowledge*, his work also makes use of conceptual tools which were introduced by French historians of science such as Bachelard and Canguilhem. These scholars oppose a continuous conception of history, and they introduce the notion of discontinuity or rupture to distinguish various scientific epochs and to underline their differences.[19] Foucault contrasts the 'new history' with previous types of history in which the task of the historian was to *efface* discontinuity – to mould it into a narrative of continuity:

> For history in its classical form, the discontinuous was both the given and the unthinkable: the raw material of history, which presented itself in the form of dispersed events – decisions, accidents, initiatives, discoveries: the material, which, through analysis, had to be arranged, reduced, effaced in order to reveal the continuity of events. Discontinuity was the stigma of temporal dislocation that it was the historian's task to remove from history.[20]

So, under the old type of history, discontinuity was at best an embarrassment for the historian at work – a failure, maybe a sign of lack of craftsmanship. In the new type of history, with which Foucault identifies himself, discontinuity, rather than being an obstruction, becomes essential to the practices of the historian:

> One of the most essential features of the new history is probably this displacement of the discontinuous: its transference from the obstacle to the work itself; its integration into the discourse of the historian, where it no longer plays the role of an external condition that must be reduced, but that of a working concept; and therefore the inversion of signs by which it is no longer the negative of the historical reading (its underside, its failure, the limit of its power), but the positive element that determines its object and validates its analysis.[21]

Foucault recognizes the twofold nature of this statement. On the one hand, it means that the historian uses the notion of discontinuity as an instrument for approaching reality. Discontinuity is a tool which allows the historian to divide up domains or periods. On the other hand, it means that the historian assumes that discontinuity is part of reality.[22]

Foucault merges structuralist notions with this concept of discontinuity, and his archaeological method thus aims at pointing out two phenomena. First, he searches for underlying structures, which are relatively unacknowledged by the individuals involved, and which are relatively stable over long stretches of time. Second, he looks for those radical transformations in history which separate the periods of relative stability – those ruptures which call an end to an epoch and which herald a new *longue durée*. Foucault's view of history indeed suggests long periods of permanence, each of which is dominated by a particular framework or set of practices. These periods are separated by relatively short intervals (often spanning only a few decades) in which the shift from the old structure to the new is accomplished. There are thus two 'rhythms' in his picture of history: the very slow rhythm of the *longue durée* (which reflects the influence of structuralist history) and the accelerated rhythm of *rupture* (which reveals very much the influence of French history of science). Note that Foucault does not always show much interest in explaining how these radical transformations came about. He occasionally justifies his lack of interest in that question by arguing that the methodological problems involved are severe.[23]

It is at this stage important to go back to the influence of structuralism on Foucault's writings, in particular the influence of the linguistic strand. Central to the linguistic strand is a holistic theory of meaning (see chapter 1). According to this theory, the meaning of a sign is dependent on its differences from the other signs currently in use within that structure.[24] Now, combined with the above Foucauldian picture of discontinuous history, this holistic theory of meaning implies that the various structures, which follow each other through time, are not simply different, but incommensurable. Indeed, every rupture leads to the emergence of a radically different structure, and given that the meaning of signs is dependent on structure (in the way described above), meaning necessarily undergoes a profound change as well. That is why, when reading Foucault, one gets the impression that with every discontinuity an entirely different world is created. This explains Foucault's reference to Borges's fictitious Chinese encyclopedia in the preface to *The Order of Things*. In that encyclopedia animals are divided into: '(a) belonging to the Emperor, (b) embalmed, (c) tame, (d) sucking pigs, (e) sirens, (f) fabulous, (g) stray dogs, (h) included in the present classification, (i) frenzied, (j) innumerable, (k) drawn with a very fine camelhair brush, (l) *et cetera*, (m) having just broken the water pitcher, (n) that from a long way off look like flies.'[25] Foucault emphasizes the extent to which this Chinese taxonomy relies upon rules and assumptions alien to us. For example, Borges's construction does not rely upon our distinction between 'the Same and the Other'. Likewise, Foucault's history, if successful, aims at presenting such bewildering discontinuities in thought and in practice throughout history.

I am now in a position to elaborate upon how Foucault's archaeology suggests a self-referential concept of knowledge, and how it draws upon the unfamiliar in order to account for the familiar. The different periods which he portrays are not only radically different from each other, they also contrast with the present day. As a matter of fact, they often stretch as far as the present day. So Foucault's portrayal necessarily involves a contrast between past and present. A number of consequences follow from this. The most obvious is that Foucault's work facilitates the awareness that, to put it epigrammatically, *the present has not always been*. That is, the portrayal of different periods allows one to become aware of the fact that some of the concepts or practices which are used today are not as universal or fixed as they might seem. For instance, reading *Madness and Civilization*, one is struck by the extent to which past definitions of madness and the ways in which the insane were then treated are alien to the conceptions, categorizations and practices of today. Second, through juxtaposition with the past, the present becomes visible. That is, structures tend to be taken for granted by the individuals who are subjected to them, and these structures are therefore unlikely to be visible to them. Juxtaposition with a different structure, whether real or imaginary, might lead to the making manifest of a previously latent structure. And this is exactly what Foucault does. His depiction of past epistemes, for instance, makes for the uncovering of contemporary conceptions surrounding epistemology or ontology. Third, it should now be clear that, in some respects, Foucault's archaeology implies the exact reverse of the realist conception of science. Realism argues that science attempts to make sense of unfamiliar phenomena by drawing upon analogies with phenomena which are familiar (see chapter 8). In contrast, Foucault's methodology attempts to draw upon knowledge about and dissimilarity with the unfamiliar (the distant past) in order to gain access to a 'familiar stranger' (the taken-for-granted present). Notice the extent to which the past, rather than a mere object of research or end-point, is a medium for access to the present. Fourth, given that Foucault's archaeology makes manifest the structures of today and shows that they are not universal, and given that structures exercise power mainly through their invisibility and through the fact that they are experienced as universal, his earlier work creates the possibility for the corrosion of the present. Once people become aware of the assumptions or rules upon which they have hitherto unconsciously drawn, and once they realize how radically different these were in the past, then the strength of these assumptions or rules is potentially undermined.

Genealogy

In the 1970s, Foucault abandons archaeology for genealogy. So *Discipline and Punish* and the three volumes of *The History of Sexuality* are offered as genealogical works.[26] It has often been pointed out that, in this period, Foucault is very much influenced by Nietzsche. I think that is a fair description. This is not to say that Nietzsche did not exercise any influence on Foucault before 1970.[27] Rather, the claim is that his influence becomes more explicit and systematic after that date. First, Foucault borrows Nietzsche's notion of genealogy – for instance, in the article 'Nietzsche, history, genealogy', where he explicitly acknowledges and quotes his mentor *in extenso*.[28] Second, in this period, Foucault, like Nietzsche, puts forward an anti-essentialist position. According to this nominalist position, the meaning of objects or practices varies according to the context in which they arise. This might explain why Foucault is reluctant to provide an explicit definition of newly introduced concepts such as power. Third, like Nietzsche, Foucault makes use of the concept of power, and this concept plays a dual role in his theory. As with Nietzsche, Foucault realizes that power struggles accompany the emergence of new meanings. Nietzsche, for instance, argues that the meanings of good and evil radically shifted with the advent of Christianity, and that this transformation of meaning was the product of a particular power struggle at the time. Foucault is also indebted to Nietzsche when he conceives of power as intertwined with knowledge; knowledge is not neutral to power, nor is it simply self-emancipatory. For instance, Foucault demonstrates in *Discipline and Punish* the extent to which the emerging social sciences and psychiatry, whilst disguised as liberating forces, were essential to the development of new, and more efficient, forms of social control.[29] Fourth, like Nietzsche, Foucault's genealogical history is opposed to any meta-narrative which would incorporate past, present and future. There is of course a story-line which runs through *Discipline and Punish* (and through *The History of Sexuality*, for that matter), but there is no overall theoretical scheme which necessarily unfolds itself through time.

I will now elaborate upon what I see as the cardinal features of Foucault's notion of genealogy. The genealogist goes back in time in order to show that at some point radically new meanings were allocated to concepts. He or she then demonstrates that the emergence of these new meanings was due to power struggles or contingency. The new meanings were subsequently transmitted across generations, and so became part of the culture. These meanings gradually came to be experienced by people as self-evident, necessary, innocuous (if not honourable) and consistent.[30] Foucault's genealogy, on the other hand, aims at demonstrating that these meanings are neither obvious, necessary, harmless, honourable nor coherent. First, the self-evident nature of the current meanings is undermined by demonstrating that radically different meanings existed in the past. Second, against any form of causal-mechanical view or teleology is the genealogist's attention to 'the accidents, the minute deviations – or conversely, the complete reversals – the errors, the false appraisals, and the faulty calculations that gave birth to those things that continue to exist and have value for us'.[31] Consequently, the genealogist breaks with any historicist view which assumes a necessary unfolding of laws or wheels of history: 'the things which seem most evident to us are always formed in the confluence of encounters and chances, during the course of a precarious and fragile history.'[32] Third, current meanings are shown to be less harmless or honourable than is assumed by demonstrating that they are interrelated with power struggles. The starting point for a genealogist is that belief systems or ethical systems appear innocuous or, stronger, ought to be held in respect; after all, they deal with matters of truth and morality. The genealogist shows that, contrary to that appearance, belief and ethical systems are very much implicated in power struggles.[33] Fourth, lack of coherence is shown by demonstrating how new meanings co-exist with old ones. It would indeed be a mistake to assume that old meanings are completely erased by new ones as if a *tabula rasa* were possible. In Foucault's own words: 'we should not be deceived into thinking that this heritage is an acquisition, a possession that grows and solidifies; rather, it is an unstable assemblage of faults, fissures, and heterogenous layers that threaten the fragile inheritor from within or from underneath.'[34]

Before elaborating on how Foucault uses genealogy in *Discipline and Punish*, let me briefly enlarge on his concept of power. Power is, after all, central to genealogy: remember that power struggles accompany and explain the emergence of new meanings. Foucault himself introduces the concept rather late. Reminiscent of Molière's Mr Jourdan who suddenly realizes that he has been speaking prose all his life, Foucault stated in an interview in 1977: 'When I think back now, I ask myself what else it was that I was talking about, in *Madness and Civilization* or *The Birth of the Clinic*, but power.'[35] In discussing power, he draws upon a counterfactual argument: it comes into play whenever people are made to do something which they would not have done otherwise. However, Foucault insists that his examination does not aim to provide a 'theory' of power, rather an 'analytics' of power.[36] The analytics of power refers to a description of the domain occupied by relations of power, and to the identification of the tools which are necessary for the analysis of that domain. Despite this 'instrumental' stance, Foucault's discussion of power is theoretical in various ways.

First, he very much rebels against what he sees as the two dominant theoretical positions with respect to power: a 'judicial-liberal' and a Marxist conception. Foucault argues that both conceptions restrict power to its economic dimension. In Marxist writings, for instance, power appears as a commodity, directed towards the maintenance and reproduction of economic relations. By contrast, Foucault's concept of power is explicitly non-economic.[37] Second, Marxists often rely upon what Foucault calls a 'descending' type of analysis. That is, power is seen as imposed on people from above. Foucault's methodological rules suggest an 'ascending' analysis of power. Here, the understanding of the local figurations contribute to the broader mechanisms at a macro-level.[38] Third, Foucault argues that several macro-analyses tend to describe power in terms of 'possession': they talk about a class or the state possessing power and imposing it on its subjects. In Foucault's micro-physics of power, power appears instead as a strategy, emerging out of the relationships between people, transmitted through the subjects, rather than imposed on them. As nobody's particular property, power cannot be localized. It is therefore dispersed, not centralized in society; there is no locus of control, no centre of gravity.[39]

Fourth, Foucault's rejection of power as something possessed by an individual or group ties in with his refusal to deal with the concept in terms of intentionality or decision. The function of power is compared to a chain in that it 'circulates' through a 'net-like' organization. The individual is not an 'elementary nucleus', a 'primitive atom' subjected to power. One of the pivotal features of power is that it identifies individuals who, instead of being the 'points of application' of power, become the 'vehicle' through which it is circulated.[40] Fifth, related to the previous point, Foucault does not wish to accept a 'negative' reading of power. In a negative view, power is merely an impediment to agency. Take the history of sexuality, for instance. According to a negative concept, power only comes into play in so far as sex and pleasure are repressed or negated: 'power can "do" nothing but say no to them'.[41] For Foucault, power does not merely operate in a negative fashion, it also constitutes things (and the latter are sometimes the vehicles for its replication); it creates, for instance, the 'individual' in the first place, or it creates sexual desires.[42] Finally, in some structuralist writings, there is hardly any role for agency. Foucault insists, instead, that power relations always involve the possibility of resistance. They are intrinsically unstable and can be reversed.[43] Genealogy might help in overturning that 'hazardous play of domination'.

So far I have dealt with the theory behind Foucault's notions of genealogy and power. Let me now return to genealogy, and show how Foucault uses it in *Discipline and Punish*. He argues that up until the late eighteenth century punishment was a public and gruesome spectacle, symbolizing the strength of the sovereign and directed towards the body of the victim.[44] He goes to some length to show that, rather than being simply a barbarous system, the form of punishment has its own logic – logic that is as sophisticated and internally coherent as ours. Be that as it may, this practice led to much disorder, because the person to be executed had, in the face of death, nothing to lose, and, confronted with an enormous audience, considerable power. It was not uncommon for someone in this situation to speak openly against the sovereign or the regime, and for the audience then to side with the condemned.[45]

Confronted with these problems of the 'society of spectacle', policy-makers and intellectuals thought of more 'efficient' forms of exercising social control. This inspired the utilitarian reforms at the beginning of the nineteenth century, which set in motion a 'disciplinary' society, in which conceptions of punishment were radically transformed. The spread of disciplinary power aims at a regular, systematic training and monitoring of the body.[46] As early as the eighteenth century, the *philosophes* had already expressed their hostility on humanitarian grounds towards the old penal system. Jeremy Bentham's new system, however, bore hardly any resemblance to that which they had in mind. The consequence of his system was anything but the reform of criminals; its effect was to implement more efficient forms of social control which could be (and were) applied outside the penal system.

Characteristic of the emerging disciplinary society was the emphasis on incarceration, 'hierarchical observation', 'examination' and 'normalization'.[47] The panopticon is Foucault's example *par excellence* of hierarchical observation in the nineteenth century. The panopticon implies a particular organization of space such that at any time the inmates are unable to know whether they *are* being watched, and they know that they *might* be monitored. This system is supposed to lead to 'self-correction': knowing that they might be watched at any time, the inmates end up monitoring themselves.[48] Besides hierarchical observation, disciplinary power implies an emphasis on what Foucault calls 'normalization'. That is, elements of behaviour are rewarded or punished depending on whether they adhere to or deviate from the postulated norm. On the basis of this penal accountancy, people are ranked depending on the extent to which they conform to standards.[49]

The combination of hierarchical observation and normalization culminates in the notion of the 'examination'. The successful implementation of the examination ultimately depended on the development of sophisticated procedures for documentation and classification. The emerging 'science of man' made possible such procedures. Hence the social sciences, although *prima facie* directed towards self-emancipation, played a crucial role in the transformation into a 'disciplinary' society. However much this society of 'surveillance' was bound up with social control, the new system gradually appeared as obvious, coherent and benevolent. So, by the late twentieth century, the disciplinary regime has permeated many realms of society:

> The judges of normality are present everywhere. We are in the society of the teacher-judge, the doctor-judge, the educator-judge, the 'social worker'-judge; it is on them that the universal reign of the normative is based; and each individual, wherever he may find himself, subjects to it his body, his gestures, his behaviour, his aptitudes, his achievements. The carceral network, in its compact or disseminated forms, with its systems of insertion, distribution, surveillance, observation, has been the greatest support, in modern society, of the normalizing power.[50]

So genealogy undercuts the present in a number of ways. First, like archaeology, it erodes the present through juxtaposition with the past. The present is made manifest, and found not to be universal: 'history serves to show that-which-is has not always been'.[51] Foucault opens *Discipline and Punish* with a significant contrast: a detailed account of the gruesome public execution of Damiens in 1757, followed by the rigid time schedule of a prison regime eighty years later.[52] The juxtaposition of public spectacle and prison system reveals the assumptions of both. The reader is struck by how different the public spectacle of former times is from the penal system of today; meanwhile, the assumptions of the latter system are revealed. Second, genealogy undercuts present meanings by demonstrating the accidents which accompanied their initial emergence. For instance, the misfortunes and unintended outcomes of the old penal regime led to the call for a different system.[53] 'What reason perceives as *its* necessity, or rather, what different forms of rationality offer as their necessary being, can perfectly well be shown to have a history; and the network of *contingencies* from which it emerges can be traced.'[54] So, these forms of rationality 'reside' upon human practice and human history, and 'since these things have been made, they can be unmade, as long as we know how it was that they were made'.[55]

Third, genealogy leads to a certain loss of innocence, since that which is hitherto experienced as innocuous is shown to be very much tainted by power struggles. Foucault sets out to show in *Discipline and Punish* that, rather than being solely emancipatory, the social sciences are not just implicated in, but essential to the emergence of a disciplinary society. Likewise, however benevolent its intentions, the carceral system is shown to be characteristic of this disciplinary regime.[56]

Fourth, genealogy undermines particular justifications of the present. Present belief systems or practices are often legitimized by indicating that they are a continuous progression from the past. Genealogy aims at demonstrating that both the assumption of continuity and the notion of progress are erroneous. Past practices and concepts appear so distinct that they cannot be moulded into a continuous narrative. Every system creates its own internal logic and justification, and it is impossible to provide an independent yardstick to judge between, for instance, different regimes of power. This explains why, after the hideous details of the execution of Damiens, Foucault takes on the difficult task of showing the internal logic of that system. And it also explains why Foucault points out that the present penal system ties in with the spread of disciplinary techniques and hence is not simply an advance in humanitarianism (compared to the *ancien régime*): 'Humanity does not gradually progress from combat to combat until it arrives at universal reciprocity, where the rule of law finally replaces warfare; humanity installs each of its violences in a system of rules and thus proceeds from domination to domination.'[57]

Fifth, genealogy undermines the apparent coherence of present belief or normative systems. That which appears to be a unitary, consistent system is shown to be heterogenous and to consist of disparate layers of meaning. This is partly because, as I mentioned earlier, previous meanings are never completely erased. In practice, however, Foucault does not always seem to be successful in applying this fifth principle. Indeed, one recurrent criticism of *Discipline and Punish* points out that, contrary to the apparent black-and-white picture painted by Foucault, the 'society of spectacle' is still prevalent today – a criticism essentially in line with the notion of genealogy. But on other occasions Foucault seems to be more sensitive to the multi-layered nature of reality. The science of man might portray itself as singularly self-emancipatory, but it is shown in *Discipline and Punish* to have other features as well.[58]

Evaluation

It has traditionally been said that Foucault's archaeological and genealogical periods are radically different from each other; just as it is commonplace to distinguish Picasso's Blue period from his Pink period, so are Foucault's archaeology and genealogy contrasted. I have suggested instead that we look at Foucault in a different way, and be sensitive to the continuity in his work. I have tried to show that through all of his work Foucault relies upon a concept of knowledge acquisition which is self-referential and which draws upon the unfamiliar to gain access to the familiar. This account exposes the significance of this concept of knowledge acquisition when applied to the study of history. Within the *contours* of the traditional consensus, the historian aims at explaining past events. That explanation can only be relevant to the present in so far as the observed regularities are not merely restricted to that period, and are thus a stepping-stone towards law-like generalizations. In contrast, once a Foucauldian self-referential concept has been adopted, the historian is in search of the present, and the past is his or her gateway towards that present. The very same act of revealing the present also undercuts that present. In Foucauldian parlance, history becomes a 'history of the present' in that he sees his own task as describing 'the nature of the present, and of "ourselves in the present"', in the light of the fact that the present 'is a time which is never quite like any other'.[59]

This way of looking at Foucault has a number of advantages, two of which are worth mentioning here. First, it allows us to conceive of his work as a coherent whole. Not only does it allow us to see the link between archaeology and genealogy, it also enables us to make intelligible several themes or ideas which would otherwise appear marginal (or unrelated) to the main project of his work. Take Foucault's notion of the role of the intellectual. It is well known that Foucault argues against what he sees as a 'traditional' conception of the intellectual. For Foucault, that traditional conception assumes that the intellectual is a messianic figure, who preaches from above, and who incites political action in the name of truth. It is also well known that Foucault substitutes this for the more modest conception of what he calls the 'new' intellectual: that is, someone who provides expertise and technical knowledge to assist in local struggles.[60] I grant that it is possible to account for Foucault's rejection of the traditional notion of the intellectual without taking on board my main argument as given above. It could, for instance, be argued that his position against the traditional intellectual is a necessary corollary of his post-modern hostility towards meta-narratives or totalizing systems. But making sense of Foucault's proposal for the *new* intellectual becomes more difficult without relying upon the view elaborated in this chapter. It is indeed difficult to conceive of what the 'advisory' role of the new intellectual consists, as long as one remains within the realm of a traditional concept of knowledge acquisition. My argument is that the tools provided by the new intellectual are exactly those I have stressed in this chapter: they are revelations about and alterations of one's own presuppositions. Foucault himself acknowledges this in his discussion of the 'ethics' of the new intellectual by distinguishing the mere academic from the academic who is also an intellectual:

> What can the ethics of an intellectual be . . . if not . . . to make oneself permanently capable of *detaching oneself from oneself* (which is the opposite of the attitude of conversion)? . . . To be at once an academic and an intellectual is to try to manipulate a type of knowledge and analysis that is taught and received in the universities in such a way as to alter not only others' thoughts, but also *one's own*. This work of altering one's own thought and that of others seems to be the intellectual's *raison d'être.*[61]

Second, this way of looking at Foucault helps to explain what appear, from the perspective of the traditional consensus, to be peculiarities, omissions and weaknesses in his work. For example, many critiques focus on his lack of interest in *explaining* discontinuity. He does indeed demonstrate radical shifts in, for instance, epistemes or systems of punishment, without always properly explaining how the changes were brought about. However, this is only problematic so long as one imposes on him *ab extra* a traditional conception of knowledge acquisition. Once it is acknowledged that Foucault adopts a self-referential conception, it is clear that the explanation of discontinuity does not necessarily fall within the scope of his enterprise. (This is not to say that explaining discontinuity *ipso facto* falls outside his enterprise.) Rather than merely accounting for why particular changes have occurred in the past, Foucault's main aim is to elucidate and undercut present belief and ethical systems. Once the traditional consensus has been abandoned in favour of the self-referential one, one cannot but be sympathetic towards his omissions. If my view on Foucault's concept of knowledge acquisition is correct, then these criticisms simply miss the point. They criticize him for failing to accomplish something which he did not set out to obtain in the first place, and which, from his perspective, should not necessarily be aimed at anyway.

This is not to say that Foucault's writings are entirely without flaws. There *are* problems with his work, and I will now elaborate on two of the more important lacunae. They concern his relativist position in his archaeological work, and the notion of power in his genealogical period. I have already touched upon Foucault's relativism in his earlier work. I argued that it relies upon two assumptions: a structuralist theory of meaning and a notion of discontinuity. If *ex hypothesi* the meaning of a concept is to be derived from its relationship with the absent totality within a language game, discourse or episteme, and if a radical discontinuity between different language games is assumed, then indeed the notion of 'incommensurability' between different language games seems to follow. This is, I think, the most plausible defence of the relativism in Foucault's archaeology. However, under close scrutiny, things become more complicated. There is, first and foremost, the obvious point made by so many that Foucault's relativist claim, like any such statement, is necessarily applicable to itself, and thus disarms itself. Even setting aside this problem of relativism in general, however, Foucault's particular version of it fails because he does not provide criteria which could justify why he considers certain language games to be discontinuous or not. More importantly, any such decision regarding the criteria is an arbitrary one. It might, of course, be argued that there is discontinuity between language games if, and only if, their underlying rules are sufficiently distinct. But there remains then an arbitrariness regarding which underlying rules are to be selected. Also, there remains the question of how much difference amounts to incommensurability. Surely, the selected discourses and epistemes still have a large number of underlying assumptions in common (there is, after all, no *tabula rasa* in the social realm).

Equally problematic is Foucault's notion of power. Remember that he argues that it is a mistake to conceive of power as merely negative. It is not just repressive or an impediment; it is also constitutive. It is productive in that it creates. Given the broad spectrum provided, it is hardly surprising to find Foucault subsequently concluding that power is everywhere.[62] I would agree with Layder's overall criticism that 'Foucault's notion of power is rather elastic and defies any definite pinning down. As a result of the vagueness or fuzziness that surrounds his notion of power, Foucault is able to evade or fend off potential criticism by stretching his notion to cover all eventualities.'[63] A concept which hardly excludes anything is a highly suspect one. Why stretch the concept of power beyond the boundaries of our daily use of the concept, and why neglect fine distinctions drawn by other theorists? Concepts, such as the Parsonian concepts of influence, socialization and internalization, suddenly fall under the imperialist heading of the catchall Foucauldian concept of power or domination. Foucault's tendency to conceive of power so broadly is not as innocuous as it might appear at first sight, since from this position it is only a small step to argue that existing power relations will necessarily be replaced by new power relations, and previous systems of domination by later systems of domination.[64]

Foucault continues with the idea that 'power relations are both intentional and nonsubjective',[65] but his exposition of the relationship between purposive action and unintended effects is confusing. His argument is that 'there is no power that is exercised without a series of aims and objectives. But this does not mean that it results from the choice or decision of an individual subject'.[66] So far so good, but this is then followed by the methodological dictum not to 'look for the headquarters that preside over its rationality; neither the caste which governs, nor the groups which control the state apparatus, nor those who make the most important economic decisions direct the entire network of power that functions in a society.'[67] It is obvious that this methodological advice does not follow from the previous statement about the incongruence between intention and effect. The fact that people want one thing and end up with another is not a sufficient reason for abandoning the study of the *relationship* between the wanting and the effect (on the contrary, it probes that question), and understanding that relationship is only possible by taking into account the purposive act in the first place. A related point is that although Foucault is essentially correct in pointing out the importance of the local or 'micro'-dimensions of power, state power (and monopoly over the use of power) can still be a necessary condition for the emergence of techniques of surveillance and so on.[68]

Foucault's statement that 'where there is power, there is resistance' is vague again.[69] Does it mean that power always entails resistance or merely that it entails the possibility of resistance? The latter is hardly a bold conjecture, while the former begs further explanation. Why should power necessarily imply resistance, especially if power is so loosely defined in the first place? Surely, if power is conceptualized such that it also incorporates those cases where individual wants are unconsciously influenced (that is, Foucault's 'positive' concept of power), then it seems even more unlikely that power always entails resistance. Foucault himself argued in an interview:

> if power were never anything but repressive, if it never did anything but to say no, do you really think one would be brought to obey it? What makes power hold good, what makes it accepted, is simply the fact that it doesn't only weigh on us as a force that says no, but that it traverses and produces things, it induces pleasure, forms knowledge, produces discourse.[70]

A similar argument can be found in *The History of Sexuality*,[71] but it goes without saying that this position weakens Foucault's claim of the necessary link between power and resistance.

Further reading

Perhaps because it is not as subtle as some of his other works, *Discipline and Punish* is probably one of Foucault's most accessible works and therefore worth starting with. I would then suggest his article 'Nietzsche, genealogy, history' (in *Language, Counter-memory, Practice*), which provides a good introduction to his methodology and his indebtedness to Nietzsche. *Madness and Civilization, The Birth of the Clinic* and *The History of Sexuality* deal with the history of, respectively, madness, medicine and sexuality. Issues related to science are dealt with in *The Order of Things* and *The Archaeology of Knowledge*. There is a huge amount of secondary literature on Foucault, but, as a simple introduction, Smart's *Michel Foucault* will do. An excellent summary of each phase in Foucault's work can be found in Sheridan's *Michel Foucault: The Will to Truth*. A more challenging attempt to link Foucault with other theoretical developments, in particular Marxism, can be found in Smart's *Foucault, Marxism and Critique* and Poster's *Foucault, Marxism and History*. Foucault's philosophy of the present, Habermas and Taylor's critique of Foucault's account of the Enlightenment are discussed in an excellent chapter of Hiley's *Philosophy in Question*. Habermas deals with Foucault in *The Philosophical Discourse of Modernity*, Taylor's argumentations can be found in his 'Foucault on freedom and truth' (*Political Theory*), and Nancy Fraser's criticisms are summarized in the article 'Foucault on modern power: empirical insights and normative confusions' (*Praxis International*).

References

Bachelard, G. 1984. *The New Scientific Spirit*. Boston: Beacon Press (originally in French, 1934).

Baert, P. 1996. Realist philosophy of the social sciences and economics: a critique. *Cambridge Journal of Economics* 20, 513–22.

Barthes, R. 1983. *The Fashion System*. New York: Hill and Wang (originally in French, 1967).

Braudel, F. 1966. *La Méditerranée et le monde méditerranéen à l'époque de Philippe II*. Paris: Armand Colin.

Canguilhem, G. 1978. *On the Normal and the Pathological*. Dortrecht: Reidel (originally in French, 1943).

Foucault, M. 1954. *Maladie mentale et personnalité*. Paris: PUF. (2nd revised edition, retitled *Maladie mentale et psychologie*, 1962).

Foucault, M. 1971. Orders of discourse. *Social Science Information* 10, 27–30.

Foucault, M. 1977a. *Discipline and Punish: The Birth of the Prison*. London: Allen Lane (reprinted, 1991; originally in French, 1975).

Foucault, M. 1977b. *Language, Counter-memory, Practice*, ed. D. F. Bouchard. Ithaca: Cornell University Press.

Foucault, M. 1979. *The History of Sexuality; Volume I, An Introduction*. London: Penguin (reprinted 1990; originally in French, 1976).

Foucault, M. 1980. *Power / Knowledge; Selected Interviews and Other Writings 1972–1977* (ed. C. Gordon). Hemel Hempstead: Harvester Wheatsheaf.

Foucault, M. 1989a. *Madness and Civilization; A History of Insanity in the Age of Reason*. London: Routledge (reprinted, 1993; originally in French, 1961).

Foucault, M. 1989b. *The Archaeology of Knowledge*. London: Routledge (reprinted, 1992; originally in French, 1969).

Foucault, M. 1989c. *The Birth of the Clinic: An Archaeology of Medical Perception*. London: Routledge (reprinted, 1991; originally in French, 1963).

Foucault, M. 1989d. *The Order of Things: An Archaeology of the Human Sciences.* London: Routledge (reprinted, 1991; originally in French, 1966).

Foucault, M. 1990a. *Politics, Philosophy, Culture; Interviews and Other Writings 1977–1984* (ed. L. D. Kritzman). London: Routledge.

Foucault, M. 1990b. *The History of Sexuality; Volume 3, The Care of the Self.* London: Penguin (originally in French, 1984).

Foucault, M. 1992. *The History of Sexuality; Volume 2, The Use of Pleasure.* London: Penguin (originally in French, 1984).

Fraser, N. 1981. Foucault on modern power: empirical insights and normative confusions. *Praxis International* 1 (3), 272–87.

Geuss, R. 1994. Nietzsche and genealogy. *European Journal of Philosophy* 2 (3), 274–92.

Habermas, J. 1987. *The Philosophical Discourse of Modernity.* Cambridge: Polity Press (reprinted, 1992; originally in German, 1985).

Hiley, D. R. 1988. *Philosophy in Question; Essays on a Pyrrhonian Theme.* Chicago: The University of Chicago Press.

Layder, D. 1994. *Understanding Social Theory.* London: Sage.

Saussure, F. 1959. *Course in General Linguistics.* London: Peter Owen (originally in French, 1915).

Sheridan, A. 1990. *Michel Foucault; The Will to Truth.* London: Routledge.

Skinner, Q. (ed.) 1985. *The Return of Grand Theory on the Human Sciences.* Cambridge: Cambridge University Press.

Smart, B. 1983. *Foucault, Marxism and Critique.* London: Routledge.

Smart, B. 1988. *Michel Foucault.* London: Routledge.

Phillip, M. 1985. Michel Foucault. In: *The Return of Grand Theory in the Human Sciences,* ed. Q. Skinner. Cambridge: Cambridge University Press, 65–82.

Poster, M., 1990. *Foucault, Marxism and History; Mode of Production versus Mode of Information.* Cambridge: Polity Press.

Poulantzas, N. 1978. *State, Power, Socialism.* London: New Left Books (originally in French, 1978).

Taylor, C. 1981. Foucault on freedom and truth. *Political Theory* 12, 152–83.

6
The Spread of Reason
Habermas's Critical Theory

Jürgen Habermas (1929–) studied philosophy, history, psychology and German literature at the universities of Göttingen, Zurich and Bonn. After completing his doctorate on Friedrich Schelling in 1954, he became a journalist, before taking up a position as Theodor Adorno's assistant at the Institute for Social Research, Frankfurt, in 1956. He subsequently taught at Heidelberg for a couple of years and then became Professor of philosophy and sociology at the University of Frankfurt. He became co-director of the Max Planck Institute in 1971, and returned to the Johann Wolfgang Goethe University of Frankfurt eleven years later to take up the chair in sociology and philosophy. Since the early 1970s, Habermas has become a leading figure in philosophy and social theory, writing widely on core themes within the field. In spite of his dense style of writing, the high level of abstraction, and occasionally the vast knowledge which he presupposes of the reader, his influence at the end of the twentieth century vastly transcends the German-speaking world. Habermas is known especially as one of the most prominent twentieth-century exponents of 'critical theory'. Critical theorists, such as Adorno, Max Horkheimer and Habermas, do not simply wish to account for or explain the social world. They intend instead to evaluate both the potential and the problems of modern society, and their ultimate aim is to contribute to people's self-emancipation.

Like Karl Popper, Habermas is convinced that knowledge progresses through open discussion and criticism (see chapter 8). In this respect, Habermas also practices what he preaches. He has indeed been embroiled in several political and academic debates, some of which arose out of his writings, and most of which have led him to reassess and redefine his previous ideas and concepts. Amongst the most memorable debates are his encounters with positivist and falsificationist philosophers of science, supporters of the German philosopher Martin Heidegger, the hermeneutic philosopher Hans-Georg Gadamer, the system theorist Niklas Luhmann, the student movement in Germany and the post-structuralist or post-modernist movement in France.[1]

There are very few philosophers or theorists who have shown such a persistent interest in differing views. There are even fewer who have been so willing, as Habermas has been, to take counter-arguments on board. As a result, Habermas's philosophy is far from static; it is constantly evolving.

Habermas's *Habilitationsschrift* was published as *Structural Transformation in the Public Sphere (Strukturwandel der Öffentlichkeit)* in 1962.[2] It depicts the emergence and spread of a 'public sphere' of open debate in the eighteenth century, and it also deals with the gradual decline of that cultural pattern in advanced capitalist society. Contrary to Habermas's later works, this book is remarkably easy to read. It is, however, truly Habermasian in that it already reveals his fascination with the communicative dimensions of a liberal democracy. For Habermas, the 'public sphere' expresses a 'discursive will-formation' or free uncoerced debate amongst equals, and the latter was to become central to his notion of a critical theory. His interest in open, unconstrained debate led eventually to his notion of communicative rationality based on an in-depth reading of American pragmatic philosophy (which Habermas referred to as 'radical democratic Hegelianism').

Shortly after the publication of his dissertation, a number of articles and essays were translated and published under the title *Towards a Rational Society; Student Protest, Science, and Politics* (originally two books: *Protestbewegung und Hochschulreform* and *Technik und Wissenschaft*). This book comments on, amongst other things, the student movement in Germany and the increase and dispersion of instrumental rationality in various aspects of life.[3] Underlying his earlier work is the notion that, in the political arena, what Mannheim called 'substantial rationality' has been substituted by 'functional rationality'. This means that ultimate values have become less of a guiding force for political practices than they were before. Instead, politics is increasingly geared towards avoiding technical problems which threaten the equilibrium or the adequate functioning of the social and economic system. The ideas in the two earlier books are obviously not far removed from his mentors, Adorno and Horkheimer.

Habermas's originality shows itself first at the level of methodology and philosophy of the social sciences. In *Theory and Practice (Theorie und Praxis)*, *Knowledge and Human Interests (Erkenntnis und Interesse)* and *On the Logic of the Social Sciences (Zur Logik der Sozialwissenschaften)* attention is focused on the epistemological foundations of critical theory.[4] Habermas advances a critical account of both functionalism and system theory, attempts to situate critical theory in relation to hermeneutics and positivist epistemology and distances himself from some positivist tendencies in the Marxist theory of society (see chapter 8). There is an obvious link with his earlier work: technical rationality goes hand in hand with those types of analysis that are indebted to a positivist or functionalist framework. But Habermas does not entirely reject the views of his opponents. Some insights of system theory are incorporated into his general social theory, and however suspicious he might be of 'empirical-analytical' modes of knowledge, they do remain an essential ingredient in his reconstruction of critical theory.

During the first half of the 1970s Habermas paid attention to a number of substantive issues. In *Legitimation Crisis* (*Legitimationsprobleme im Spätkapitalismus*) he directs his attention towards societal problems related to the advent of modernity. He deals in particular with different types of crisis under advanced capitalism, in particular crises of motivational commitment and normative integration. Then followed *Communication and the Evolution of Society* (*Zur Rekonstruktion des Historischen Materialismus*), an attempt to provide a contemporary reassessment of Marx's theory of history, and to deal with the homology or structural identity between personality development and changes at a social level.[5] Gradually, however, Habermas's interest turned towards the accomplishments of the linguistic turn in philosophy, and by the mid-1970s he had worked out the cornerstones of his theory of universal pragmatics – the prelude to his theory of communicative action.

In 1981 Habermas published his *magnum opus:* two volumes of *The Theory of Communicative Action* (*Theorie des Kommunikativen Handelns*). This is a *tour de force* in grand social theory, in which, amongst other things, he reworks the concept of rationality whilst overcoming some of the shortcomings of an originally Cartesian philosophy of consciousness (*Bewusstseinsphilosophie*) and its attendant subject–object conception of cognition.[6] Habermas's notion of communicative rationality and his criticisms of Marx are not unrelated. Marx paid exclusive interest to the concept of 'labour', and Habermas insists that linguistically mediated interaction is as vital to social reproduction and evolution as is labour. So, the concept of labour needs to be supplemented with the notion of 'interaction'. Whereas labour ties in with instrumental reason, interaction refers to communication geared towards mutual understanding.[7] Likewise, Habermas's concept of communicative rationality (central to his attempt to develop a critical theory) is embedded in linguistically mediated interaction.

Having been exposed to various criticisms, Habermas has retreated from some of the more extreme positions in *The Theory of Communicative Action*. Despite this, it is fair to say that he is still committed to the broad outline of the theory. Indeed, his more recent contributions share roughly the same assumptions. *The Philosophical Discourse of Modernity* (*Der Philosophische Diskurs der Moderne*), for instance, consists of a staunch defence of the project of the Enlightenment against anti-modernist, post-modernist and poststructuralist authors such as Nietzsche, Heidegger, Foucault, Derrida and Jean-François Lyotard (see chapter 5).[8] For Habermas, these critiques of the Enlightenment have basically failed to recognize its emancipatory potential.

Enlightenment thinkers stood for open debate and criticism, and thus for communicative rationality. Most recently, *Justification and Application* (*Erläuterungen zur Diskursethik*) is Habermas's contribution to ethics and legal theory. This work is again very much in line with the theoretical outline of his theory of communicative action.[9]

Influences and early writings

The early Frankfurt School, of which Adorno and Horkheimer were the most eminent members, was founded in the early 1920s, and dissolved approximately ten years later because of the radically changing political scene in Germany at the time. Adorno et al. embarked upon an ambitious project aimed at reconstructing Marxist social theory whilst taking on board some Weberian and Nietzschean insights. They considered Marx too much enmeshed in, and thus not critical enough towards, the project of the Enlightenment. The members of the Frankfurt School left their home country in the mid-1930s for safer regions (in particular the United States), but a number of them, including Adorno, returned after the Second World War. Habermas, originally a student of Adorno and later his assistant, is considered to be the main successor of that generation – a leading intellectual, whose work, although from varied sources, is still in some respects faithful to the spirit of the early Frankfurt School.

There are a number of continuities running from the Frankfurt School to Habermas's work. Some commentators argue that, because of its interdisciplinary nature, Habermas's *oeuvre* comes particularly close to the research conducted in the early years of the Frankfurt Institute of Social Research.[10] More substantively, Habermas shares with Adorno and Horkheimer a concern with the extent to which the *Aufklärung*, in spite of its liberating potential, has led to the spread and dispersion of means–end rationality in the West.[11] Furthermore, the early Frankfurt School and Habermas are highly critical of the epistemological assumptions of positivist sociology. They emphatically deplore the technical nature of positivist knowledge (see chapter 8).[12] Habermas obtains from Adorno et al. a conception of critical theory as geared towards the self-emancipation of human beings. In this view, social scientific knowledge ought to help lift up past social and psychological restrictions.

Amongst the differences with, for instance, Adorno is that Habermas's penchant for developing a 'grand social theory' in a traditional mould is at odds with the former's criticisms of identity thinking. Adorno coined the term 'identity thinking' to designate any attempt to impose a unitary system of concepts and general definitions onto the particularity and idiosyncrasy of objects.[13] This ties in with yet another difference: whereas Adorno's view of rationality is still deeply embedded in the philosophy of consciousness,

Habermas prefers to ground reason in the intersubjective context of daily linguistic usage. Whereas for Adorno the only safe haven for reason against the spread of instrumental rationality resides in the aesthetic realm, Habermas opts for a dialogical notion of reason. Also, whereas the Frankfurt School, following Weber, portrays a single and irreversible direction towards increasing instrumental rationality (*Zweckrationalität*) in the West, Habermas points out the twofold and selective nature of that rationalization process. For Habermas, one aspect of this process is indeed the alleged means–end rationality; another is the extension of judicial liberties and communicative rationality. The latter is worth defending.[14] Finally, whereas the early critical theorists seem to reject bourgeois society *in toto*, Habermas argues that there are some formal features of bourgeois political institutions which are worth preserving. By contrast with Horkheimer and Adorno, Habermas indeed demonstrates how his notion of communicative rationality is already presupposed in the main institutions of our liberal democracy, and *mutatis mutandis* how an immanent critique of contemporary society becomes feasible.[15]

Habermas is also widely acquainted with the broader German philosophical tradition. During his university training, he became familiar with Immanuel Kant, Hegel, Schelling, Johann Gottlieb Fichte, Marx and Georg Lukács. Amongst sociological influences are Marx's historical materialism, Durkheim's theory about the transition from mechanical to organic solidarity, Weber's theory of rationalization, Parsons's notion of social differentiation and Garfinkel's ethnomethodology. Further influences include the American pragmatism of Peirce, Dewey and Mead, Gadamer's hermeneutics, post-Wittgensteinian 'ordinary language philosophy' of Oxford's J. L. Austin, John Searle and Peter Strawson, and Jean Piaget and Lawrence Kohlberg's stage theory. Given the wide variety of Habermas's sources, it is remarkable that his own project is nevertheless unified thematically. Whether he is discussing Weber's concept of rationality or Mead's notion of a symbolically constituted social world, whether he is arguing against the excesses of logical-positivism or against the relativist inclinations of the French postmodernist wave, underlying his *oeuvre* one always finds a fierce belief in the project of the philosophy of the Enlightenment and in the principles of political liberalism. Most of his writings are centred around this deeply held conviction.

It should already be clear that, in some aspects, Habermas's project is not dissimilar to that of Giddens (see chapter 4). Indeed, they both attempt to integrate a wide variety of intellectual traditions in order to develop a post-empiricist, though explicitly non-relativist, contribution to social theory. Furthermore, both warn against the dangers of adopting a one-sided argument, whether it is so-called structure-related or actor-orientated. Each aims instead at linking different levels of social analysis and at overcoming previously held dualisms. Like Giddens, Habermas wants to transcend the opposition between the functioning at the system level on the one hand, and the workings at the symbolic, intersubjective realm on the other. In this respect, Habermas introduces two central concepts: the 'social system' and the 'life-world' (Schutz's *Lebenswelt*). The life-world refers to the shared meanings and taken-for-granted nature of our daily activities. Habermas states that the life-world is central to social reproduction; by that he means that society is constantly made and remade through these routine practices. The life-world has, in particular, received close attention from 'internalist' viewpoints such as phenomenology and ethnomethodology (see chapter 3). The social system refers to the way in which social structures and functional imperatives constrain people's actions through the media of money and power. It has been the object of study from externalist perspectives such as structural-functionalism or system theory (see chapters 1 and 2). Whereas the life-world raises issues of communication, the social system relates to the forces and relations of production. Habermas's work pays attention both to the social system and to the life-world and aims to demonstrate their interplay. The life-world is dependent on the adequate functioning of the social system, especially the efficient use of resources and state-governed organization and co-ordination of activities. The social system needs properly socialized individuals and a certain degree of permanence at a cultural level. This is provided by the life-world.[16]

For Habermas, critical theory should be seen as residing at the intersection between philosophy and science. Critical theory intends to uncover the structural conditions of people's actions, and it is ultimately directed towards transcending these conditions. Habermas goes to some lengths to define critical theory and to specify how it relates to other forms of knowledge. Relying partly upon Peirce's pragmatic philosophy and its attendant link between science and action, Habermas distinguishes in his earlier work three distinct forms of knowledge: empirical-analytical knowledge, hermeneutics and critical theory. These types of knowledge are related to three anthropologically distinct forms of *a priori* interests. Interests are understood as 'basic orientations' embedded in 'fundamental conditions' of reproduction and self-constitution of the human species.[17] Whereas the empirical-analytical or positivist approach ties in with technical control and prediction through nomological knowledge, hermeneutics seeks understanding within a context of intersubjective meaning. Finally, critical theory, as a combination of hermeneutics and empirical-analytical types of knowledge, is aimed at emancipation. It endeavours to question assumptions that previously have been taken for granted, and to remove psychological or social constraints and dependencies. Note that each of these interests is related to different means of social organization and media. Empirical-analytical types of knowledge have an affinity with 'instrumental action' or 'work', hermeneutics is relevant to 'language' or 'interaction', and critical theory deals with 'asymmetrical relations' or 'power'.[18]

I will deal with each type of knowledge in turn. What Habermas calls empirical-analytical knowledge is basically a positivist notion of knowledge. Positivism is a broad term, and includes, for instance, Comte's holistic thinking and his unilinear evolutionism on the one hand, and Mill's methodological individualism and his ahistorical approach on the other. Positivism is exemplified more recently in Hempel's or Nagel's deductive-nomological model. Originally an ambitious attempt to ban all metaphysics and religion, positivism now covers a large number of different assertions or themes. Amongst the latter are the assumptions that there is a unity of method between the social and the natural sciences; the notion that the social sciences ought to search for eternal law-like generalizations; the belief that the same format which allows phenomena to be explained also allows the prediction of the very same phenomena, and vice versa; a rejection of explanations which refer to subjective states of individuals such as motives or purposes; a predilection towards quantification; and a view of the social sciences as exclusively aimed at solving technical problems of society (see chapter 8). Habermas rejects the positivist claim that it is the only form of valid knowledge, and he also repudiates the positivist tendency to ignore the intersubjective and social dimension of scientific knowledge.[19] In his view, there is a residual positivism in Marxism in so far as it reduces social interaction to mainly (if not exclusively) a mechanical outcome of the productive forces.[20] Like Giddens and Bourdieu, Habermas recognizes that some hermeneutic insights are indeed relevant to the workings of the social world: people attribute meaning to their surroundings, and act accordingly (see chapters 1 and 4).

This brings me to the second type of knowledge. Hermeneutics, or the method of *Sinnverstehen*, postulates a qualitative difference between the methods of the social and the natural sciences. This argument goes back to Wilhelm Dilthey's appeal for a distinctive method of interpretative understanding (*Verstehen*) for the human sciences (*Geisteswissenschaften*). Dilthey clearly articulated the hermeneutic position in the so-called *Methodenstreit* at the end of the nineteenth century. According to him, whereas the natural sciences deal with questions like 'why' and 'how', the social sciences and history try to answer 'what' questions. Although Dilthey initially presented an individualistic version of the method of *Verstehen*, in which re-enactment takes a prominent position, he later came to recognize the public-collective and linguistic features of this re-enactment process. Habermas argues that, due to its emphasis on descriptive analysis, Dilthey's hermeneutics is incapable of critically assessing the validity of statements. Furthermore, against Dilthey's assumption of a neutral or virginal re-enactment of the past and in line with Gadamer's notion of prejudice (*Vorurteilsstruktur*), Habermas argues that interpretations are only possible through the medium of implicit preconceptions. For him, the more recent developments within hermeneutics (for example, Schutz's sociological interpretation of Husserl's phenomenology,

Peter Winch's interpretation of Wittgenstein's *Philosophical Investigations*, or Garfinkel's ethnomethodology) do not entirely overcome some of the shortcomings of Dilthey's work. Habermas finds more inspiration in the work of Gadamer, in particular his *Truth and Method*. Gadamer argues against the Enlightenment notion of value-free and theory-independent knowledge. According to him, tradition and prejudice should not be seen as obstacles to the acquisition of knowledge, but rather as the precondition for the possibility of that knowledge. As the historicity of traditions is intrinsic to knowledge formation, knowledge is temporal and open to future reassessments. Understanding the world is not merely a one-way process – our very preconceptions are reconstructed in the encounter with the world. Most of these conceptual insights are taken over by Habermas, whilst he criticizes Gadamer for his alleged lack of a critical dimension. People's knowledge or interpretation, he argues, necessarily rely upon a number of implicit assumptions which are embedded in history and tradition, but it does not follow that different sets of assumptions are equally valid. What sociology needs in addition, Habermas continues, is a 'depth hermeneutics' which provides a yardstick enabling us to evaluate different traditions critically and to identify ideological distortions and their relationship with power relations.[21]

Habermas's depth hermeneutics falls under the third type of knowledge: critical theory. Critical theory rests upon a combination of causal explanation and *Sinnverstehen* and is ultimately aimed at self-emancipation. Self-emancipation takes place whenever people are able to challenge past restrictions which are a result of distorted communication.[22] Although Freud defined his theory in close association with the natural sciences, Habermas conceives of psychoanalysis as the example *par excellence* of critical theory. The hermeneutic dimension enters a psychoanalytic encounter whenever the psychoanalyst helps the patient to re-enact previously repressed memories and experiences. Habermas talks about 'depth hermeneutics' here, since the psychoanalyst attempts to move behind the surface meaning and to delve further at the level of repressed needs and wishes. One of the aims of this interaction is, of course, to reveal to the patient the previously hidden causal mechanisms which have hitherto influenced behavioural patterns; this then is the empirical-analytical dimension. However, the ultimate goal of the psychoanalytic encounter is the removal of these restrictions of the past, which Habermas calls the emancipatory dimension of psychoanalysis.[23] Another example of critical theory, but at a societal level rather than at a psychological one, is historical materialism. Like psychoanalysis, historical materialism is directed towards reflection and critical awareness.

Habermas's earlier writings, and in particular *Knowledge and Human Interests*, suffer from a number of weaknesses. First, as he later acknowledges himself, his earlier thought is still embedded in what he calls a Cartesian 'philosophy of consciousness' (or philosophy of the subject) in that it overlooks the social nature of communicative practices. Second, although Habermas demonstrates persuasively that psychoanalysis can be self-emancipatory for the *individual*, this does not imply, as he seems to assume, that psychoanalysis is a stepping-stone for a critical theory of *society*. Many doubts have since emerged regarding such potential for psychoanalysis.[24] Third, the early Habermas regularly conflates reflection upon socially induced constraints on the one hand, and liberation from these constraints on the other. When later pressed on this issue, he recognizes that self-reflection is a necessary, though not sufficient, condition for negating past restrictions. But in his early writings the two notions are not always properly distinguished. Fourth, Habermas uses the term 'reflection' with at least two different meanings. One refers to the Kantian concept of 'critique' as reflection upon the conditions of possibilities of knowing or acting. Another refers to the Hegelian emancipatory notion of *Bildung* as reflection upon hitherto unconscious or hypostatised constraints.[25] Habermas later recognizes this ambiguity in these writings, calling the latter self-criticism and the former rational reconstruction. He has devoted an important part of his work in the 1990s, including *The Theory of Communicative Action*, to the phenomenon of rational reconstruction. In this context, he relies upon what he calls 'reconstructive sciences', referring to Chomsky's generative grammar, Piaget's theory of cognitive development and Kohlberg's theory of moral development. These reconstructive sciences reveal the underlying rules of our pre-theoretical 'knowing how'. Habermas's theory of communicative action or universal pragmatics is itself such a reconstructive science. This theory allows him to follow Kant in his notion of reason, reflecting upon the universal conditions of its own functioning, whilst avoiding the *a priori* nature of Kant's enterprise.[26]

The theory of communicative action

This brings me to his seminal work on rationality. For Habermas, an action or a statement is rational if it can, in principle, be justified on the basis of an open debate with equal participation for each individual. This working definition can be used to address three aspects of the concept of rationality. One component is epistemological. Its leading question is whether or not each culture incorporates its own rationality. Habermas's conceptualization of rationality as procedural leads him to reject relativist notions such as those of Winch, who relies upon Wittgenstein's *Philosophical Investigations*. A second component of rationality operates at the level of social theory. It deals with the rationality claims which are made in one's explanations of social conduct (see chapter 7). The third component, to which Habermas pays most attention, refers to the sociology of culture and particularly the cultural process of transition which the West has undergone since roughly the sixteenth century.

By focusing on this third component, Habermas reacts partly against Weber's notion of disenchantment (*Entzauberung*) and Adorno and Horkheimer's concept of instrumental reason. According to these authors, modern civilization is characterized by an increase in the logic of means–end rationality. As such, they are highly critical of the project of modernity. For Habermas, however, rationalization is not a single, but a twofold process. On the one hand, it indeed involves instrumental rationality, as it has been conceptualized by Weber and the Frankfurt School. Like them, Habermas is highly critical of excessive means–end rationality. On the other hand, there is undoubtedly a more positive component to the rationalization process in the West. Habermas decides to call this positive aspect of the Enlightenment 'communicative rationality'. Communicative rationality refers to the institutionalization of mechanisms of open criticism and defence. Whereas instrumental rationality links in with the imperative of the social system, communicative rationality refers to the level of the life-world. Communicative rationality becomes the corner stone of Habermas's contribution to critical theory.[27]

Central to Habermas's 'universal pragmatics' is the notion of competence. He argues that people possess specific practical skills which allow them to draw particular distinctions. One of these distinctions is between three types of action: 'instrumental', 'strategic' and 'communicative action'. Instrumental and strategic action are both orientated towards success, but whilst the former refers to a relationship with external nature, the latter deals with strategic situations between people. Strategic and communicative action are both social, but the latter is social action orientated towards reaching 'understanding' (*Verständigung*) with respect to all 'validity claims' (*Geltungsansprüche*).[28] Obviously influenced by Popper (see chapter 8), Habermas argues that people are able, in principle, to make an additional distinction between three different worlds: external nature, society and internal nature. Whereas the world of external nature refers to issues of a correct representation of facts, society refers to issues of moral rightness of social rules, and internal nature deals with issues of sincerity.[29] As will be obvious from what follows, the ability of people to make these various distinctions is central to Habermas's notion of communicative action.

One of Habermas's central claims is that the notion of rationality presupposes communication. To elaborate this argument, Habermas relies on speech act theory. He draws heavily upon Austin's distinction between illocutionary and locutionary speech acts. Austin introduces these terms to draw a distinction between saying something on the one hand, and doing something by saying something on the other. Following Austin, Habermas claims that every speech act can be divided up into a propositional level and an illocutionary level. Habermas combines this with his tripartite frame of worlds according to which there are three uses of language: cognitive, interactive and expressive.

The cognitive use of language points to something in the objective world and draws upon constatives as a type of speech action. The interactive use refers to the social world, aims at establishing legitimate interpersonal relations and draws upon regulatives (like commands or promises). Finally, the expressive use refers to the subjective world, the intention or self-representation of the speaker, whilst drawing upon avowals. As will become clear in the following, these three uses of language tie in with three 'validity claims'.[30]

I am now in a position to elaborate on the core of Habermas's theory of communicative action. One of his pivotal assertions is that whenever people are involved in a conversation with one another four culturally invariant 'validity claims' are implicitly presupposed. These are 'intelligibility', 'truth', 'moral rightness' and 'sincerity'. Intelligibility (*Verständlichkeit*) refers to the presupposition that whenever one speaks, what one says has meaning and is not gibberish. As intelligibility is fulfilled within language use itself, it is not part of the subject-matter covered within Habermas's universal pragmatics. Truth (*Wahrheit*), the second validity claim, refers to the fact that, by saying something, there is the implicit idea that the 'factual content' of what is said is true. Moral rightness (*Richtigkeit*) refers to the implicit claim that, by saying something, one has the right to say it at a given moment within a given context. Finally, sincerity (*Wahrhaftigkeit*) is the implicit claim that, by saying what one says, one is not intending to deceive the other participants in the interaction.

The ability of people to differentiate beween the three worlds ties in with the latter three validity claims. Truth belongs to the world of external nature; Habermas calls it the 'cognitive-instrumental sphere'. Moral rightness links in with the world of society; in Habermasian parlance, this is the 'moral-practical sphere'. Sincerity concerns the world of internal nature; Habermas calls it the 'evaluative or expressive sphere'. Although the validity claims are implicitly presupposed in communication, all are also potentially open to argumentation. Each validity claim is associated with a different form of argumentation. Theoretical discourse refers to the truth-validity of propositions or efficacy of actions; Habermas calls this form of discourse the 'cognitive use of language'. Practical discourse refers to the rightness of norms; Habermas coins it 'interactive use of language'. Aesthetic criticism and therapeutic critique refer to adequacy of value standards and truthfulness and sincerity of expressions; this is the 'expressive use of language'.[31]

'Undistorted communication' differs from 'distorted communication' in that the people involved can openly defend and criticize all validity claims. This is especially the case in an 'ideal speech situation', which is an uncoerced debate between free and equal individuals, and as such it is entirely dominated by one principle: the 'force of the better argument'. Furthermore, all individuals involved have equal right to enter the discussion, and there is no repressed motive or self-deceit which might affect the outcome. The ideal speech situation is an ideal type in the Weberian use of the word, and one of Habermas's bold claims is that it is inherent in the nature of language. He refers to it as a 'counterfactual' ideal which can operate as a yardstick for critically evaluating and comparing real-life situations and as a critique of distorted communication.[32] Of the four validity claims, only truth and moral rightness can be redeemed in discourses which approximate an ideal speech situation. The intelligibility of a statement tends to be demonstrated by putting it differently, and sincerity can only be shown by subsequent actions. But truth and moral rightness can be redeemed in discourse. It follows that Habermas's notion of rationality and truth is a *procedural* one: his notion of rationality does not adhere to absolute foundations of knowledge, but to *procedures* of reaching knowledge.[33] One of the upshots of this is that, analogous to Popper's rejection of a 'first philosophy', our knowledge is temporal – to be held until a better argument compels us to think otherwise (see chapter 8). Contrary to, for example, Tarski's notion of a correspondence theory of truth, Habermas's consensus theory of truth refers to agreements reached on the basis of an open unrestrained debate amongst equals.

Hitherto, I have mainly dealt with the Habermasian notion of a rational 'conduct of life' (*Lebensführung*); but what about the differences between societies as to whether their 'form of life' (*Lebensform*) allows for such rational conduct? For Habermas, some societies are more predisposed to *Lebensführung* than others. In particular, the *Lebensform* of earlier civilizations seems less conducive to rationality. In this context, Habermas develops a theory of homology or structural identity between individual and societal development. For this he relies, in part, upon Piaget's work on the cognitive and moral development of children, distinguishing, as does Piaget, four stages of the child's development: the symbiotic, the egocentric, the sociocentric and the universalistic. Each phase leads to a 'decentring' of an egocentrically distorted view of the world. The child gradually learns to distinguish the objective, the social and the subjective realm. Before children enter the egocentric stage, they are unable to differentiate themselves from the environment, and it is only during the sociocentric stage that children gradually learn to distinguish physical and social reality. Finally, during the universalistic stage they learn to reflect critically upon their actions or values from the perspective of alternative arguments. This unilinear perspective ties in with Kohlberg's three stages of consciousness in ontogenesis: the pre-conventional, the conventional and the post-conventional.[34]

Consistent with his interpretation of, amongst others, Lévi-Strauss, Piaget and Kohlberg, Habermas argues that societal development goes through analogous stages to personal development. As opposed to modern world-views, mythical world-views do not allow people to distinguish between the external world, the social world and internal nature – they tend to conflate nature and culture, or language and the world. Analogous to individual development, there is a trend towards increasingly discursive rationality in the transition from mythopoietic, cosmological and religious cultures, to metaphysical and modern societies. Habermas adheres to a unilinear evolutionism in that he sees this trend towards increasing rationality as the inevitable and irreversible outcome of a collective learning process.[35] Rationality becomes a possibility once a differentiation of the system and life-world takes place, plus a differentiation of the cognitive-instrumental sphere, the moral-practical sphere, the evaluative and the expressive sphere.

However, with the differentiation of the system and life-world, two problems occur. First, the maintenance of the economic and political dimensions of the social system might become eroded. This ties in with a 'motivation crisis' in the work sphere and a 'legitimation crisis' at the political level. Broadly speaking, Habermas's argument is that in advanced capitalism, politics is reduced to its pragmatic dimension; it is mainly in charge of macro-economic issues. However, if it fails to pursue its economic functions, it cannot rely upon legitimate authority, loyalty or commitment on the part of the citizens. Once politics is largely reduced to the solving of economic problems, recurrent economic crises are sufficient to erode its legitimacy.[36] Second, the system imperatives tend to instrumentalize the life-world, and this 'colonization of the life-world' leads to what Durkheim diagnosed as 'anomie' and Weber as a general loss of meaning. The subordination of the life-world to system imperatives is exemplified in Marx's theory of labour where the commodification of labour leads to the erosion of its life-world dimension. It is worth mentioning, however, that Habermas's theory of colonization differs significantly from the view of classical social theorists and their followers. He differs from Weber in that he does not conceive of the colonization of the life-world as part of an internal logic of modernization. In Habermas's view, the colonization of the life-world is not inevitable. This differs from a Marxist view in that Habermas's hope rests with the new social movements, and the latter do not operate within a traditional Marxist agenda. The new social movements are concerned with issues relating to quality of life and self-realization. Although these values are not incompatible with Marx's earlier writings, contemporary Marxists are reluctant to attribute such priority to these goals.[37]

Evaluation

There is no doubt that Habermas's enterprise is a courageous one. At a time when the project of the Frankfurt School has been widely abandoned, Habermas aims at finding new philosophical grounds for critical theory. Whilst post-modernism has been so much in the ascendant in the last quarter of the twentieth century, Habermas attempts to redefine and defend precisely the project of modernity. Furthermore, he also sets out to argue against all those who, whether influenced by Nietzsche, Wittgenstein or Kuhn, court the doctrine of relativism. Despite the controversial nature of Habermas's work, its sheer breadth and depth are achievements in themselves. The latter accomplishments are probably unrivalled in the twentieth century. Habermas incorporates an impressive range of philosophies and sociological theories. He deals with a wide spectrum of issues, from traditional philosophical topics to the intricacies of contemporary politics.

Given the enormous scope of his work and given the difficult tasks he sets out to achieve, it would be inconceivable for his project to be without any significant lacuna. I will not even attempt to provide here an exhaustive list of all the criticisms which have been levelled against his writings. It is simply too long, and Habermas has incorporated some of these arguments in his work anyway. I will instead mention what I personally see as major weaknesses in his project. I deal especially with his central writings on communicative rationality because they have been the most influential so far. I think the deficiencies listed seriously compromise the validity of Habermas's argument as a fruitful contribution to critical theory.

First, there is the rather tedious, though not insignificant, point that some aspects of his work lack a solid empirical grounding. Habermas's contribution to critical theory relies on a number of 'reconstructive sciences'. The latter have been regularly subjected to criticism on empirical grounds, and rightly so. For example, the empirical basis of Piaget's or Kohlberg's work does not remain uncontested, neither does Lévi-Strauss's *oeuvre* (see chapter 1). The lack of empirical support for these theories may jeopardize the core of his theory of communicative action, which in its procedure of rational reconstruction draws heavily upon them. A similar criticism applies to Habermas's theory of societal evolution, which he backs by his personal and selective reading of the work of other theoreticians of evolution (Weber, Marx and Durkheim, to name only a few), who in their turn often rely upon secondary sources. Habermas's reconstruction of others' accounts of evolution clarifies and illustrates his position very well indeed, but, as a defence of that very same position, it is inevitably unconvincing. This is certainly not to say that Habermas's theoretical frame of reference cannot be sustained by empirical evidence, but more research is needed to pass a judgement on this issue.

Second, there are problems with Habermas's statement that communicative action is orientated towards reaching understanding or agreement. It is, in Habermas's own terms, *verständigungsorientiertes Handeln*. However, the German word '*Verständigung*' is confusing since it incorporates both understanding and agreement. Of course, it could be argued that agreement presupposes at least a minimal form of understanding. If two people agree upon something, then they necessarily must have some understanding upon what they agree. Understanding, however, does not presuppose agreement: if two people understand each other, it does not follow that they agree upon what has been understood.[38] This weakens Habermas's argument that communication presupposes the possibility of *Verständigung*. He might have compelling reasons for arguing that communication indeed requires as a condition the possibility of understanding, but this does not imply that there is such a tight link between the two as he thinks there is. This problem comes to the surface especially when communication takes place between individuals belonging to different cultures. This brings me to the next point.

Third, deeper criticism applies to the concepts of communicative rationality and of the ideal speech situation, as conceived and conceptualized by Habermas. Even if, hypothetically, one can imagine an ideal speech situation to exist, it is rather difficult to grasp how people would reach an understanding, let alone consensus, when radically different forms of life (and thus different underlying assumptions) are at stake. Under these conditions even Habermas's notion of 'the force of the better argument', however innocuous at first sight, appears problematic. The rules of valid argumentation themselves are indeed part of a cultural heritage and tradition, and therefore, in Habermas's own terms, open to debate and criticism. One enters a vicious circle here, since deciding upon the better argument is dependent on Habermas's 'force of the better argument', and this in turn will be decided upon by the force of the better argument, and so on, *ad infinitum*. Leaving these analytical problems aside, it is sufficient to notice that the ideal speech situation fails to serve its practical purposes in the confrontation between different cultural settings – especially obvious in the case of competing theoretical systems or paradigms in science.[39]

Fourth, it has often been argued against Habermas that his notion of an ideal speech situation is shockingly unreal. Critics are indeed sceptical about the value of grounding critical theory on utopian grounds. This criticism needs further qualification though. It is, of course, true that the ideal speech situation is an ideal type, and as such it cannot be found in reality. But from this observation alone, it does not follow that the counterfactual notion of unconstrained communication is useless as a foundation for critical theory. Habermas would be correct to counter-argue that it can still be employed as a yardstick to compare and judge between real settings. What is an unsurmountable problem for Habermas, however, is that the ideal speech situation rests upon an extremely impoverished notion of self and personhood. Note that Habermas insists that, apart from external constraints, any psychological barrier to open criticism and defence ought to be lifted as well. However, it is difficult to see how any being, referred to in the counterfactual, can be described as an individual at all. The notions of self and personhood are so intertwined with the very same psychological features (for example, deference to authority or self-doubt) of which Habermas is willing to dispose. Several features, normally associated with the notion of personal being, cannot legitimately be attributed to the 'individuals' depicted in Habermas's unconstrained communication. To put it bluntly, the problem with his utopia is not that it promotes an unreal setting, but that it is devoid of people. Even leaving this argument aside (and assuming that Habermas's counterfactual is not a deserted place after all), any individual would still have a very different psychological make-up from his or her counterpart in the counterfactual. There are strong arguments to say that, rather than being the same individuals with different features, they are simply different individuals. This again seems to jeopardize the usefulness of the counterfactual.[40]

Fifth, there is a remarkable lack of sociological awareness in Habermas's notion of communicative rationality. Remember that equality is one of his central concerns. After all, the ideal speech situation rests not only upon open unconstrained debate, but also upon equal opportunity for all to participate. But problematic for Habermas's notion of equality is the pedestrian observation that not all people are equally well equipped to participate successfully in these open communicative practices. Habermas indeed fails to recognize the extent to which communicative rational practices rest upon a vast amount of cultural and educational resources, which are unevenly distributed across the globe and across various sections of the same society. One does not need much exposure to the intricacies of the sociology of education to realize that educational and cultural capital are very much monopolized by the educated, upper-middle class. It is not terribly convincing to found critical theory, as Habermas does, upon an ideal type in which these people (or any section of society for that matter) hold such a privileged position. This does not imply that a viable critical theory cannot be based on the theory of universal pragmatics. But it does mean that the latter theory needs to be supplemented by a reflection upon the structural conditions which would secure more equal allotment of the communicative skills concerned.

Sixth, Habermas's 'consensual' theory of truth is problematic as well. He differs from Popper or Bhaskar in rejecting a realist account of science (see chapter 8), but he desperately attempts to avoid the more radical implications of that position. Distancing himself from both a correspondence theory of truth and a redundancy theory of truth, Habermas links the cognitive validity of a statement to its warrantability within procedures of a 'court of appeal' in which only 'the force of the better argument' prevails.[41] However he remains suspiciously vague about what counts as evidence or what counts as the better argument within an open debate.[42] More importantly, it seems obvious that, however much the actual debate approximates Habermas's ideal speech situation (and for the sake of the argument, let us assume that it *is* an ideal speech situation in the Habermasian sense), people's agreement upon the truth or falsehood of a statement can still potentially be mistaken. Hence, as a prescriptive contribution to the philosophy of science Habermas's procedural concept of rationality compares unfavourably with, for instance, Popper's. However problematic Popper's notions of falsification and verisimilitude might be, they do provide us with tools for establishing which claims are more desirable than others (see chapter 8).

Further reading

Those who wish for a historical introduction to the Frankfurt School can consult Held's *Introduction to Critical Theory*. For a fine analytical approach to the project of critical theory, I would suggest Geuss's excellent *The Idea of a Critical Theory*. For a brief, but comprehensible introduction to Habermas's work in general, Bernstein's introduction to his edited volume *Habermas and Modernity* and Giddens's contribution to the same volume (entitled 'Reason without Revolution') are both a good start. Also recommendable, though more difficult, is Dews's *Autonomy and Solidarity*, an edited collection of interviews with Habermas. Part III of Held's *Introduction to Critical Theory* discusses Habermas's work within the context of critical theory in general. McCarthy's *The Critical Theory of Jürgen Habermas* is an excellent introduction to his earlier work, but does not fully incorporate Habermas's theory of communicative action. The latter is summarized very well in Ingram's *Habermas and the Dialectic of Reason*. Habermas's universal pragmatics is critically evaluated in *Habermas: Critical Debates*, edited by Thompson and Held. Outhwaite's *Jürgen Habermas* is a solid, well-balanced overview of Habermas's work and includes not only his writings on communicative rationality, but also his latest work on legal theory. *Habermas and Modernity*, edited by Bernstein, is an excellent series of articles dealing with Habermas's defence of the project of the Enlightenment. Habermas's own writings are difficult to read, and this, unfortunately, does not improve with time: his earlier works are more accessible (*Towards a Rational Society*, for instance), whilst his most influential contributions so far (*Knowledge and Human Interests* and *The Theory of Communicative Action*) are pitched at an extremely high level of abstraction. It is ironic that for someone who grounds critical theory primarily in communicative practices aimed at *understanding*, Habermas has been remarkably unsuccessful in addressing his audience in an intelligible, let alone accessible manner.

References

Adorno, T. W. 1973. *Negative Dialectics*. London: Routledge (originally in German, 1966; reprinted, 1990).

Adorno, T. W. and Horkheimer, M. 1973. *Dialectic of Enlightenment*. London: Allen Lane (originally in German, 1947).

Adorno, T. W., et al. 1976. *The Positivist Dispute in German Sociology*. London: Heinemann.

Bernstein, R. J. 1978. *The Restructuring of Social and Political Theory*. Philadelphia: University of Pennsylvania Press.

Bernstein, R. J. (ed.) 1985a. *Habermas and Modernity*. Cambridge: Polity Press.

Bernstein, R. J. 1985b. Introduction. In: *Habermas and Modernity*, ed. R. J. Bernstein. Cambridge: Polity Press, 1–32.

Dallmayr, F. R. and McCarthy, T. A. (eds.) *Understanding and Social Inquiry*. Notre Dame: University of Notre Dame Press.

Dews, P. (ed.) 1986. *Autonomy and Solidarity; Interviews with Jürgen Habermas*. London: Verso.

Fahrenbach, H. (ed.) 1973. *Wirklichkeit und Reflexion: Festschrift für Walter Schulz*. Pfüllingen: Neske.

Geuss, R. 1981. *The Idea of a Critical Theory*. Cambridge: Cambridge University Press.

Giddens, A. 1985a. Jürgen Habermas. In: *The Return of Grand Theory in the Human Sciences*, ed. Q. Skinner. Cambridge: Canto, 121–40 (reprinted, 1990).

Giddens, A. 1985b. Reason without Revolution, In: *Habermas and Modernity*, ed. R. J. Bernstein. Cambridge: Polity Press, 95–121 (reprinted, 1991).

Giddens, A. and Turner, J. (eds) 1987. *Social Theory Today*. Cambridge: Polity Press (reprinted, 1990).

Habermas, J. 1970a. On systematically distorted communication. *Inquiry* 13(3), 205–18.

Habermas, J. 1970b. Towards a theory of communicative competence. *Inquiry* 13(4), 360–75.

Habermas, J. 1973a. Wahrheitstheorien. In: *Wirklichkeit und Reflexion: Festschrift für Walter Schulz*, ed. H. Fahrenbach. Pfüllingen: Neske, 211–65.

Habermas, J. 1973b. *Theory and Practice*. Boston: Beacon Press (originally in German, 1963).

Habermas, J. 1976. *Legitimation Crisis*. Cambridge: Polity Press (originally in German, 1973).

Habermas, J. 1977. A review of Gadamer's *Truth and Method*. In: *Understanding and Social Inquiry*, eds F. R. Dallmayr and T. A. McCarthy. Notre Dame: University of Notre Dame Press, 335–63.

Habermas, J. 1979. *Communication and the Evolution of Society*. Cambridge: Polity Press (originally in German, 1976; reprinted, 1991).

Habermas, J. 1987a. *Knowledge and Human Interests*. Cambridge: Polity Press (originally in German, 1968; reprinted, 1989).

Habermas, J. 1987b. *The Philosophical Discourse of Modernity*. Cambridge: Polity Press (originally in German, 1985; reprinted, 1992).

Habermas, J. 1987c. *The Theory of Communicative Action, Volume 2: Lifeworld and System: A Critique of Functionalist Reason*. Cambridge: Polity Press (originally in German 1981; reprinted, 1991).

Habermas, J. 1987d. *Toward a Rational Society; Student Protest, Science, and Politics*. Cambridge: Polity Press (originally in German, 1969; reprinted, 1989).

Habermas, J. 1988. *On the Logic of the Social Sciences*. Cambridge: Polity Press (originally in German, 1970; reprinted, 1990).

Habermas, J. 1989. *Structural Transformation of the Public Sphere: An Inquiry into a Category of Bourgeois Society*. Cambridge: Polity Press (originally in German, 1962; reprinted, 1992).

Habermas, J. 1991. *The Theory of Communicative Action, Volume 1; Reason and the Rationalization of Society.* Cambridge: Polity Press (originally in German, 1981).

Habermas, J. 1993. *Justification and Application.* Cambridge: Polity Press (originally in German, 1989).

Habermas, J. and N. Luhmann. 1971. *Theorie der Gesellschaft oder Sozialtechnologie.* Frankfurt: Suhrkamp.

Held, D. 1980. *Introduction to Critical Theory: Horkheimer to Habermas.* Cambridge: Polity Press (reprinted, 1990).

Hesse, M. 1982. Science and objectivity. In: *Habermas: Critical Debates,* eds J. Thompson and D. Held. London: Macmillan, 98–115.

Holub, R. C. 1991. *Jürgen Habermas; Critique in the Public Sphere.* London: Routledge.

Honneth, A. 1987. Critical theory. In: *Social Theory Today,* eds A. Giddens and J. Turner. Cambridge: Polity Press (reprinted, 1990).

Ingram, D. 1987. *Habermas and the Dialectic of Reason.* New Haven: Yale.

Lukes, S. 1982. Of gods and demons: Habermas and practical reason. In: *Habermas: Critical Debates,* eds J. Thompson and D. Held. London: Macmillan, 134–48.

McCarthy, T. 1984. *The Critical Theory of Jürgen Habermas.* Cambridge: Polity Press.

McCarthy, T. 1985. Reflections of rationalization in the theory of communicative action. In: *Habermas and Modernity,* ed. R. J. Bernstein. Cambridge: Polity Press, 176–91.

Ottmann, H. 1982. Cognitive interests and self-reflection. In: *Habermas: Critical Debates,* eds J. Thompson and D. Held. London: Macmillan, 79–97.

Outhwaite, W. 1994. *Jürgen Habermas,* Cambridge: Polity Press.

Pusey, M. 1987. *Jürgen Habermas,* London: Tavistock.

Roderick, R. 1986. *Habermas and the Foundations of Critical Theory.* London: Macmillan.

Skinner, Q. (ed.) 1985. *The Return of Grand Theory in the Human Sciences.* Cambridge: Canto.

Thompson, J. B. and Held, D. (eds) 1982. *Habermas: Critical Debates.* London: Macmillan.

Wellmer, A. 1985. Reason, utopia, and enlightenment. In: *Habermas and Modernity,* ed. R. J. Bernstein. Cambridge: Polity Press, 35–66.

7
The Invasion of Economic Man
Rational Choice Theory

Individualistic and economic approaches to social life were amongst the *bêtes noires* of Durkheim's sociological project. Part of the constitution of the new discipline of sociology was to distinguish it clearly from psychology and economics, not only in terms of subject-matter, but also in terms of theoretical approach. In opposition to individualistic approaches, society was considered to be an entity *sui generis* – not a mere aggregate of its component parts. Furthermore, rational calculative attitudes were seen as limited to particular spheres of social life, and, even in cases where these attitudes were prevalent, a precondition for their existence was identified in shared norms and values.

Sociology has long been dominated by this Durkheimian perspective. In its weak version, sociological reasoning is seen as alien to the picture of actors rationally pursuing their individual interests. A stronger version presumes that reason is, in John Wilmot's terms, 'an *ignis fatuus* of the human mind': that behind the surface level of rational action lies a deeper more fundamental level of unacknowledged social structures. That Durkheimian perspective, advocated in either of its versions, has permeated twentieth-century sociology: there is indeed a consensus amongst otherwise very different theorists such as Parsons, Dahrendorf, Garfinkel, Bourdieu and Giddens on the irreducibility of social life to economic logic (see chapters 1, 2, 3 and 4). Even Weberian action theorists, who have traditionally been hostile to holistic types of explanation, are keen to distance themselves from any form of economic reductionism. The emergence of rational choice theory in social and political science in the course of the 1980s has therefore been all the more surprising and revolutionary. Rational choice theory in the study of politics and sociology is nothing short of the invasion of economic man. It is the ultimate imperialist assault of economics on sociology – the subordination of *homo sociologicus* to *homo economicus*.

Of course, it could be argued that economic man has been expansionist in the past. After all, Hobbes's political theory relied heavily upon the view that the world is inhabited by rational, self-interested agents, and Adam Smith occasionally employed economic reasoning to account for political action. Furthermore, the utilitarian reforms of the early nineteenth century drew upon an economic logic postulating that, at all times and places, people tend to avoid pain for pleasure, and that institutions should be directed towards these utilitarian principles. Some rational choice theorists go even further and argue that Tocqueville's and Marx's methodologies adumbrated a rational choice perspective.[1]

However, only recently has the economic approach been employed in such a sophisticated way as to encompass so many different aspects of social life, ranging from church attendance and marriage to war situations and suicide patterns.[2] Both the sophistication and the broad applicability of current economic reasoning is partly due to the emergence and development of game theory. Game theory aims at dealing conceptually with situations in which individuals make decisions whilst being aware that their choices may (and usually will) be affected by the choices of the other players.[3] As to its sophistication, game theory has provided several fine counter-intuitive insights: for instance, that, in certain situations, people might be worse off by acting in the pursuit of self-interest. The abstract nature of game theory lends itself to wide application, further encouraging its popularity.

In this chapter I deal with the economic approach and its usage in explaining non-economic phenomena. Sections one, two and three help to provide the stage setting. In the first section, I discuss the assumptions which underlie the economic approach. This involves outlining what the advocates of the economic approach mean by rationality and rational behaviour. In the second section, I discuss game theory, which is often used by rational choice theorists. In the third section, I discuss some examples of rational choice applications in social and political science. I elaborate on the work of Downs, Olson, Becker and Coleman. In the fourth section I set out to discuss the main limitations of the economic approach.

Before doing so, let me briefly elaborate on what I wish to discuss or, more importantly, what I will not discuss. This chapter obviously deals with the economic approach or what is nowadays called 'rational choice theory' (henceforth RCT). I use the term as it is commonly employed, that is, defined as a sociological theory which tries to explain social and political behaviour by assuming that people act rationally. However non-controversial, a number of consequences follow from this definition. First, I deal with the rational choice perspective as a theory which attempts to explain social and political phenomena, not economic behaviour. Some of the criticisms which I raise against RCT might also apply to its usage in economics, but I would prefer to leave to economists to judge whether the points raised here are also relevant for their discipline. Second, RCT (at least according to my definition) is to be distinguished from philosophical reflections regarding rationality and rational choice. These philosophical views occasionally inform RCT, but the latter certainly does not incorporate all these philosophical reflections. Hence, my criticisms against RCT (infra) are not necessarily criticisms of Elster's or Hollis's philosophical writings.[4] Third, RCT is distinct from decision theory. Decision theory is a normative theory in that it informs one about that which an individual should do if he or she were rational. RCT occasionally relies upon insights from decision theory, but I do not intend to focus on the latter, and will deal with it only in so far as my critique of the rational choice perspective necessitates this. Fourth, rational choice theorists develop *sociological* theories, and they aim at explaining and predicting behavioural patterns of groups of people. RCT should not be understood as a theory which simply explains or predicts individual behaviour. For instance, some rational choice theorists purport to explain and predict voting patterns – not each (or any) individual's vote.

Rational choice explanations[5]

The myriad versions of RCT notwithstanding, most followers of the theory take on board the following key notions: the assumption of intentionality; the assumption of rationality; the distinction between 'complete' and 'incomplete' information, and, in the case of the latter, between 'risk' and 'uncertainty'; and the distinction between 'strategic' and 'interdependent' action. I will deal with each in turn.

First, rational choice theorists assume intentionality. Rational choice explanations are indeed a subset of so-called 'intentional explanations'. Intentional explanations do not merely stipulate that individuals act intentionally; rather they *account* for social practices by referring to beliefs and desires of the individuals involved. Intentional explanations are often accompanied by a search for the unintended (or so-called 'aggregation') effects of people's purposive action. Contrary to functionalist forms of explanations (see chapter 1), the unintended effects of social practices are not employed to explain the persistence of the very same practices. Rational choice theorists pay particular attention to two types of negative, unintended consequences or 'social contradictions': counterfinality and suboptimality. Counterfinality refers to the 'fallacy of composition' which occurs whenever people act according to the mistaken assumption that what is optimal for any individual in particular circumstances is necessarily simultaneously optimal for all individuals in these circumstances.[6] Take Sartre's example of deforestation: every peasant intends to get more land by cutting down trees, but this leads to deforestation and thus erosion, so that, in the end, the peasants have less cultivable land than at the outset.[7] Suboptimality refers to individuals who, faced with interdependent choices, choose a particular strategy, aware that the other individuals will do the same, and also aware that everybody could have obtained at least as much if another strategy had been adopted.[8] Take the example of Sartre's peasants again. Suboptimality occurs when a peasant is aware of the possibility of the aggregated outcome, but nevertheless realizes that, whatever the others decide, it is to his or her advantage to cut down trees. The so-called Prisoner's Dilemma, which will be discussed later, is a clear example of suboptimality with two people involved.

Second, besides intentionality, rational choice theories assume rationality. Rational choice explanations are indeed a subset of intentional explanations, and they attribute, as the name suggests, rationality to social action. By rationality, it is meant, roughly speaking, that, whilst acting and interacting, the individual has a coherent plan, and attempts to maximize the net satisfaction of his or her preferences whilst minimizing the costs involved. Rationality thus implies 'the assumption of connectedness', which stipulates that the individual involved has a complete 'preference ordering' across the various options. From such a preference ordering social scientists may infer a 'utility function' which attributes a number to each option according to its rank within the preference ordering. For a person to be rational, his or her preference ordering needs to fulfil certain requirements. The principle of transitivity is an obvious example of such a precondition: the preference of X over Y and Y over Z should imply the preference of X over Z. In case both connectedness and transitivity are met, rational choice theorists talk about 'a weak ordering of preferences'.[9]

Rational choice explanations account for an individual's behaviour by referring to the *subjective* beliefs and preferences of that individual – not by the *objective* conditions and opportunities faced by that individual. So it is possible for someone to act rationally whilst relying upon false beliefs *vis-à-vis* what are the best means to achieve his or her goals or desires. However, for someone to be called rational, he or she is expected to gather, within the boundaries of what is possible, enough information such that his or her beliefs are substantiated. Endlessly gathering information can be a sign of irrationality as well, especially if the situation has a certain urgency. For example, confronted with an imminent military attack, a prolonged examination of possible strategies would have disastrous consequences.

Third, there is the distinction between uncertainty and risk. I have so far assumed that people know with certainty the consequences of their actions, but in reality people often possess only partial information regarding the relationship between particular actions and consequences. Some theoreticians even take the position that there are no real-life settings in which people are able to draw upon perfect information because, as Burke spelled out two centuries ago, 'you can never plan the future by the past'. There is a distinction within 'imperfect information' between 'uncertainty' and 'risk' – a distinction first introduced by both J. M. Keynes and F. Knight – and RCT tends to treat choice under uncertainty as choice under risk.[10] Faced with risk, people are able to attribute probabilities to various outcomes, whereas confronted with uncertainty they are unable to do this. Rational choice theorists tend to focus upon risk for two reasons: either because they argue that situations of uncertainty do not exist, or because they argue that, if they do exist, RCT might be unhelpful in accounting for people's actions. Faced with risk, RCT assumes that people are able to calculate the 'expected utility' or 'expected value' for each action. To grasp the meaning of the concept 'expected utility', one needs first, for each outcome, X_i, to multiply the utility, U_i, of that outcome with the probability, P_i, that it will occur. The expected utility then stands for the sum of these multiplications: $U_1.P_1 + U_2.P_2 + \ldots + U_i.P_i + \ldots U_n.P_n$ (with n standing for the number of possible outcomes).[11]

Fourth, there is the distinction between strategic and parametric choices. With the exception of the above two types of social contradiction (which are indicative of 'strategic or interdependent choices'), I have concentrated hitherto on 'parametric choices'. These refer to choices faced by individuals confronted with an environment independent of their choices. Suboptimality and counterfinality are examples of strategic choices in that individuals need to take into account choices made by others before deciding their own course of action. To give another example, people who buy and sell shares on the stock market tend to take into account the choices of others before making a decision themselves. As part of RCT, game theory deals with the formalization of interdependent or strategic choices. It constructs ideal-type models which anticipate the rational decision for each player in a game where other players also make choices and where each player needs to take into account the choices of the other. I elaborate on game theory in the next section.

Game theory

Hitherto I have presented a rough picture of what game theory stands for. Since it is crucial in modern rational choice explanations, it is now time to spell out its main features. A game consists of at least two players who develop strategies in order to obtain certain outcomes or rewards. Games consisting of two players are called 'two-person games'; games for more than two players are referred to as 'n-person games'. The reward to each player depends not only on his or her own strategy, but also on the strategies and rewards of all the others involved in the game. Likewise, the strategy of each player is dependent on the strategy of the others. With the preferences of each player for various outcomes or rewards as given, game theory attempts to predict the strategies of the players were they to act rationally on the basis of the information available. Obviously, there might be a discrepancy between that game theoretical anticipation and people's actual choices in experimental or life settings.

A distinction is often drawn between 'co-operative' and 'non-cooperative' game theory.[12] The non-cooperative version is that which is commonly understood by game theory. It is assumed that people act within their own interests, and they only choose to co-operate with others if it furthers their individual interests. In co-operative games each individual pursues the best outcome for the group, and that choice does not necessarily coincide with the best strategy if mere self-interest were at stake. As RCT tends to treat people as maximizing their individual interests, and given that the co-operative version is a far less developed branch of game theory, I will in the following focus on non-cooperative game theory.

In some cases, called 'variable-sum' or 'non-zero-sum' games, the net total of the rewards of all players is dependent on the strategy of each player. This is not the case in 'constant-sum' or 'zero-sum' games: here the gain of one player implies an equal loss for the others. Whereas constant-sum games involve pure conflict and rarely occur in real life, variable-sum games involve either pure collaboration or a combination of conflict and collaboration. Variable-sum games which involve only collaboration are called co-ordination games, whereas the combination of conflict and collaboration is exemplified in the Prisoner's Dilemma, the battle of the sexes, the chicken game and the assurance game. I will elaborate on these shortly.

Within non-cooperative game theory, two types of game can be distinguished: 'strategic form' games and 'extensive form' games.[13] In the strategic form game (sometimes referred to as the normal form game) players are considered to choose strategies simultaneously. The extensive form game takes into account the sequence of choices and the information gathered by the players each time. Thus, synchronic analysis is typical for strategic form games, whereas extensive form games imply a diachronic analysis. It is technically possible for any extensive form game to be converted into a strategic form game. There could be good reasons for doing so: for example, the snapshot provided in the strategic form game is simple and lends itself easily to analysis. Things are more complicated the other way around: any strategic form game can be converted to an infinite number of extensive form games. Given that the underlying logic is roughly the same in both cases, I will here, for the sake of clarity, only consider strategic form games.

All this sounds rather complicated, but a few examples will demonstrate the simplicity of the basic assumptions of game theory. I will start with the Prisoner's Dilemma, an example of a variable-sum game with mixed conflict and collaboration. This is probably the most well known of all games, not only because of its relevance in various areas of social and political life, but also due to some of its counterintuitive implications. Imagine that you and somebody else have committed a crime together, you are both arrested, but the police fail to provide conclusive evidence against either of you. You are put in separate cells, and you are cross-examined by the police. You are told the following: 'You have two choices: you either confess or you deny any involvement in the crime. If you confess and your accomplice does not, you will go free and your accomplice will get a life sentence. If you confess and so does your accomplice, you will both get twenty years. If you both deny involvement in the crime, you will both get five years. Your accomplice has been set the same conditions.'

Now, to clarify the argument which follows, imagine that you care more about the length of your own sentence than that of your accomplice; assume, in fact, that your relationship with your accomplice is purely 'professional', and that you have not developed any special bond whilst being jointly involved in criminal activities. The same applies to your accomplice, whom you therefore have no reason to trust any more than he or she can trust you. His or her concerns are first and foremost with the length of his or her sentence, and only then with yours.

Assuming that you care more about your sentence than that of your accomplice, your choice is straightforward. After rational reflection, you decide to confess to involvement, because this will be the most advantageous choice *whatever* the choice of your accomplice. This is easily proven. Your accomplice has two possibilities: confession or denial. Take the case where your accomplice denies: your confession then allows you to go free, whereas your denial would have led to your imprisonment for five years. A similar argument applies were your accomplice to confess: in that case you will both get twenty years, whereas had you denied, a life-sentence would be waiting for you. So whatever your accomplice decides upon, it is to your advantage to confess.

Remember, too, that your accomplice has been told the same story, and, assuming that he or she decides on a rational basis and that the length of his or her own sentence is the priority, the decision will the same as yours: confession. Now a situation has arisen where you both decide to confess, and this means that you both end up with twenty years. But notice that it would be better for both of you to deny since each of you would then serve only five years instead of twenty. The Prisoner's Dilemma thus demonstrates that the rational pursuit of individuals can lead to unintended, suboptimal results. Notice also that your (or your accomplice's) awareness of this paradox does not help to alleviate the problem: it still remains advantageous for you to confess, whatever the choice of your accomplice, and vice versa. In other words, the suboptimal result, although unintended, is not necessarily unforeseen.

I take the opportunity to introduce some technical notions related to game theory: pay-off, dominant strategy and Nash-equilibrium. In table 7.1 the pairs in each box refer to the pay-offs for you and your accomplice, depending on the decision of each. A payoff or utility number is a numerical indication of how desirable a particular outcome is for each player. The first number of each pair refers to the pay-off of the 'row' player (you in this

Table 7.1 Prisoner's Dilemma

		accomplice	
		deny	confess
you	deny	3,3	1,4
	confess	4,1	2,2

case), the second number indicates the pay-off of the 'column' player (your accomplice in this case). Say your pay-offs are either 1 (which stands for the undesirable life sentence), 2 (twenty years), 3 (five years) or 4 (free).

Now, some caution is needed here: in statistical terms, a utility number is an ordinal variable and nothing more than that. That is, what matters is merely that 4 is higher than 3, that 3 is higher than 2, and 2 higher than 1 – that is all there is to it. It is not the case that a score of 4, for example, is twice as desirable than a score of 2. Our example demonstrates this: it does not make sense to say that being set free is twice as good as being imprisoned for twenty years.

In terms of pay-offs the following picture emerges: if your accomplice confesses any involvement, you score 2 by confessing as well and 1 by denying; if your accomplice denies, you get the highest score by confessing and 3 by denying. The same argument applies to your accomplice. Hence, confessing is your 'dominant strategy'; it is also that of your accomplice. A dominant strategy is one that is beneficial to you *whatever* the other player decides. Some games do not provide a dominant strategy, but all have at least one Nash-equilibrium. A Nash-equilibrium (sometimes referred to as simply 'equilibrium') is a pair of strategies where each represents the best strategy, given the other's strategy.[14] In the Prisoner's Dilemma the Nash-equilibrium refers to the pair (confess, confess) – the dominant strategies of both you and your accomplice. However, the equilibria of some games do not consist of dominant strategies. In our example there is only one Nash-equilibrium, but certain games have multiple equilibria.

Hitherto I have only discussed a single instance of the Prisoner's Dilemma. However, what happens when one is confronted with the same partner in various such dilemmas through time? The answer, it seems, depends on whether the number of games is finite or not, and whether the players in-volved know how many games are being played. If the game is played *ad infinitum*, or if the players do not know how many times the game will be repeated, the 'tit for tat' strategy seems to be one of the more effective procedures.[15] According to this strategy, in general you co-operate, unless the other player defects in which case your next move will be defection as

Table 7.2 Co-ordination game

		other person	
		wait	go
you	wait	0,0	1,1
	go	1,1	0,0

well. But if the game is played a finite number of times and if both players know the exact number of times, then it can be shown that the co-operative tit for tat strategy breaks down. The reason is that in the last round the usefulness of one's co-operative strategy is eroded because there will be no further games. One's last game then becomes like a single Prisoner's Dilemma, and the rational decision is therefore to defect rather than co-operate. However, this also means that one's decision in the last game is fixed and is not affected by any of the previous games. Therefore one's decision for the penultimate game will not be affected by the last game, since that choice is already fixed. So the same logic applies here as well, and so on *ad infinitum*. One ends up deciding to defect throughout the sequence of games. The principle employed here is that of 'backward induction': one imagines the last game and then moves towards the first game.

A second type of dilemma can be found in the co-ordination game – a variable-sum game with pure collaboration. This game differs from the previous one in that it is in the interest of the players to co-ordinate – hence the name. Imagine the situation where you and somebody else are taking a lift. There is enough space for both of you in the lift, but you cannot *enter* the lift simultaneously – somebody needs to go first. You are not particularly in a hurry, and you are quite courteous: therefore you do not mind if the other person goes through first. What you want to avoid, though, is for both of you to attempt to go through first, or for both of you to wait for the other. Let us assume that the game is again symmetrical in that the person coming from the opposite direction has similar preferences to you. Table 7.2 represents such a co-ordination game. There are two equilibria: (wait, go) and (go, wait). Any other combination is less preferable.

As there are two equilibria, it is *prima facie* not altogether clear what each player needs to do. But in reality co-ordination games tend to be repeated. Imagine that you encounter that tortuous situation with the same person every day. The first encounter might be embarrassing, but it is likely that after a few encounters a certain rule or convention becomes established. You might, for instance, take turns – that is, if you went first yesterday you would expect the other person to go first today. Or you might follow the rule that

Table 7.3 Battle of the sexes

		woman	
		dinner	cinema
man	dinner	4,3	2,2
	cinema	1,1	3,4

the older person always goes first. As neither you nor the other person minds who goes first, the nature of the arrangement is not important. But however arbitrary, once established, it is in your favour and in the other person's favour to stick to it. The rule or convention makes for the relative predictability of social life, and it is in your and the other person's interest to keep to it.

Like the Prisoner's Dilemma, the battle of the sexes (see table 7.3) is an example of a variable-sum game, with mixed collaboration and conflict. Here again, it is in the interest of both players to co-ordinate up to a certain point. The game is exemplified through a common dilemma faced by couples – hence the provocative name. Imagine a couple planning their evening. They want to do different things, though not if it means doing it without the other. The man prefers to go out for dinner rather than go to the cinema, but he would rather be with the woman even if she insists on going to the cinema. The woman prefers to go to the cinema rather than to go out to eat, but she would rather be with the man than go to the cinema alone. The two equilibria are (dinner, dinner) and (cinema, cinema). Any other combination would be worse, because most important for both is to avoid being alone.

Game theory is relevant for understanding a number of sociological phenomena. I have only dealt with examples of the Prisoner's Dilemma, but the other games have applications as well. In reality, the players do not have to be individuals; they can, for example, be 'decision-making' bodies such as firms or governments. Two types of empirical application can be distinguished here. First, there are straightforward cases, where one is dealing with only two players. Second, there is the extended case where more than two (and often many) players are involved; the similarities with the original game are nevertheless striking enough to make the use of the analogy fruitful. To take an example of the first type, the arms race between two superpowers is often conceived as a Prisoner's Dilemma: even if it is preferable for each superpower to disarm completely, it is in the interest of each to be fully armed *whatever* the other one does. Hence the suboptimal result.[16] Or take two countries opting for protectionist policies since this is the best choice *whatever* the policy of the other country, although an agreement to abandoning protectionism would be beneficial to both. Second, the extended version with a large number of players elucidates the so-called 'free-rider' problem. Free-riders are rational decision-makers who benefit from the efforts of others without making any effort themselves. An example might be students who fail to attend lectures, and who count on their colleagues to provide them with the necessary lecture notes. Another concerns those who prefer not to strike for a pay rise but who still benefit from the rise once it is achieved through the efforts of others.

Examples of rational choice applications

With the key notions of RCT and game theory in mind, I can now introduce examples of RCT applications in social and political science. I have selected for this purpose four books which have contributed to a more sophisticated economic approach, and which made for its wider acceptance in social and political science. Anthony Downs's *An Economic Theory of Democracy* was one of the first books to explore the applications of RCT to political phenomena. Mancur Olson's *Logic of Collective Action* attempted to use the same argument for the understanding of organisations. Gary Becker's *The Economic Approach to Human Behavior* was a collection of essays attempting to demonstrate the wide applicability of the economic approach to a variety of phenomena, ranging from drug abuse to marriage. Finally, James Coleman's *Foundations of Social Theory* is a contribution to social theory from the perspective of RCT. I will deal with each in turn.[17]

First, there is Downs's *Economic Theory of Democracy*. The assumption in this is that politicians and voters act rationally. The motivations of politicians are personal desires such as income, prestige and power derived from holding office. Since these attributes cannot be obtained without being elected, the actions of politicians are aimed at maximizing political support, and their policies are merely a means towards this end. Voters establish a preference amongst competing parties based on a comparison between the 'utility income' from the activities of the present government and the 'utility income' if the opposition parties had been in office. Their choice is also dependent on the electoral system. In a two-party system the voter simply votes for the party which he or she prefers. In a multiparty system, however, the voter needs to take into account the preferences of others. For instance, if the preferred party has no chance of winning, then the voter opts for another party that might possibly keep the least preferred party out of power. Governments can gain votes by spending and lose votes by raising taxes. They will continue to spend until the marginal vote gain from their spending activities equals the marginal vote loss as a result of the taxes they had to impose to finance them. Vote gain and loss depend on the utility incomes of all voters and the strategies of opposition parties. Downs's work signalled a breakthrough for the economic approach in some areas of political science.

Second, I will turn to Olson's *Logic of Collective Action*. What Downs managed to do in political science, Olson did for organizational theory. Olson deals with those organizations that further the *common* interests of their members. For example, all members of a union have a common interest in better working conditions or higher wages.[18] He focuses upon 'public goods': that is, those that having been provided for one or several persons in a group, cannot be withheld from the other members of that group.[19] The following problem then emerges. Assume that it is in the interest of all members of a large group to obtain the public good. Obtaining the public good, however, takes time and energy, so it is in the interest of each member not to contribute his or her effort, but to leave it up to the others to do so. Once the public good is obtained, it is available to all anyway. Furthermore, in large groups, one person's effort often does not make much difference. But if everybody operates on that basis, then nobody will obtain the public good. So, although it is in the interest of everybody to pursue the good, the group does not necessarily achieve this. All this explains why large groups tend to employ incentives and negative sanctions to make people contribute towards obtaining the public good.[20]

Third, Becker's *The Economic Approach to Social Behavior* is a collection of articles with a bold and provocative introduction. Underlying this work is the belief that what distinguishes economics from related disciplines is not the subject-matter, but its approach.[21] Becker's aim is to demonstrate that what he calls the 'economic approach' is extremely powerful in that it can be applied to a wide variety of phenomena. Others have shown the usefulness of that approach for explaining economic life, but Becker sees it as his task to show the applicability of the economic approach to a wide range of non-economic behaviour. He is the clearest exponent of 'economic imperialism' in that he goes as far as saying that the economic approach 'provides a valuable unified framework for understanding *all* human behavior'.[22] Becker sees the following assumptions as central to the 'economic approach'. First, people's preferences are relatively stable, and they do not differ substantially between various categories of the population, nor between different cultures or societies. Second, people exhibit maximizing behaviour on the basis of an optimal amount of information. Third, markets exist which facilitate the co-ordination of the actions of the people involved and for the mutual consistency of their behaviour.[23] The strength of Becker's work lies in the technical sophistication of the modelling in his empirical work.

Fourth, there is Coleman's *Foundations of Social Theory*. Like Parsons's *Social System*, Merton's *Social Theory and Social Structure* and Giddens's *Constitution of Society*, Coleman's book aims at developing a treatise in general social theory (see chapters 2 and 4).[24] Like Merton, Coleman backs up his theory with empirical research, which aims to demonstrate the usefulness of his research programme. Like Parsons and Giddens, Coleman attempts to transcend the traditional opposition between the macro- and micro-levels of society.[25] His contribution to social theory therefore operates at three levels: it aims at explaining how the properties of the system level affects the individual level; it attempts to account for what happens at the individual level; and it deals with how people's action affects the system level.[26] The basic idea is simple. Culture generates particular values in the people involved, which make them act in the pursuit of these values, and, whilst doing so, they affect society. The further elaboration of this proposition is complex and takes almost a thousand pages. Especially important for this survey is Coleman's notion of purposive and rational action. In his view, people do not merely act intentionally, they also choose actions or goods which maximize utility.[27] He provides two reasons for this assumption. First, a theory which assumes that people maximize utility has higher predictive power than a theory which simply postulates intentionality. Second, assuming that people maximize utility adds to the simplicity of the theory.[28] Equally important, though, is Coleman's notion that purposive action affects the macro-level. He pays special attention to the role of unintended effects. People act purposefully, but they might produce results which they did not intend or which they did not foresee. Sometimes these effects might even counter the initial intentions.[29]

Problems with rational choice theory

It is not difficult to see the attraction of RCT for social and political scientists. One, in contrast with the complexity of the philosophical accounts of rationality, rational choice explanations in social and political science are remarkably simple. The core of Becker's and Coleman's accounts can be summarized in a few elementary lines. Two, some of the presuppositions of the rational choice explanations appear commonsensical and thus beyond dispute. One takes for granted that people act purposefully, that they act knowingly, though produce unanticipated effects. Three, some of the results of rational choice applications are nevertheless counter-intuitive. Take, for example, the insight that what is rational for each individual is not necessarily rational for all simultaneously. Four, RCT fuels the hope that a united social science is feasible. For two centuries sociologists and economists have been speaking different languages. RCT would allow for renewed communication across the disciplines.

Whatever the attraction, the problems with RCT are probably too severe for it to be considered as a viable alternative to 'sociological' reasoning. I will discuss four major problems: the tendency of rational choice theorists to develop *post hoc* explanations; their mistaken assumption of a culturally free notion of rationality; the fallacy of the so-called 'internalist' rational choice theorists; and the fallacy of 'externalism'.

I will deal first with the issue of *post hoc* reasoning. Rational choice theorists tend to make sense of social practices by attributing rationality to them *ex post facto*. Indeed, they often conceive of their task as demonstrating the fact that social practices which are *prima facie* irrational are actually rational after all.[30] The more that practices appear to be irrational, the more significant the attempt to show that they are in fact rational. For instance, however irrational at first sight, some social psychologists, like Brown, use game theory to demonstrate that panic behaviour is rational after all.[31] Sociological examples include the attempts to show that marriage patterns and criminal behaviour operate according to an economic logic.[32] Notice the analogy with early functionalism (see chapter 2). Whereas the functionalist tendency was to attribute social rationality retrospectively to practices which are *prima facie* irrational, rational choice explanations attempt to make sense of practices by attributing individual rationality *ex post facto*. Not dissimilar to the early functionalist tendency to legitimize existing practices, RCT is often invoked as a *deus ex machina*, suggesting that people live in Leibniz's or Voltaire's 'best [or at least the most rational, PB] of all possible worlds'.

However, there are severe problems related to this *post hoc* theorizing. From the mere fact that these practices *can be* moulded into a rational narrative, it does not follow that, in this instance, RCT has been empirically validated or corroborated. For most, if not all, practices can be reconstructed in that way, especially given that rational choice theorists tend to attribute the preferences and beliefs which suit their theory to their research subjects. Rational choice theorists indeed often rely upon *ex post facto* reasoning to immunize their theory against potential falsifications. First, confronted with the fact that people do not always adjust their behaviour to new opportunities, rational choice theorists tend to argue that 'because adjustment is not costless, it may be rational to postpone it until one knows for certain that the change is a durable one'.[33] Second, confronted with the fact that people often contribute more to the achievement of collective goods than is predicted by the theory, rational choice theorists tend to argue that the individuals involved simply overestimate the impact of their actions.[34] Third, there is the well-known 'paradox of voting'. Given that voting takes time and given that each vote is unlikely to be decisive, RCT would expect people not to make the effort to vote. But a significant number of people *do* vote. Rather than treating this as a falsification, rational choice theorists tend to mould this counter-intuitive phenomenon into a rational narrative as well. It was argued that people vote because they overestimate the impact of their vote or because voting provides them with some psychological satisfaction not accounted for by early rational choice theorists like Downs. They get psychological satisfaction from expressing allegiance to a political system or from contributing to a potentially successful enterprise.[35]

In short, the problem with this form of *post hoc* theorizing is twofold. First, it rests upon *post hoc* assumptions which are empirically not validated (for example, the assumption that people overestimate the impact of their actions). Second, it accommodates mutually exclusive observations (for instance, adjusted and unadjusted behaviour; co-operative action and defection; non-voting and voting), and is thus non-falsifiable. Whilst rational choice theorists tend to situate themselves within a falsificationist tradition (see chapter 8), they fail to acknowledge that *post hoc* reconstructions do not serve as empirical corroboration of the theory.

The second problem is that most rational choice theorists tend to ignore or efface cultural diversity. First, some of the theorists do so rather obviously by making the contentious claim that preferences are stable across cultures.[36] This fits rather well with their tendency to attribute preferences to the subjects involved without checking empirically whether this attribution is justified. (If preferences are stable, then researchers can indeed trust themselves in attributing preferences to others.) Various unsatisfactory justifications are given for assuming that preferences are stable. The oddest one is the claim that economics knows little about preference formation, and that this is a sufficient reason for assuming preferences to be invariant.[37] The absurdity of this logic is striking: the weakness of the approach (its inability to account for how people's preferences are formed) is used as its justification. A more convincing reason for assuming preferences to be fixed is that it adds to the simplicity of the model. Besides empirical testing, rational choice theorists often use the criterion of simplicity to judge between rival theories.[38] But although it could indeed be argued that simplicity is desirable, it should not be adopted at any cost, especially if doing so implies making empirically unsubstantiated or even false assumptions. And this is often the case here. In some areas of economics, preferences might be relatively invariant, but in many others they are not. Simply assuming that they are (and, in some cases, discounting the empirical counter-evidence) represents a lack of intellectual honesty.

Second, there is the more far-reaching presupposition in RCT that, confronted with the same situation and assuming constant preferences, there exists a single, culturally free 'rational course of action'. For instance, rational choice theorists introduce the notion of people's 'rational belief', without fully taking into account that the cultural context, in which these people find themselves, affects what counts as a rationally founded belief and what does not. The problem for RCT is that it deals with beliefs about the relationship between action and outcome which necessarily rely upon culturally embedded notions, for instance, regarding causality or agency. It is a mistake to reduce causality or agency, as RCT does, to only one of those notions. Take, for instance, two people, A and B, who observe that action x tends to be followed by outcome y. A holds a regularity notion of causality, and person B holds a realist view.[39] A might assume that the observation is sufficient (and necessary) evidence to conclude that x causes y; B does not. But it would be erroneous to say that A's belief is more rational than B's belief, or vice versa, simply on the basis of the particular notion of causality which A and B hold, especially given the fact that, even in academic literature, there is no consensus regarding the superiority of one notion over the other. (This is not to say that A or B might not have better arguments for defending his or her notion.)

It is important to mention that this second argument can also be used against decision theory. Let me remind the reader that, as a normative theory, decision theory indicates what, in a particular instance, is the rational course of action to take. It does not assume that people act as such (neither does it assume that people do not act in that way). My previous objections to RCT (the argument against internalism and externalism, the argument against *post hoc* theorizing) do not affect the validity of the normative theory. In contrast, however, the argument that RCT rests upon a mistaken notion of culturally free rationality does not merely threaten RCT, but also the normative theory.

The third problem refers to the distinction between acting as if one is rational on the one hand, and acting because one is rational on the other. Rational choice theorists often defend their theories by showing that they are confirmed by empirical findings. It is important to understand exactly what rational choice theorists mean by the notion of corroboration or empirical confirmation. To justify their framework, they typically refer to the fact that the model, which is inferred from that framework, allows for accurate predictions about people's actions and the effects of their actions. Underlying this reasoning is the epistemological assumption that the validity of a theory depends on its predictive power.

Congruence between the model and reality is, however, not sufficient to corroborate the rational choice theories that form the basis of that model. First, recent developments in the philosophy of science undermine the notion that the strength of a theory depends on its predictive power (see chapter 8). Given that social systems tend to be open systems, corroboration and falsification of a theory are less relevant because they might be due to other generative mechanisms which potentially intervene.[40] Second, there is a distinction between acting rationally on the one hand, and acting *as if* one is rational on the other. From the observation of a congruence between the model and reality (and the attendant predictive power of the theory), it might be legitimate to infer that people generally act in accordance with the basic principles of rationality. But it would be erroneous to conceive of that congruence as empirical evidence that people generally act rationally. For individuals to act *as if* they are rational does not necessitate any rational decision process remotely similar to the one attributed to individuals by RCT. Take, for instance, a rival theory T' according to which the individuals involved tacitly acquire skills and practices, and these skills and practices result in outcomes that appear to be rational on average. If M is the model derived from RCT, and M' is the model derived from the rival theory T', then M is identical to M' because RCT and T' only differ in whether they account for human action in terms of conscious calculation or tacit knowledge. But this means that the very same empirical evidence which was used to support RCT can equally well be used to support the rival theory T': if M proves to yield accurate predictions, then M', being identical to M, does as well.

Some rational choice theorists might, of course, reply that their particular version of RCT is an 'externalist' one.[41] Contrary to internalists, externalists abandon the intentionality requirement. Becker, for instance, states that his economic approach 'does not assume that decision units are necessarily conscious of their efforts to maximize or can verbalize or otherwise describe in an informative way reasons for the systematic patterns in their behaviour'.[42] This externalist position introduces a theoretical argument which says that people in general act rationally, and that they do so *either* because they have tacitly acquired skills or practices (which are found to have a rationale) *or* because the skills or practices are the outcome of conscious calculation.

There are two problems with this counter-argument. First, given that the requirement of (necessarily) conscious calculation has been abandoned, this externalist position (T'') becomes remarkably similar to rival arguments such as T', and it is no more justified to call say T'' a 'rational choice perspective' than it is to describe T' as such. The only justification for doing so might be that T'' leaves open the *possibility* that people's skills and practices are the product of rational calculation, whereas T' sees it exclusively in terms of tacitly acquired knowledge. Moreover, once one leaves the realm of artificial theories (such as T'), one realizes that rival theoretical arguments (which draw upon tacit or practical knowledge) do not even exclude the possibility of intentionality; they simply deny the regularity or typicality of its occurrence. Take, for instance, Bourdieu's perspective on social theory (see chapter 1).[43] Bourdieu postulates that people's *habitus* is adjusted to the objective conditions in which they are situated, and that the *habitus* is not typically acquired consciously. He would not exclude the fact that the *habitus* is occasionally arrived at consciously; he would simply deny that it is the norm. I do not wish to argue that the explanatory format provided by Bourdieu and the one provided by the externalists are completely identical, but that they are not substantially different with regard to the issue of whether it is possible that the practices are the product of conscious calculation. Stated concisely, there are no obvious reasons which justify calling the externalist viewpoint – but not Bourdieu's – a rational choice perspective. But it is plainly nonsensical to call Bourdieu's theory a RCT, and it follows that it is equally absurd to call the externalist view a RCT.

Second, the explanatory power of the externalist argument is weak. Let me clarify this by invoking the Weberian notion that both 'causal adequacy' and 'adequacy of meaning' are a *sine qua non* for the validity of a social explanation. Whereas causal adequacy is fulfilled if, and only if, the explanation provided is supported by observed regularities, adequacy of meaning is fulfilled if, and only if, the explanation provided makes intelligible the observed regularities. Given that the social sciences deal with open systems, I would not attribute such significance to regularity conjunctions as Weber did. Neither do I wish to commit myself to his further specifications regarding how adequacy of meaning can be fulfilled through *Verstehen* (interpretative understanding). However, it is difficult to deny his general view that adequacy of meaning is essential to explanation in social and political science. To explain is indeed to make observed phenomena intelligible. And it is exactly on this score that the externalist view falls short. However high they might score on adequacy of causality, externalists are weak on adequacy of meaning due to the fact that they do not wish to commit themselves to explaining *how* the observed patterns come about.

It is then not surprising that those who position themselves in the externalist camp tend to invoke intentionality and related notions (such as knowledge and foresight), once they discuss the results of their research. Take, for instance, Becker (a self-declared externalist) who argues that people live an unhealthy lifestyle not out of ignorance of its consequences, but because other things are more important to them than maximizing their life span. Smoking heavily or working hard 'would be unwise decisions if a long life were the only aim, but as long as other aims exist, they could be *informed* and in this sense "wise"'.[44] If one stuck to an externalist view (to which, theoretically, Becker subscribes), notions such as 'aims', 'informed decisions' and 'wise decisions' should be excluded. But given that, at the level of adequacy of meaning, externalism is weak, self-declared externalists have only two options. Either they stick to the externalist doctrine, and then they fail to say anything other than that people generally act as if they are rational; or they slip back into internalism when they discuss their results. It is no wonder that most, like Becker, are driven towards the second option (in spite of its difficulties, mentioned earlier).

Further reading

For a simple introduction to RCT and its applications to social and political science, I suggest chapter 2 of Hindess's *Choice, Rationality and Social Theory*, and Becker's introduction to *The Economic Approach to Human Behaviour*. It is worth bearing in mind that Becker is an advocate of RCT and Hindess is not. I would then suggest Elster's introduction to his edited volume *Rational Choice*: it is an excellent state-of-the-art compilation of advanced philosophical issues related to RCT. Introductions to the philosophy of the social sciences from the perspective of rational choice are Elster's *Nuts and Bolts for the Social Sciences* and Hollis's *The Philosophy of the Social Sciences*. Standard works on RCT and its applications for empirical research are Becker's *The Economic Approach to Human Behavior* and Coleman's *Foundations of Social Theory*. Most books on game theory are written by and for economists, and Kreps's *Game Theory and Economic Modelling* is one of the best introductions. Worth reading is Olson's *The Logic of Collective Action*, one of the first systematic applications of RCT to empirical topics in politics and sociology. A further attempt to apply this approach to a broad range of empirical phenomena can be found in Boudon's *The Unintended Consequences of Social Action*. Abel's *Rational Choice Theory*, Elster's *Rational Choice* and Moser's *Rationality in Action* are edited collections with seminal articles on rational choice. Hindess's *Choice, Rationality and Social Theory* is a well-balanced and readable critique of RCT. A more convincing critique is Green and Shapiro's *Pathologies of Rational Choice Theory*.

References

Abel, P. (ed.) 1991. *Rational Choice Theory*. Aldershot: Edward Elgar.

Arrow, K. 1951. *Social Choice and Individual Values*. New Haven: Yale University Press.

Axelrod, R. 1984. *The Evolution of Co-operation*. New York: Basic Books.

Becker, G. C. 1976. *The Economic Approach to Human Behavior*. Chicago: Chicago University Press.

Bhaskar, R. 1979. *The Possibility of Naturalism*. Hemel Hempstead: Harvester.

Boudon, R. 1982. *The Unintended Consequences of Social Action*. London: Macmillan (originally in French, 1977).

Bourdieu, P. 1977. *Outline of a Theory of Practice*. Cambridge: Cambridge University Press (originally in French, 1972).

Bourdieu, P. 1990. *The Logic of Practice*. Cambridge: Polity Press (originally in French, 1980).

Brown, R. 1965. *Social Psychology*. New York: Free Press.

Cartwright, N. 1989. *Nature's Capacities and their Measurement*. Oxford: Clarendon Press.

Cohen, G. A. 1982. Reply to Elster on Marxism: functionalism and game theory. *Theory and Society* 11, 483–95.

Coleman, J. 1990. *Foundations of Social Theory*. Cambridge, Mass.: Harvard University Press.

Downs, A. 1957. *An Economic Theory of Democracy*. New York: Harper.

Elster, J. 1978. *Logic and Society; Contradictions and Possible Worlds*. Chichester: John Wiley and Sons.

Elster, J. 1979. *Ulysses and the Sirens*. Cambridge: Cambridge University Press.

Elster, J. 1983. *Sour Grapes: Studies in the Subversion of Rationality*. Cambridge: Cambridge University Press.

Elster, J. 1985. *Making Sense of Marx*. Cambridge: Cambridge University Press.

Elster, J. (ed.) 1986a. *Rational Choice*. New York: New York University Press.

Elster, J. 1986b. Introduction. In: *Rational Choice*, ed. J. Elster. New York: New York University Press, 1–33.

Elster, J. 1989. *Nuts and Bolts for the Social Sciences*. Cambridge: Cambridge University Press.

Friedman, M. 1953. *Essays in Positive Economics*. Chicago: University of Chicago Press.

Giddens, A. 1984. *The Constitution of Society; Outline of the Theory of Structuration*. Cambridge: Polity Press.

Green, D. P. and Shapiro, I. 1994. *Pathologies of Rational Choice Theory; A Critique of Applications in Political Science*. New Haven: Yale University Press.

Hacking, I. 1983. *Representing and Intervening; Introductory Topics in the Philosophy of Natural Science*. Cambridge: Cambridge University Press.

Hardin, R. 1982. *Collective Action*. Baltimore: John Hopkins University Press.

Hindess, B. 1988. *Choice and Rationality in Social Theory*, London: Unwin Hyman.

Hinich, M. J. 1981. Voting as an act of contribution. *Public Choice* 36, 135–40.

Hollis, M. 1984. *The Philosophy of the Social Sciences*. Cambridge: Cambridge University Press.

Hollis, M. 1988. *The Cunning of Reason*. Cambridge: Cambridge University Press.

Hollis, M. 1994. *The Philosophy of the Social Sciences*. Cambridge: Cambridge University Press.

Jervis, R. 1978. Co-operation under the security dilemma. *World Politics* 30 (2), 167–214.

Keynes, J. M. 1921. *A Treatise on Probability*. London: Macmillan.

Knight, F. 1921. *Risk, Uncertainty and Profit*. Boston: Houghton Mifflin.

Kreps, D. 1990. *Game Theory and Economic Modelling*. Oxford: Clarendon Press.

Lawson, T. 1989. Abstraction, Tendencies and Stylised Facts: A Realist Approach to Economic Analysis. *Cambridge Journal of Economics* 1 (13), 59–78.

Merton, R. 1968. *Social Theory and Social Structure*. New York: The Free Press (enlarged edition).

Moser, P. K. (ed.) 1990. *Rationality in Action; Contemporary Approaches*. Cambridge: Cambridge University Press.

Nash, J. 1950. The Bargaining Problem. *Econometrica* 18, 155–62.

Olson, M. 1965. *The Logic of Collective Action*. Cambridge: Harvard University Press.

Parsons, T. 1951. *The Social System*. London: Routledge and Kegan Paul.

Posner, R. A., 1980. The ethical and political basis of the efficiency norm in common law adjudication. *Hofstra Law Review* 8, 487–551.

Riker, W. H. 1992. The entry of game theory into political science. In: *Toward a History of Game Theory; Annual Supplement to Volume 24 of History of Political Economy*, ed. E. R. Weintraub. London: Duke University Press, 207–24.

Riker, W. and Ordershook, P. C. 1973. *Introduction to Positive Political Theory*. Englewood Cliffs, NJ: Prentice Hall.

Sartre, J.-P., 1960. *Critique de la raison dialectique*. Paris: Gallimard.

Schwartz, T. 1987. Your vote counts on account of the way it is counted. *Public Choice* 54, 101–21.

Weintraub, E. R. (ed.) 1992. *Toward a History of Game Theory; Annual Supplement to Volume 24 of History of Political Economy*. London: Duke University Press.

8
Eroding Foundations
Positivism, Falsificationism and Realism

It might seem rather unusual for a book on social theory to devote a chapter to philosophy of science. Indeed, the development of social theory is often treated as if it resides within a philosophical vacuum. Underlying this book is the presupposition that a grounding in the history of philosophy of science is a *sine qua non* for fully capturing the fortunes and vicissitudes of modern social theory. There are good reasons for making this assumption. Any form of theoretical reflection upon the workings of society necessarily relies upon a number of explicit or tacit philosophical presuppositions regarding, for instance, what is a successful explanation, or the nature of causality. These philosophical assumptions affect which theories are considered to be acceptable, meaningful or preferable. For example, if it is assumed that explanations should only refer to entities which are immediately accessible to observation, some social theories such as structuralism (see chapter 1) and ethnomethodology (see chapter 3) would be deemed unacceptable. Contrast this with the realist assumption that explanations should allude to generative mechanisms which, whilst accounting for the observable phenomena, are not necessarily immediately accessible to observation themselves. From this perspective, structuralism and some versions of ethnomethodology are regarded as acceptable, if not desirable.

'Sociology' (or 'social physics' as it was initially termed) and 'positivist philosophy' were both Comtean offspring, and this is symptomatic of the extent to which positivist epistemology dominated the sociological scene for such a long time.[1] The positivist straitjacket implied hard and fast rules *vis-à-vis* which types of theorizing and research are plausible, acceptable and to be recommended. The initial popularity of positivism can at least partly be explained by the fact that many of its features, however erroneous, at first sight appear to resonate with common sense. Even today, many positivist tenets (and their implications for social theory) appear self-evident: for instance, the notion that science (and hence social science) should avoid explanations which refer to non-observables, and the notion that a successful explanation aims at predicting phenomena. Towards the middle of the twentieth century, however, the citadel of positivism had come under fierce attack, its major building blocks removed. The fact–value distinction, the distinction between theoretical and observational statements, the Humean concept of causality, the verificationist theory of meaning, the notion of symmetry between explanation and prediction are only a few of the proud pillars of positivism which one by one have been eroded. Again, these philosophies had significant effects on which forms of theorizing were to be considered acceptable or preferable. This chapter deals with the grand ambitions of positivism, its demise, and the development of post-positivist philosophies of social science.

The link with the social theories discussed so far will, I hope, become clear. First, as can be inferred from the previous chapters, most social theorists in the twentieth century have positioned themselves in opposition to positivist epistemology. Their work both reflected and contributed to the demise of positivism in philosophy. However different, structuralists, interpretative micro-sociologists and critical theorists all distance themselves from a positivist conception of social science (see chapters 1, 3 and 6). Otherwise radically different theorists like Parsons, Habermas and Giddens all emphasize the extent to which positivist epistemology is either an inadequate philosophy of science in general, or inapplicable to the understanding of the social realm (see chapters 2, 4 and 6). Only a few functionalists and rational choice theorists remained loyal to the old creed, but even they gradually incorporated ideas from falsificationist philosophy of science (see chapters 2 and 7).

Second, of all the theories considered in this book, the rational choice perspective in particular relies upon a falsificationist view of social science (see chapter 7). Popper himself, the founding father of falsificationism, had a view in mind of social science which was remarkably similar to rational choice theory. But there are also obvious affinities between Habermas's communicative rationality and the falsificationist notion of an open society (see chapter 6). Both emphasize the desirability of institutionalizing procedures of unrestrained discussion and criticism. Third, realism has become rather popular amongst social theorists and practising social scientists. Many of the social theories discussed in this book can be made compatible with a realist philosophy of science. Realism provides a philosophical backbone for both structuralist and hermeneutically informed social theories.

Positivism

Originally only associated with Comte's project, the term positivism is now widely used, often as a term of abuse for any reductionist conception of the social sciences. Going through the literature in the social sciences since 1945, one is indeed struck by the frequency with which the label is used by commentators to discredit the empirical or theoretical works of their colleagues. This contrasts sharply with the remarkably small number of people who publicly admit to adhering to the old dogma. The concept of positivism has thus become so loose that it might mean very different things for different people. For the sake of clarity, I will list a number of features which are regularly associated with positivism, bearing in mind that no single author, however committed to the positivist cause, would embrace all characteristics. I start with features which, at least in my view, are essential to positivism. Gradually I move on to propositions which, although compatible with positivism and likely to follow from it, are not necessitated by that position.

As part of an attempt to sweep away the metaphysical burden of our western philosophical heritage, positivism conceives of sensory observations as a solid foundation (if not the *only* foundation) for the development of scientific knowledge.[2] The epistemological primacy attributed to the realm of sensory observations does not, as is sometimes mistakenly assumed, *ipso facto* imply a commitment to inductivist principles. According to inductivism, a large, but finite number of observations, gathered under a wide variety of circumstances, enables one legitimately to infer laws or law-like generalizations. Nineteenth-century positivists often relied upon an inductivist logic (and this probably explains the conflation between the two), but, in the course of the twentieth century, positivism gradually abandoned its allegiance to inductivism in favour of deductivism. According to the latter, science operates by inferring deductively empirical hypotheses from a theory and then empirically testing these hypotheses.[3] Here again, sensory observations are the stepping-stone for sound scientific practices. Whether inductivist or deductivist, notice that positivists are inclined towards a clear-cut distinction between 'observational language' and 'theoretical language'. That is, given a Lockean conception of the human mind, it is assumed that observational statements (i.e. statements recording what one has observed) are devoid of theoretical presuppositions. Observation statements are impregnated with the empirical world, and this is precisely what makes them so reliable.

A corollary of this is the positivist preoccupation with the empirical testability of scientific knowledge. Science can be distinguished from non-science by virtue of providing statements which are, if not *de facto*, at least in principle, empirically testable. Some positivists preferred verifiability as a criterion for demarcation, some alluded to the importance of falsifiability – although the latter is inevitably associated with Popper's critical rationalism which deviates in many respects from mainstream positivism.[4] A statement is verifiable if it is constructed in a way that makes it possible to find empirical evidence to support it, whereas a statement is falsifiable if its logical structure allows one to find empirical counter-evidence. From a positivist perspective, propositions which are not testable (that is, non-verifiable or not falsifiable) are not part of the scientific realm. Some hard-core positivists go even further in their attempt to eradicate any metaphysics by considering untestable propositions as not only non-scientific, but also meaningless.

One of the central concepts in a positivist outlook is a Humean concept of causality.[5] A Humean concept of causality conceives of the regular succession of X by Y to be a necessary and sufficient condition for claiming that X causes Y. One might be psychologically compelled to refer to *how* Y is caused, but such references do not belong to empirical reality, and they ought therefore strictly speaking not to enter into the discussion whether X causes Y. One of the upshots of this is the positivist tendency, as is sometimes reflected in social science research, to reduce explanation to a matter of constant event conjunctions. Hence, positivist explanations avoid references to entities which are not immediately accessible to observation. References to theoretical entities, such as molecules, genes, viruses or social structures, cannot be part of the explanatory format, because they do not belong to the empirical, immediately accessible realm.

From the positivist adherence to a regularity concept of causality follows another of their central assumptions – widely known as the symmetry of explanation and prediction. That is, the same format which allows one to explain a phenomenon also enables one to predict that phenomenon, and vice versa. A closely related, though analytically distinct, positivist assertion is that the explanatory strength of a theoretical construction depends on its predictive abilities, and *vice versa*. Predictive power is regarded as both necessary and sufficient for a theory to be considered as scientific. Theories which allow for accurate predictions are highly desirable, even if they fail to account exactly for *how* these regularities and predictions come about.

Positivists adhere to naturalism. That is, they believe in a unity of method between the natural and the social sciences. In the case of positivism, the naturalist assumption is often accompanied by the belief that knowledge in the social realm is less advanced than in the natural sciences. Hence, to become mature disciplines on a par with the natural sciences, the social sciences need to adopt those methods which are already successfully employed in the natural realm. Now, although positivism implies a belief in the unity of method, adhering to naturalism does not therefore mean accepting positivist epistemology. It is possible, for instance, to hold to naturalism whilst relying upon a realist (and not a positivist) philosophy of science. Like positivists, realists such as Bhaskar, Cartwright, Hacking and Harré search for an underlying method which cuts across the distinction between the natural and the social sciences, and like positivists they reconstruct the methods employed in the natural sciences in order to infer prescriptions for the social sciences.[6] But given their particular philosophical orientation, their prescriptions for the social sciences are different from those of the positivists. For the latter, for example, interpretative approaches in the social sciences need to be avoided. Positivist naturalism avoids any reference to subjective states of individuals, such as purposes, motives and so forth. Again, naturalism in itself does not necessitate this position, and late twentieth-century realist philosophers of science, for instance, have attempted to merge naturalism with insights from hermeneutics. According to orthodox positivists, this realist argument is an illegitimate move. In contrast with, for instance, behaviour patterns, subjective states of individuals are not immediately accessible to observation, and this is a sufficient reason for excluding them from social explanations.

Finally, most positivists adhere to a hard and fast distinction between facts and values. They basically accept the Humean dictum that that which ought to be cannot be inferred from what is, and *vice versa*. In the social sciences this position was strongly advocated by Weber, who argued that although values inevitably play a role in the choice of one's research topic, they are not to play any part in the process of carrying out the research itself. A related position (also taken up by Weber, who was influenced by Nietzsche in this respect) is that whilst the social and natural sciences allow one to judge and evaluate which means are more appropriate for reaching particular goals, they do not (and can never) help one in deciding between the ultimate values themselves. So the social sciences cannot inform people of which ultimate goals they should aim at.[7]

To complete the above introduction to positivism, three reservations have to be made regarding the secondary literature in this area. First, some critiques mistakenly associate the term 'positivism' with a particular deterministic outlook in which attention is paid mainly to the extent to which external factors influence people's conduct.[8] It is true that positivist epistemology and determinism are compatible, as can be inferred from the above discussion about the Humean concept of causality and the symmetry of explanation and prediction. It is also true that positivist social science in its early stages *was* closely related to a search for social or environmental influences. Comte and, later, Durkheim tried to demonstrate the extent to which external social forces constrain people's conduct. Likewise, early behaviourists attempted to show the extent to which human conduct is caused by external stimuli. What is mistaken, however, is the assumption that working within a positivist epistemology *necessarily* implies the absence of a theory of action. Rational choice theorists, for instance, accept a significant number of positivist principles, including the notion that a satisfactory explanation allows for accurate predictions (see chapter 7). However, by demonstrating the extent to which social life can be explained as the product of a cost-benefit analysis on the part of the individuals involved, their approach is very much opposed to a Durkheimian research programme.

Second, too often quantitative researches have been dismissed as lying within a positivist framework. It is undoubtedly true that within the *contours* of positivist epistemology, certain forms of multivariate analysis are regarded as legitimate, if not encouraged. It is equally valid to argue that early forms of positivism were closely accompanied by systematic attempts to make use of statistical data, Durkheim's *Suicide* being a case in point.[9] However, it is erroneous to assert that positivist-inspired research cannot draw upon other methods or techniques. It is also equally mistaken to argue that any form of research which employs statistics necessarily falls within a positivist framework. All too often sophisticated quantitative researches have fallen victim to misguided critiques.

Third, positivism has often been portrayed as a unified doctrine. However, with a history approximately as long as that of sociology, positivist thought has changed substantially through time. Although the features discussed in the above are shared by the different forms in which positivism has appeared during the nineteenth and twentieth centuries, it is worth recalling their differences as well. Roughly speaking, three forms of positivism can be distinguished. First, there is nineteenth-century positivism, initially introduced by Auguste Comte, and further developed by J. S. Mill, Herbert Spencer and Émile Durkheim.[10] Inspired first by Newton's accomplishments in physics and subsequently by Darwinian evolutionary theory, these authors argued for the implementation of methods from the natural sciences in the social sciences. This positivist knowledge was thought to be the basis for scientifically planning and steering society – hence Comte's dictum 'to know in order to predict and to predict in order to control'. Steering society was considered to be necessary in order to restore social order – that very social order which was thought to have been eroded due to political and economic changes at the time (in particular the French Revolution and the industrial revolution). The methods employed were generally inductivist.

Second, there is logical positivism as developed first by the members of the Vienna Circle at the beginning of the twentieth century. Moritz Schlick, Rudolph Carnap and Otto Neurath were amongst the core members; A. J. Ayer, Kurt Gödel, Karl Popper, and Ludwig Wittgenstein had some affiliation with them. But logical positivism was not a solely Austrian enterprise. Bertrand Russell worked in a similar vein, and after Ayer's return to England and the subsequent publication of his highly influential *Language, Truth and Logic*, many Anglo-Saxon philosophers converted to and worked within the logical positivist tradition. There is quite a sharp contrast between nineteenth-century positivism and logical positivism. Whereas the former was preoccupied with the foundation of sociology as a separate discipline, the latter abandoned the close link with sociology. Whereas the former thought that a positivist study would be essential in order to direct society, the latter failed to attribute any such role to the social sciences. In an attempt to eradicate metaphysics, members of the Vienna Circle developed a logical system aimed at separating

Table 8.1 Hempel's DN model

explanans	L1 L2 . . . Ln	Laws
	C1 C2 . . . Cn	Antecedent conditions
explanandum E		

meaningful and non-meaningful statements. Given the logical positivist commitment to atomism, meaningful statements were considered to be reducible to an aggregate of descriptions of elementary facts. Employing a nominalist framework, meaning was only attributed to concepts as long as they referred to concrete objects, whereas abstract or metaphysical notions do not exist except as names. More relevant for the social sciences, logical positivists, and especially Neurath, adhered to a 'physicalist' notion of sociology. Physicalism reduced the social world to a mere aggregate of behavioural expressions, whilst eradicating any references to mental states of individuals.[11]

Third, more recently there has been the deductive-nomological (DN) method, very much associated with Carl Hempel's work. Heavily influenced by logical positivism, Hempel attempted to merge the logical and the empirical dimensions of positivism. His central notion was that all sciences draw upon a theoretical format (containing laws and initial conditions) from which hypotheses are then deduced which are eventually put to the test (see table 8.1). By pointing out the universality of that format across disciplines, Hempel's work epitomized the positivist notion of unity of method between the social and the natural sciences. Nevertheless, he did acknowledge two ways in which the social sciences are distinct.[12] On the one hand, some of the laws are embedded within people's tacit common-sense knowledge, and they therefore do not lend themselves easily to be put discursively. On the other hand, as often not enough empirical evidence has been accumulated, historians and other social scientists tend to rely upon 'explanation sketches' which are not identical to, but nevertheless approximate the DN model. In sociology, Hempel's work in this area was welcomed by theoreticians ranging from Homans to Merton (see chapter 2). Whereas Homans built his laws on behavioural psychology and utilitarian economics, Merton reconstructed Durkheim's argument in *Suicide* in terms of Hempel's hypothetico-deductive methods.[13]

Positivism has been criticized from many angles. Rather than presenting an exhaustive list of problems, I will only discuss those criticisms raised by three major rival theoretical traditions. The first problem to be discussed was initially raised by theorists working in the hermeneutic tradition, the second was introduced by members of critical theory, and the third was made by critical realists.

Authors within the hermeneutic tradition argued that although positivism might be applicable to the natural sciences, it fails miserably in dealing with the social realm. The reason is that hermeneutics is absent in positivist epistemology, whilst being essential for understanding the social realm. This is roughly Winch's position in his influential *The Idea of Social Science*.[14] Influenced by the later Wittgenstein, Winch views the social world as pregnant with meaning. People differ from innate objects in that they attribute meaning to the world which surrounds them and then act in accordance with that meaning. Meaning, so Winch continues, is embedded in implicit rules shared by members of the same community. Regularities in the social and in the natural realm are thus to be treated very differently. Any observed regularity presumes criteria of identity: the observed regularity that all Xi are followed by Yi rests upon criteria of identity which make one decide that all Xi are identical and that all Yi are of the same kind. In the social realm, however, these criteria of identity are provided by the shared rules of the community in which the observed behaviour is situated. The researcher needs to learn the implicit rules gradually, and this enterprise is obviously far removed from the positivist preoccupation with Humean causality.

Although Winch's critique of positivist sociology has widely been accepted, most commentators do not accept the entirety of his argument. Two reservations have usually been made. First, there is the realist view that Winch mistakenly assumed that positivist epistemology is an appropriate philosophy of the natural sciences. As will be shown later in this chapter, realists argued that the nature of explanatory formats in the natural sciences differs from that assumed in positivism. Once a realist account of scientific explanations is provided, so they argued, Winch's position as to the impossibility of naturalism does not hold.[15] This issue will be discussed in a further section. Second, it has been argued that, although Winch is correct in arguing that issues related to meaning and rule-following are important, if not essential, to the social sciences, sociological analysis surely does not end there. In addition, it is the task of the researcher to draw attention to mistakes in the perceptions and evaluations of the individuals under investigation. It is also his or her task to pay attention to the unacknowledged conditions and unintended consequences of people's actions (see chapter 4).[16] So whereas the first form of criticism questioned the naturalism in Winch's work, the second accused him of writing an apology for mere descriptive forms of social research. Importantly, though, neither of these aimed at eroding the strength of his argument against a positivist view of the social sciences.

Doubts have been expressed, especially by adherents of critical theory, over the positivist distinction between facts and values (see chapter 6). The arguments are manifold, but two of them are, I think, especially damaging and therefore worth recalling. First, it has been counter-argued that, even when social researchers pursue 'objectivity', values and interests necessarily affect the entire research process (and not merely the choice of the topic). Second, the position of many critical theorists has been that, independent of the question of whether or not values *ipso facto* enter into social research, it is not a desirable strategy to aim at value-free social science anyway. The reasons for supporting this critique can be negative or positive. The positive proposition is that, rather than simply representing or explaining social reality, one of the central goals of social research is to contribute to the self-emancipation of the individuals under investigation. The negative proposition refers to the argument that, disguised as a value-free enterprise, social research tends to serve particular values in society – often conservative ones. According to the Frankfurt School, in particular, positivist social research is indicative of and contributes to the spread of instrumental rationality in various areas of life (see chapter 6). Instead of aiming at emancipatory goals, the task of the social sciences within a positivist framework is reduced to the identification and avoidance of technical problems with the smooth functioning of society.[17]

From a realist point of view, the positivist notion of scientific explanation seems problematic. There are two points to the argument. First, the positivist tendency to reduce causality to regularity conjunctions fails to establish a distinction between laws and accidental generalizations. Realists have argued that observed regularities are not sufficient for making claims about causality – most realists would even argue that they are not necessary either. What is needed instead is a reference to hidden mechanisms which explain *how* the observed regularities are brought about.[18] Second, most realists have felt uncomfortable with the positivist notion of symmetry between explanation and prediction. There are indeed numerous theories (such as evolutionary theory and recent developments in quantum physics and thermodynamics) which are widely regarded as successful, though which do not allow for precise predictions. Conversely, many formats which allow for prediction are not explanations at all: readings of a barometer allow one to make predictions regarding the weather, without alleviating one's ignorance in this area.[19]

So positivism has been criticized from very different corners: by hermeneutics for ignoring the meaningful dimension of social life, by critical theory for clinging on to a mistaken distinction between facts and values, and by realists for an erroneous concept of scientific explanation. I certainly do not wish to suggest that the criticisms of positivism end here. There are numerous other problems with the concept – so many that positivist epistemology and, even more so, positivist social science are not any longer viable positions. As far as the former is concerned, its weakest point is probably its assumption that there is a hard and fast distinction between observation and theory. In philosophy and psychology, the notion of the mind as a *tabula rasa* has now been abandoned, and a consensus has emerged that any observation is only possible by relying upon theoretical presuppositions. If theoretical presumptions are essential for observations, the latter are fallible, and thus fail to provide the reliable foundation which positivists hoped for.

Falsificationism

Karl Popper has been one of the most influential philosophers in the twentieth century. The range and scope of his writings is extraordinarily broad, dealing with diverse issues from straight epistemology and philosophy of science, to political and social theory. In spite of the wide spectrum of his interests, one is struck by the consistency and coherence of his arguments. A number of themes recur throughout his writings. There is, above all, his belief, in whatever context, in the value of open debate and criticism – a belief that he obviously shared with Habermas (see chapter 6). Popper saw this principle as underlying, for instance, our liberal parliamentary democratic systems and our scientific activities, and most of his writings are devoted to elaborating upon and defending this principle. He also warned people of the many attempts which have been made to restrict these procedures of open discussion. These restrictions may be imposed structurally (for instance through totalitarian regimes) or intellectually (for instance through the promotion of non-falsifiable and historicist approaches). Popper's philosophy of science should be seen within this wider context.

In order to understand the rationale behind Popper's critical rationalism, one needs to grasp the underlying assumptions of the inductivist programme. I have mentioned inductivism earlier, and it is now time to delve deeper. According to inductivism, universal statements can be inferred from a finite number of singular observational statements. 'All ravens are black' is, for instance, a universal statement, and 'this raven is black' is a singular observational statement. Notice that inductivism draws upon the positivist belief in a clear-cut distinction between theoretical and observational language. That is, it is thought that observations are independent of one's theoretical presuppositions to such an extent that these observations are a reliable basis for inferring universal statements. Of course, inductivism states that the inference (of the universal statement from the singular statements) can only be made if a number of conditions are fulfilled. First, the number of observations needs to be sufficiently high: the observation of two black ravens, for instance, is obviously not sufficient to infer that all ravens are black. Second, the observations have to be gathered under a wide variety of different conditions. So an inductivist will observe ravens in different seasons, at different times of the day, in different countries, and so on and so forth. Third, none of the single observations conflicts with the universal law. Obviously, any observation of a raven which is not black makes the statement that all ravens are black implausible.[20]

One can easily understand the initial attraction of many philosophers and scientists towards inductivism. It meant a significant break with the metaphysics of the time, and it also fuelled the hope that through unbiased experiments and observations a superior understanding of the world would be achieved. Philosophically, however, inductivism ran into a number of difficulties. To begin with, from a finite number of observations one cannot infer universal statements, because there always exists the possibility of a future observation which contradicts that universal statement; this is commonly known as the problem of induction.[21] To consider the same example again, however many black ravens have been observed hitherto, from these observations it can never be inferred that all ravens are black since there is always the possibility of a future encounter with a raven whose colour is not black. The problem of induction can also be rephrased by contrasting inductive and deductive reasoning. Deductive reasoning is such that if the premises of the argument are correct, then it follows that the conclusion is also correct. For instance, if 'all ravens are black' is correct, and if 'this particular animal is a raven' is also correct, then it follows that the conclusion 'this animal is black' cannot be false. This does not apply to inductive reasoning: here the premises might be correct and the conclusion false. Consider, for instance, 'raven 1 is black' to be a correct statement, and 'raven 2 is black', etc. It is still possible, however, for the universal statement 'all ravens are black' to be incorrect, in spite of the fact that all premises are correct. So whereas deductive reasoning provides certainty regarding the validity of the conclusions as long as the premises are correct, inductivism does not.

Various attempts have been made to rescue the case of inductivism, but all in vain. Some philosophers have argued that although a number of observations can never be sufficient to infer universal statements, the former does increase the probability of the latter. However, this argument does not hold, because the number of observations is finite, whereas the universal statements refer to an infinite (or unknown) number of cases. Confirmation from a finite number of cases (however great that number) does not add to the probability regarding an infinite (or unknown) number of cases.

A second attempt to defend inductivism drew upon empirical evidence. Although inductivist method cannot be defended on logical grounds, it can be vindicated with the help of the history of science. The argument is then that the history of science demonstrates, first, that scientists nearly always employ inductivist method, and second, that they have been successful in so doing. This argument is flawed as well, for three reasons. First, the fact that through induction scientists have achieved some progress or success does not take away the possibility that, if different methods of research had been employed, more would have been accomplished. Second, most contemporary scholars like Kuhn and Popper have demonstrated that, in the history of science, scientists rarely draw upon induction.[22] Third, even if scientists were to operate in an inductivist fashion, the argument would not be convincing because of its circularity: it attempts to defend inductivism by employing inductivist method itself. As part of its proof, it assumes what is to be proven.[23]

Popper's philosophy of science becomes intelligible against this background. Against the doctrine of inductivism, he argued for the importance of deductive methodology in scientific practices, as did Liebig and Duhem before him and Hempel roughly simultaneously.[24] For Popper, scientists do not merely observe and then infer from that. Instead, they start with a problem, from which they construct a feasible theoretical construction which allows them to infer deductively testable hypotheses. These hypotheses are tested through observation, and theories are abandoned if they do not survive the test.

There are other differences between Popper and inductivism. Remember that inductivists assumed that there is a clear-cut distinction between theoretical language and observational language. The mind is considered to be a *tabula rasa*, with the external world imposing itself on it, and thus observational statements are theory-independent. More recent studies in psychology have shown this conception to be mistaken: people draw upon a number of theoretical presuppositions whilst getting access to the world. Likewise, Popper rejected the naïve distinction between observational and theoretical statements. One of the recurring themes in his writings is the extent to which theoretical assumptions are a precondition for the acquisition of knowledge.[25]

Popper tried to overcome the problem of induction. Although universal statements cannot be inferred from a finite number of observations, it is also true that one single refutation is sufficient to abandon a universal statement. One yellow raven is enough to conclude that not all ravens are black. Popper saw scientific theories and progress very much in this light. From a problem which puzzles them, scientists develop a plausible theory, and from that theory they infer a hypothesis. One single refutation on the basis of observation is sufficient to abandon the theory. A new theory is then tried out which will eventually be refuted as well. In Popper's view, scientific theories are temporary constructions, and they succeed one another through 'trial and error'.[26]

From Popper's notion that refutation is central to scientific progress, something important follows. To clarify this, Popper reminded the reader that a hypothesis can only be refuted if it is constructed such that it is refutable. For example, compare the statement '2 + 2 = 4' with the proposition 'the higher the rate of industrialization in a country, the more likely its birth rate will decrease'. The former can never be refuted, whilst the latter can, in principle, be falsified if empirical evidence shows otherwise. Here, Popper's philosophy acquires a normative dimension. He stipulated that theories can only be considered as scientific in so far as they allow one to infer falsifiable hypotheses, that is, hypotheses which are constructed such that they can be proved wrong. Theories which are non-falsifiable in that sense might still operate as heuristic devices and they might provide a first step towards future scientific understanding, but it would be a mistake to conceive of them as scientific theories themselves. Falsifiability is indeed Popper's line of demarcation between science and non-science.[27] However, as much as falsifiability is important, so are the *degrees* of it: certain propositions are highly falsifiable, others less so. Popper not only wanted to eradicate non-falsifiable theories from scientific discourse, he also very much praised highly falsifiable statements. He wanted scientists to lead a dangerous life, developing 'bold conjectures' which can easily be refuted.

Theories have to be falsifiable not only because they are then not immune to refutation, but also because falsifiability goes hand in hand with precision and information. Compare two statements: 'somebody may or may not kill himself today' and 'suicide is committed more frequently by men than women'. The former is non-falsifiable: whether somebody commits suicide or not, the statement can never be refuted. The latter is falsifiable: if suicide is found to be higher amongst women than men or if there is no significant difference across gender then the statement will be refuted. The first statement is not only non-falsifiable; it also fails to provide information about the world, because it fails to exclude any possibilities. The second statement is falsifiable; it excludes possibilities (for instance, that there is no difference between men and women with regard to suicide) and therefore provides information about the world. In general, falsifiability and information go together. Likewise, degrees of falsifiability go together with precision and information. The more falsifiable a statement, the more precise it is and the more information it provides.[28]

Popper's notion of falsifiability lay at the core of his assault on Marx, Freud and Adler. Although, for Popper, it is perfectly feasible to approach the social realm scientifically, many swindlers have infiltrated this domain. In his autobiography, Popper pointed out that, from an early age, he was struck by the difference between relativity theory on the one hand, and Marxism and psychoanalysis on the other.[29] From Einstein's theory, bold conjectures were inferred, which allowed for accurate predictions to be made and which allowed for either corroboration or falsification. Nothing like this applies to either Marxism or psychoanalysis. On the contrary, both doctrines can accommodate mutually exclusive scenarios and are therefore immune against refutation. Whether the communist revolution has occurred as yet or not, whether you act in this or that way towards your father – the doctrines fit with mutually exclusive possibilities. So a potential source of attraction towards Marxism and psychoanalysis reflects, in Popper's view, exactly their weakness: their ability to account for very diverse actions or outcomes, even mutually exclusive ones.

Popper's critique of Marx tied in with his assault on historicism. By historicism, he meant 'an approach to the social sciences which assumes that *historical prediction* is their principal aim, and which assumes that this aim is attainable by discovering the "rhythms" or the "pattern", the "laws" or the "trends" that underlie the evolution of history'.[30] Marx's historical materialism is clearly indicative of a historicist perspective. Popper's argument becomes rather complex here, but it seems to have roughly three components. First, historicism fails to distinguish between laws and trends.[31] Whereas the former are conditional statements ('if . . . then . . .'), the latter merely refer to a sequence of events in a not too distant period in the past. In contrast with the claim to universal validity of a law, no justification could be provided as to why a particular trend is to continue in the future. Second, historicist prophecies often draw upon non-falsifiable propositions. If the prophecy has not yet occurred, then historicists can always argue that it might come about at a later stage. Third, there is Popper's argument with regard to the growth of knowledge. The future depends on the growth of knowledge, but it is impossible for one to know the future of scientific knowledge (because if one is able to predict that knowledge, then surely one would have it now). Hence, one cannot make prophecies with regard to the future.[32]

Critical as Popper was of historicism, he also attacked utopian conceptions of society. Once implemented, a utopian scheme, like any human intervention, leads to unintended (and often unforeseen) effects which potentially contradict some aspects of the utopia. Often, authoritarian measures are employed to defend the utopia against criticism. It is thus not surprising that utopias tend to be non-falsifiable and hence immune to rational criticism. Instead of utopias, Popper argued in favour of piecemeal engineering in which policies are gradually implemented and people learn from their mistakes – here again, his notion of progress was one of trial and error. Obviously, the social sciences play an important role in this process: through scientific investigation people learn from their mistakes and rationally steer their society on that basis.[33]

Although Popper's philosophy of the social sciences shared the emphasis on deduction with Hempel's DN-model, critical rationalism differed substantially from positivist epistemology. Whereas inductivist and positivist conceptions of science adhered to a cumulative conception of knowledge, Popper's falsificationism conceived of scientific theories as temporal – to be superseded at a later stage. In Popper's view, paradoxically, one can only be certain about that which one holds to be false, and one can never be certain about that which one holds to be true. The picture presented was far removed from the old certainties advocated by previous perspectives on science.

Three main criticisms have been levelled against Popper's philosophy. The first focused upon his notion of the theory-laden nature of observations. By this, Popper meant that observations can only be made by making a number of assumptions, some of which might be mistaken. However, given that falsifications are based on observation statements, if (as Popper rightly acknowledged) observations are theory-laden, then falsifications must be theory-laden and thus fallible. If this is the case, though, then not only can nobody be certain about what they hold to be true, but they cannot even be certain about what they hold to be false.

A second issue relates to relatively recent findings in the history of science. Kuhn and many others have demonstrated that Popper's critical rationalism does not correspond to the way in which scientists normally operate. Kuhn's argument was that in periods of 'normal science' scientists do not question the paradigm (that is, a set of implicit rules and assumptions shared by members of a scientific community) which guides their research. Instead, they try to articulate that paradigm. Once confronted with results which might undermine the paradigm, they tend to blame auxiliary assumptions or the test situation – not the paradigm. Compare this with Popper's adventurous picture of the scientists who live dangerously – who develop bold conjectures ready to be refuted. In Kuhn's portrait, scientists are more cautious and modest, attempting to develop further details of the paradigm and initially blind to revolutionary results. Only at a later stage (once confronted with many results which contradict the paradigm, and apprised of an alternative), do they start questioning the underlying paradigm.[34]

Popper's reply to Kuhn was predictable: ultimately Popper's philosophy of science is prescriptive, not descriptive. If there is some truth in Kuhn's historical reconstruction, so Popper argued, then all there is to say is that these scientists were not properly trained.[35] Popper's argument could not be sustained. It became difficult for Popper to sustain a prescriptive philosophy of science once it was demonstrated that scientists in the last couple of centuries rarely followed these principles, especially given that Popper himself praised the progress made by the very same scientists. The historical case against Popper became even stronger in Feyerabend's counterfactual thinking. He argued that in a significant number of cases it could be shown that not only had scientists rarely followed Popper's principles, but if they had, then significant progress (which they did actually make) would not have taken place.[36]

Third, Popper has been criticized by realists for mistakenly assuming the existence of closed systems. Scientists create closed systems in laboratory experiments: one causal factor is isolated and the others are controlled for. Realists insisted that closed systems are rare in reality, and that open systems are frequent, especially in the social realm. The existence of open systems means that various generative mechanisms intervene and they might cancel each other out. The inductivist search for regularities is therefore in vain, but so is the positivist or Popperian preoccupation with verification and falsification, since they rely upon the chimerical assumption of closed systems. A falsification of a proposition might be due to the falsehood of the proposition, but it might also, because of the openness of systems, be due to intervening mechanisms. The same argument applies to the corroboration of a statement which, although possibly indicative of the truth of a proposition, could also be explained by the interference of other generative mechanisms.[37]

Imre Lakatos's sophisticated falsificationism was the most elaborate attempt to save a Popperian perspective, whilst taking into account some of the above mentioned criticisms by historians of science. Like Kuhn, Lakatos conceived of theories in a broader sense: Lakatos's research programme referred to a set of assumptions and rules shared by members of the same community about how to carry out empirical research. One falsification is obviously not sufficient to abandon a research programme, because that falsification might, instead of indicating the falsehood of the hypothesis, be due to the fact that one or more of the auxiliary assumptions are mistaken. So Lakatos's main point was that the core of a research programme needs to be protected against such swift refutations. In this context, he distinguished between the hard core and the protective belt of a research programme. By the hard core, he meant the basic theoretical assumptions shared by all scientists who work within that research programme. For social scientists working within a Durkheimian framework, for example, 'social facts have to treated as things and are to be explained by other social facts' would be part of the hard core. The protective belt, in Lakatos's terminology, refers to a set of auxiliary assumptions and initial conditions about how to carry out research. Now, as long as scientists work within a particular research programme, the hard core needs to remain intact (Lakatos called it the 'negative heuristic'), whilst the protective belt can be altered whenever necessary (the 'positive heuristic'). Once scientists decide to change the hard core, a new research programme has emerged. Lakatos argued that this should only be done once the initial research programme is no longer 'progressive' but 'degenerating'. A research programme is progressive if it allows for theoretical or empirical progress. The former refers to successful application to new domains, the latter to novel empirical findings and corroborations. A research programme is 'degenerating' if it fails to make either empirical or theoretical progress.[38]

The critique of Popper regarding the fallibility of falsifications did not apply to Lakatos, because the notion of the theory-laden nature of our observational statements lies at the core of his version of critical rationalism. Compared to Popper, Lakatos's writings were also less susceptible to criticisms regarding historical inaccuracy, since he incorporated some of Kuhn's insights into his philosophical construction. However, the realist critique of falsificationism still stands. In addition, Lakatos cannot but acknowledge that a research programme might for a while appear to be degenerating and then suddenly re-emerge as progressive. A common pertinent critique has indeed been that he failed to specify when a research programme is to be considered as unequivocally degenerating. This is indeed a problem given that he, like Popper, sees his main task as developing a prescriptive philosophy of science.

But there are deeper problems with critical rationalism, whether Popper's version or Lakatos's. Both rightly believed in the fruitfulness of the implementation of procedures of open discussion and criticism. Both rightly believed that these procedures are necessary for scientific progress. But both then set out to define the exact parameters within which the discussion should take place. For instance, Popper insisted that the discussion regarding the validity of scientific theories should focus upon empirical corroboration or falsification. However, three problems emerge. First, the stipulation of these strict rules (regarding what is meaningful, fruitful and legitimate scientific communication) contradicts the initial commitment to open debate and criticism. To institutionalize an open debate and criticism in science necessitates a similar open discussion at a meta-level. Second, scientific communication often proceeds by adopting different rules from the ones which were stipulated by Popper and Lakatos. Whether a theory allows for successful predictions or not is only one criterion (amongst many) used by scientists. Other criteria also come into play: the simplicity of the theory, whether it is wide-ranging or not, its perceptiveness, etc. Third, especially in the social realm, Popper's (and even Lakatos's) prescriptions would lead to highly impoverished procedures for theory evaluation. They would lead to the abandonment of highly informative theories (like Freud's or Marx's) and the survival of insignificant theories. It is indeed not difficult to conceive of numerous (real or imaginary) theories, which are highly falsifiable, which have been corroborated, but which lack any depth or breadth.

Realism

It is generally fair to say that, since the 1970s, realist philosophy of the social sciences has been *in statu ascendi*. Realist philosophy of science was originally introduced by philosophers like Mary Hesse and Rom Harré in order to avoid some of the rigidities and inconsistencies of both the then prominent logical positivist model and its falsificationist alternative. The significance of realism for the social sciences soon became obvious, so obvious that second generation realists, such as Roy Bhaskar and Nancy Cartwright, dealt almost exclusively with the social sciences. Three publications were central to the spread of realist social science: Harré and Secord's *Explanation of Social Behaviour*, Keat and Urry's *Social Theory as Science*, and Bhaskar's *The Possibility of Naturalism*.[39] I will briefly discuss each in turn.

First, Harré's commitment to the realist cause exercised a profound impact on social psychology, especially since the publication in the early 1970s of the widely influential *Explanation of Social Behaviour*.[40] In this book, Harré and Secord argued against the dominance of positivist episte-mology in social psychology, its attendant Humean concept of causality and mechanistic model of human conduct, whilst appealing for a realist inspired 'ethogenics'. Drawing upon, *inter alios*, Mead and Wittgenstein, ethogenics attempted to explain human action in terms of self-monitoring and rule-following. By introducing these notions, Harré and Secord argued against what they saw as the dominant view in social psychology, according to which people's conduct is determined by external forces. Harré and Secord argued instead that people constantly monitor their actions in accordance with shared, implicit rules.

Second, if *Explanation of Social Behaviour* introduced realism to social psychology, Keat and Urry's *Social Theory as Science* fulfilled the same function for sociology.[41] Published shortly after *Explanation of Social Behaviour*, the underlying philosophy of *Social Theory as Science* is very much inspired by Harré. In addition, Keat and Urry set out to explore the affinities between Harré's realism, structuralist sociology and hermeneutics. Positiv-ism is again the main target. Keat and Urry saw it as the task of sociology to account for observed regularities by invoking underlying mechanisms which might or might not be directly open to observation. Structuralist and hermen-eutic authors were then shown to be realists *avant la lettre* – companions in the struggle against the dominance of positivist epistemology. From the realist perspective, both structuralism and hermeneutics indeed attempt to explain *how* the observed regularities come about by invoking entities which are not necessarily immediately accessible to observation.

Third, the growing sociological interest in realism culminated in Bhaskar's *The Possibility of Naturalism*.[42] This realist manifesto, originally published in the late 1970s, had significant ramifications for the social sciences. Like Keat and Urry, Bhaskar endeavoured to merge realism with structuralist and hermeneutic notions, but his overall project was more ambitious than Keat and Urry's. Not unlike Bourdieu and Giddens, he attempted to transcend a number of dichotomies: subjectivism versus objectivism, agency versus struc-ture, etc. (see chapters 1 and 4). His core notion was the transformational model of social action, according to which structure is a *sine qua non* for agency, whilst the reproduction of structure is dependent on the very same agency. Partly due to the widespread influence of Bhaskar's work, many publications have now emerged which argue for a realist perspective on the social sciences, ranging from realist-inspired empirical investigations to text-books on research methodology.[43] Bhaskar's work has been influential not merely in sociology, but also in economics.[44]

Given that it is impossible to take into account all variations within real-ism, I will focus on what is called 'critical realism', which has been inspired by Bhaskar, and which has become highly influential in sociology. To start with, I will spell out the cardinal characteristics of this realist perspective, both as a general philosophy of science and as a contribution to social theory. I will then discuss some of its inadequacies.

Like positivism, realism adheres to 'naturalism'. That is, realists advocate a unity of the sciences, or, more precisely, a unity of *method* between the natural and the social sciences. Realists and positivists disagree as to what is the nature of 'scientific method'. The latter draw upon a Humean concept of causality, and they refuse to attribute reality to entities which are not immediately accessible to observation (see above). The former propose a non-Humean conception of causality, and they do allocate 'reality' to theoretical entities (see below). By arguing for naturalism, realists distance themselves from most hermeneutic-inspired philosophies of social sciences, such as that espoused by Winch. Realists agree with Winch that the social world is endowed with meaning, but argue that to infer from this (as Winch and others have done) the 'impossibility of naturalism' is a *non sequitur*. Realists acknowledge that there are differences between social and natural structures; for instance, the reproduction of social structures is, unlike natural structures, dependent on the actions which the very same structures help to constitute. However, this does not mean that a different scientific method is at stake.[45]

Realists argue for a 'stratified conception of reality'. That is, they believe that there are three realms of reality: the actual, the empirical and the deep. The actual level refers to events or states of affairs. These events are real in that they occur and exist independently of the empirical level. The empirical level consists of people's perceptions, observations and experiences of the actual level. Finally, the deep level involves underlying mechanisms or powers which generate these events. The deep level is not necessarily accessible to observation, but nevertheless it exists.[46]

Realists argue that these different realms are not necessarily 'synchronized', and, as a matter of fact, they are often 'out of phase' with each other. Let me spell out what realists mean by 'synchronization' (versus 'being out of phase') in this context. There would, in realist parlance, be synchronization between the actual and the empirical if people's observations of events corresponded to the events in an unproblematic fashion. If a hard and fast distinction between observational language and theoretical language (a position taken up by some positivists) pertained, then the actual and the empirical would be in synchrony. Indeed, if observations were theory-neutral, then one's observational statements would correspond unproblematically to that which has been observed. Similarly, still within a realist vocabulary, a synchronization between the actual and the deep level would imply that the underlying mechanisms reveal themselves in a straightforward manner at the phenomenal level. If scientific laws were mere regularity conjunctions (a position taken up by most positivists), then the actual and the deep would therefore be synchronized. The laws would then appear unconcealed at the phenomenal level.

But the realist argument is that synchrony is rare and should certainly not be assumed; this contention is central to the realist programme and to its assault on other philosophies of science. First, the actual and the empirical are usually non-synchronic because observations *are* theory-laden (that is, observations can only be made by drawing implicitly or explicitly upon theoretical presuppositions) and therefore fallible. Inductivism is thus mistaken in assuming that scientists can rely upon a solid bedrock of observations. Second, and more importantly, the actual and the deep are often out of phase with each other. Realists tend to resort to the example of the falling leaf to illustrate this point. If the actual and the empirical were synchronous, then the law of gravity would show itself in an unproblematic fashion, and all leaves would fall down in a straight line (according to the mathematical formulation of the same law). However, needless to say, leaves tend not to fall in a straight line. This is because they occupy open systems: as well as the law of gravity, other generative mechanisms are at work (for example, aerodynamic forces), which might interfere with the law of gravity and potentially cancel it out. This example indicates the extent to which, once open systems are in operation, verification loses its relevance and so does falsification. It would indeed be foolish to conclude that the law of gravity does not hold simply because the leaf fails to fall in the way stipulated by that law. The realist position is that closed systems are rare in general, and that *a fortiori* social systems are likely to be open systems. The actual and the deep are often out of phase with each other, especially in the social realm. By drawing upon a Humean concept of causality (see below), positivists fail to acknowledge this lack of synchrony, and erroneously attribute too much significance to verification and falsification.[47]

Positivists tend to subscribe to what is often referred to as a 'Humean concept of causality'. It is called 'Humean' because it depends on a particular reading of Hume's ideas on causality. I leave aside to what extent this notion actually corresponds to Hume's sophisticated reflections upon causality. According to the positivists' Humean concept of causality, regularity conjunctions are both necessary and sufficient for attributions of causality. So if (and only if) X is found regularly to be followed by Y, it is justifiable to say that X causes Y. A positivist explanation for the high fertility rate of a given country might be, for instance, that it has been regularly observed that under-industrialized countries tend to have high fertility rates, and that this particular country happens to be at a low stage of industrialization. One of the upshots of this Humean concept of causality is that causal explanations do not include references to generative mechanisms.

The realist position could not be more different. First, this positivist notion of causality, descriptive as it is, demands an explanation, rather than providing one. From a realist perspective, to explain something entails explaining *how* it is brought about, and regularity conjunctions do not fulfil this function.

Second, given that most systems are open systems in which, by definition, various countervailing mechanisms come into play, regularities are neither necessary nor sufficient for making claims about causality. So, given these objections, realists plead for a different notion of causality. For them, explanations must also include assertions about causality, but explaining the causes of phenomena at the empirical level can only be accomplished by appealing to mechanisms or causal powers at the non-actual level. These mechanisms or causal powers are not necessarily immediately available to observation, but some certainty about their existence can still be obtained. One arrives at these mechanisms through 'retroduction', to which I will now turn.[48]

Modern philosophy of science tends to be either inductivist or deductivist. Inductivism assumes that one can infer general laws from a finite, though large, number of observations – as long as these observations are made under various circumstances. Deductivism starts with a theory which consists of general laws or assumptions, plus initial conditions. From this theory hypotheses are deduced, and are then tested. Instead of both inductivism and deductivism, realists appeal for 'retroduction', in which phenomena that are unfamiliar are explained by drawing upon analogies and metaphors with phenomena that are familiar. For example, Charles Darwin's evolutionism drew upon analogies with the notion of survival of the fittest in economics, and the role of variation in domestic breeding. Likewise, nineteenth-century sociologists, such as Spencer or Durkheim, tried to explain long-term societal changes by drawing upon analogies with biological evolution. Other examples include Levi-Strauss's explanation of social life by drawing upon analogies with linguistic systems (see chapter 1), or the use of evolutionary models in contemporary economics (see chapter 7). Realists advocate retroduction for two reasons. First, they argue that it allows one to surpass some of the philosophical problems which are commonly associated with either inductivism or deductivism. Second, it is thought to account for the creative dimension of scientific activity, whereas previous philosophies of science did not score well on this.[49]

By discussing the realists' commitment to naturalism, I have already mentioned some aspects of their social theory. It is now time to elaborate on this.[50] One of the leitmotivs of realist social theory is, like structuration theory, the necessity of moving beyond the age-old dualism between the individual and society, or between action-orientated and structural theories (see chapter 4). In order to transcend this dualism, they argue in favour of the transformational model of social action (henceforth TMSA). Like Giddens's 'duality of structure', TMSA postulates that structure is a precondition for the emergence of agency, and agency makes for the unintended reproduction of that very same structure. An example of this recursive model – already cited in chapter 4 – can be found in language. When people speak in English, they cannot help drawing upon the structural properties of the English language, but the act of speaking also contributes to the reproduction of that very same structure. Three important issues follow from this. First, contrary to some structuralist approaches which see structure as an impediment to agency (see chapter 1), TMSA sees it as the *sine qua non* of agency. Like Giddens, realists tend to put this epigrammatically by saying that structures are not merely constraining, but also enabling (see chapter 4). Second, contrary to the structuralist tendency to reify structure and to downplay agency (see chapter 1), realists explain the reproduction of structures as dependent on actions which the very same structures make possible. Third, as opposed to those hermeneutic approaches which tend to portray human actions as creations *de novo*, one of the ramifications of TMSA is that there is no *tabula rasa* in the social realm. In some respects, Persius' *de nihilo nihil* (from nothing, nothing can come) summarizes the realist position very well, because any transformation can only be made by relying upon (and hence reproducing) certain structural properties.

Notice that, partly by drawing upon a particular reading of Wittgenstein, some realists tend to emphasize, like Giddens, that people are knowledgeable individuals who know a great deal about social life, though in a practical manner (see chapters 3 and 4). For example, one knows one's native language in that one knows how to speak in accordance with the rules of grammar; to speak one's native language, one does not need to know the rules of grammar explicitly. (As a matter of fact, discursive forms of knowledge could be an impediment in this instance.) Likewise, one knows how to behave in accordance with the local rules of proper conduct without necessarily being able to set out these rules discursively. To summarize, the knowledge involved is *practical* knowledge concerning *tacit rules* of social life.

The main weakness of realism is that it fails as a prescriptive philosophy of science. Whereas initially realists tried to reconstruct what (natural) scientists actually do, some subsequently went further and allocated a prescriptive value to realism. They argue or assume that realism can inform scientists about that which *needs* to be done. For instance, Harré not only dismisses what he regards as a positivist view of psychology, but also introduces a new perspective on psychological theory and methodology – one inspired by realism. Similarly, Lawson not only condemns most research in mainstream economics as embedded in an outmoded and erroneous positivist epistemology (see chapter 7), but he also appeals for a realist-informed economics. In their attempt to extract methodological prescriptions from realism, Harré and Lawson are not alone any longer: a significant number of new textbooks on social research methodology have emerged which take an explicit realist stance.

However, as a prescriptive philosophy, the realist programme is quite limited for a number of reasons. First, the only type of research which, for realists, seems to be ruled out is an extreme form of positivism. Contrary to what realists presume or state, most research in the social sciences does *not* operate according to positivist principles anyway. It is indeed rare for social scientists merely to search for regularity conjunctions and to remain at the phenomenal level. Even Durkheim's *Suicide*, often seen as the example *par excellence* of positivist empirical research in sociology, is not a mindless pursuit of regularities.[51] Second, most realist guidelines are already followed by social scientists, who account for observed phenomena by alluding to underlying mechanisms, which are often considered not to be directly accessible to observation. In *Suicide*, for example, Durkheim searches for underlying societal forces. The people who are subjected to these forces are not necessarily aware of their existence, nor are such forces instantaneously available to social researchers. Now, given that most empirical social research already operates according to realist, not positivist, principles, and given that positivist enquiry is the only type of research which, from a realist perspective, is to be excluded, then the prescriptive value of realism as a philosophy of social sciences must seriously be in doubt.

It could, of course, be counter-argued by realists that the prescriptive value of any philosophy of science does not merely rest upon its ability to exclude certain practices from the realm of science. Indeed, the prescriptive value of a philosophy also depends on the capacity to inform scientists about how to conduct research, and to provide criteria for judging between different theories. However, here the realist programme falls short as well. Let me start by considering the realist suggestions for deciding between rival theories. Realists argue that theories need to be judged on the basis of whether they survive empirical testing, and, if they do, on the basis of their explanatory power. Empirical testing will be dealt with later, and I will, *ad interim*, concentrate on the notion of explanatory power. The realist argument is that, when confronted with two theories with equal empirical cogency, one should opt for the one with the higher explanatory power. Realists are evasive when it comes down to defining the notion of explanatory power, but it would seem reasonable to suppose that the explanatory power of a theory is dependent on the range of phenomena which can be explained by that theory. The more that can be explained by a theory, the greater its explanatory power. However, highly non-falsifiable theories have huge explanatory power, so the realist argument seems to imply that highly non-falsifiable theories are highly desirable. Popper would turn in his grave, and the realist argument becomes more problematic given that realists consider themselves to be fallibilists.

I will now move to the realist guidelines regarding how to carry out research. Realists suggest that one should start with 'stylized facts'; that is, observed regularities of nature. Examples of stylized facts are the observation that leaves tend to fall to the ground, or, sociologically more relevant, that Protestants have a higher suicide rate than Catholics. From a realist perspective, these stylized facts are then explained by invoking underlying mechanisms, which are arrived at through retroduction. The existence of these mechanisms is then falsified or corroborated through empirical testing.

Taking into account the other premises of realism, the argument concerning stylized facts does not bear close scrutiny. Given that the realists postulate the openness of systems and, *mutatis mutandis*, a lack of synchrony between the actual and the empirical level, they should not, as they do, put so much weight on observed regularities. From their assumption of the openness of systems, they should instead infer that stylized facts are highly unreliable sources for uncovering underlying mechanisms. Likewise, given the very same postulate regarding open systems and the lack of synchrony between the actual and the empirical, they should not, as they do, rely upon empirical testing to such an extent.

To put it differently: from the realist notion of open systems, it should be inferred that verification and falsification are highly problematic for deciding whether or not a theory is acceptable. So the realist programme falls short in two ways. First, whilst initially taking a strict philosophical position, realists ignore the obvious consequences of that view when dealing with research methodology. One cannot have it both ways. To promote the notion of an open system necessarily argues against unconditional reliance upon observed regularities and empirical testing. Second, realists fail to recognize the radical consequences of their own position. Once the notion of open systems is taken on board, empirical grounds for judging the existence of underlying mechanisms are undermined. So, realists might well be right when they claim that there are underlying structures which exist independently of one's experience or perception, but, given their notion of the openness of systems, they must be incorrect in asserting that it is possible for scientists to acquire that level of certainty regarding the existence of these structures.

It could, of course, be argued that the strength of the realist programme as a prescriptive philosophy of science lies in its contribution to the social sciences. It could, in particular, be held that, although empirical social research already operates according to the principles of realist philosophy of science, realism presents a novel and fruitful theoretical perspective on the individual and society (and that the latter has repercussions for the methodology of social research). I think that, on the contrary, the realist perspective on social theory has serious limitations. First, the core presuppositions of the critical realist programme are not exceptionally new, and unquestionably not as original or unseasoned as they have sometimes been presented. The cardinal assumptions of realist social theory were anticipated by others. Bourdieu and Giddens, for instance, attempted earlier to transcend the opposition between the individual and society, between agency and structure and between objectivist and subjectivist approaches.[52] Giddens's duality of structure is very similar, if not identical, to Bhaskar's TMSA (although they differ in their definition of structure). Like Bhaskar, both Bourdieu's notion of *habitus* and Giddens's concept of practical consciousness focus on the interrelationship between tacit knowledge and rule-following (see chapters 1 and 4). Second, whilst the core propositions of the realist programme are bordering on the self-evident, hardly any attempt is made to go further than that. It is worth recalling some of these propositions: people act purposively but they bring about unintended effects; people exercise agency but they can only accomplish this by drawing upon structures; and hence, although people are knowledgeable, their knowledge is always bounded by unacknowledged conditions and unforeseen effects. Not many people would question the validity of these propositions, because they are as self-evident as mathematical axioms.

Third, in spite of the differences between realists and Giddens, the core of their theories are similar. And that core, I would argue, is problematic. Realists describe their theory as transformational, but realist social theory is anything but. TMSA (like Giddens's concept of the duality of structure) is strong in accounting for the *reproduction* of structures, but not in accounting for their *transformation*. In short, the realist contribution to social theory has a particular bias towards order, not change. Fourth (and very much related to the previous point), realists fail to acknowledge people's ability to stand back from structures, and to develop discursive knowledge regarding previously tacit rules and assumptions. I call this ability 'reflection of the second order' as opposed to 'reflection of the first order', the latter referring to practical, tacit knowledge, and the former to theoretical, discursive knowledge. Reflection of the second order arises through the confrontation with unanticipated experiences: for instance, with unforeseen consequences of previous actions, or with different forms of life. Once reflection of the second order acquires public-collective features, it can become an important source of planned change, or deliberate maintenance.[53] It should be clear from the above that the realist bias towards order goes hand in hand with its neglect of reflection of the second order (see chapter 4).

Further reading

For a broad introduction to the history of the philosophy of science, Chalmers's *What is this Thing Called Science?* is very accessible and lucid. For a general introduction to the philosophy of the social sciences, I suggest Hollis's *The Philosophy of Social Science*. Kolakowski's *Positivist Philosophy* is an excellent historical overview of positivism. Giddens's 'Positivism and its Critics' in his *Studies in Social and Political Theory* provides a more sociological angle. For a good introduction to Popper, the relevant chapters in Chalmers's *What is this Thing Called Science?* will be very useful. Chapter 8 in O'Hear's *Karl Popper* provides a concise and accurate account of Popper's views on the social sciences. Of course Popper's own writings are clear and provocative – in particular,

The Logic of Scientific Discovery still makes a good read. For those interested in the polemic between Popper, Kuhn and Lakatos, their contributions to Lakatos and Musgrave's *Criticism and the Growth of Knowledge* summarize the debate well. Bhaskar's critical realism is spelled out in his *A Realist Theory of Science* and *The Possibility of Naturalism*. Keat and Urry's *Social Theory as Science* captures very well the essential features of the realist perspective once applied to the social sciences. Outhwaite's *New Philosophies of the Social Sciences: Realism, Hermeneutics and Critical Theory* explores the link between critical theory, hermeneutics and realism.

References

Adorno. T. W. et al. 1976. *The Positivist Dispute in German Sociology*. London: Heinemann (originally in German, 1962).

Ayer, A. J. 1946. *Language, Truth and Logic*. London: Victor Gollancz (2nd edition, 1970).

Ayer, A. J. (ed.) 1959. *Logical Positivism*. Glencoe, Ill.: Free Press.

Baert, P. 1992. *Time, Self and Social Being; Outline of a Temporalised Sociology*. Aldershot: Avebury.

Bhaskar, R. 1978. *A Realist Theory of Science*. Brighton: Harvester Press.

Bhaskar, R. 1989. *The Possibility of Naturalism*. Brighton: Harvester (2nd edition).

Bourdieu, P. 1977. *Outline of a Theory of Practice*. Cambridge: Cambridge University Press (originally in French, 1972).

Bryant, C. G. A. 1985. *Positivism in Social Theory and Research*. New York: St Martin's Press.

Carnap, R. 1959. The elimination of metaphysics through logical analysis of language. In: *Logical Positivism*, ed. A. J. Ayer. Glencoe, Ill.: Free Press, 60–81 (originally in German, 1932).

Cartwright, N. 1989. *Nature's Capacities and their Measurement*. Oxford: Clarendon Press.

Chalmers, A. 1976. *What is this Thing Called Science?* St Lucia: University of Queensland Press.

Comte, A. 1969. *System of Positive Polity; Volumes 1–4*. New York: Burt Franklin (originally in French, 1830–42).

Duhem, P. 1954. *The Aim and Structure of Physical Theory*. Princeton, NJ: Princeton University Press (originally in French, 1906).

Durkheim, E. 1952. *Suicide*. London: Routledge (originally in French, 1897; reprinted, 1992).

Durkheim, E. 1982. *The Rules of Sociological Method, and Selected Texts on Sociology and its Method*. London: Macmillan (originally in French, 1895; reprinted, 1992).

Faris, R. E. L. (ed.) 1964. *Handbook of Modern Sociology*. Chicago: Rand McNally.

Feyerabend, P. 1975. *Against Method; Outline of an Anarchistic Theory of Knowledge*. London: Humanities Press.

Giddens, A. 1977. *Studies in Social and Political Theory*. London: Macmillan (reprinted, 1979).

Giddens, A. 1984. *The Constitution of Society; Outline of the Theory of Structuration*. Cambridge: Polity Press.

Giddens, A. 1993. *New Rules of Sociological Method*. Cambridge: Polity Press (2nd edition, 1993).

Hacking, I. 1983. *Representing and Intervening; Introductory Topics in the Philosophy of Natural Sciences*. Cambridge: Cambridge University Press (reprinted, 1992).

Harré, R. 1975. *Causal Powers; A Theory of Natural Necessity*. Oxford: Blackwell.

Harré, R. 1985. *The Philosophies of Science; An Introductory Survey*. Oxford: Oxford University Press (2nd edition; reprinted, 1986).

Harré, R. and Secord, P. 1972. *Explanation of Social Behaviour*. Blackwell: Oxford.

Hempel, C. G. 1965. *Aspects of Scientific Explanation; and other Essays in the Philosophy of Science*. New York: Free Press.

Hempel, C. G. 1966. *Philosophy of Natural Science*. Englewood Cliffs, NJ: Prentice Hall.

Hollis, M. 1994. *The Philosophy of Social Science*. Cambridge: Cambridge University Press.

Homans, G. C. 1964. Contemporary theory in sociology. In: *Handbook of Modern Sociology*, ed. R. E. L. Faris. Chicago: Rand McNally, 951–77.

Homans, G. C. 1967. *The Nature of Social Science*. New York: Harcourt, Brace and World.

Hume, D. 1975. *Enquiries Concerning Human Understanding and Concerning the Principles of Morals*. Oxford: Clarendon (3rd edition).

Hume, D. 1978. *A Treatise of Human Nature*. Oxford: Clarendon.

Keat, R. and Urry, J. 1982. *Social Theory as Science*. London: Routledge and Kegan Paul (2nd edition).

Kolakowski, L. 1972. *Positivist Philosophy; From Hume to the Vienna Circle*. London: Penguin (originally in Polish, 1966).

Kuhn, T. 1970a. *The Structure of Scientific Revolution*. Chicago: University of Chicago Press (2nd edition).

Kuhn, T. 1970b. Logic of discovery or psychology of research. In: *Criticism and the Growth of Knowledge*, ed. I. Lakatos and A. Musgrave. Cambridge: Cambridge University Press, 1–24.

Lakatos. I. 1970. Falsification and the methodology of scientific research programmes. In: *Criticism and the Growth of Knowledge*. eds I. Lakatos and A. Musgrave. Cambridge: Cambridge University Press, 91–196.

Lakatos, I. and A. Musgrave (eds) 1970. *Criticism and the Growth of Knowledge*. Cambridge: Cambridge University Press.

Lawson, T. 1994. A Realist Theory for Economics. In: *New Perspectives on Economic Methodology*, ed. R. Backhouse. London: Routledge.

Layder, D. 1992. *New Strategies for Social Research*. Cambridge: Polity Press.

Mill, J. S. 1891. *System of Logic; Ratiocinative and Inductive*. London: Longmans (8th edition).

O'Hear, A. 1980. *Karl Popper*. London: Routledge.

Outhwaite, W. 1987. *New Philosophies of Social Science: Realism, Hermeneutics and Critical Theory*. Basingstoke: Macmillan.

Popper, K. 1950. Indeterminism in quantum physics and in classical physics. *British Journal of Philosophical Science* 1, 117–33, 173–95.

Popper, K. 1966. *The Open Society and its Enemies; Volume 1: The Spell of Plato*. Princeton, NJ: Princeton University Press (5th edition; reprinted, 1971).

Popper, K. R. 1968. *The Logic of Scientific Discovery*. London: Hutchinson (2nd edition; originally in German, 1934).

Popper, K. R. 1970. Normal science and its dangers. In: *Criticism and the Growth of Knowledge*, eds I. Lakatos and A. Musgrave. Cambridge: Cambridge University Press, 51–8.

Popper, K. 1986. *The Poverty of Historicism*. London: Routledge (2nd edition; reprinted, 1991).

Popper, K. R. 1989. *Conjectures and Refutations; The Growth of Scientific Knowledge*. London: Routledge and Kegan Paul (5th edition; reprinted, 1991).

Popper, K. R. 1992. *Unended Quest; An Intellectual Autobiography*. London: Routledge (2nd edition).

Russell, B. 1967. *The Problems of Philosophy*. Oxford: Oxford University Press (reprinted, 1991).

Spencer, H. 1961. *The Study of Sociology*. Ann Arbor: University of Michigan Press (revised edition).

Weber, M. 1949. *The Methodology of the Social Sciences*. New York: Glencoe.

Winch, P. 1990. *The Idea of Social Science and its Relation to Philosophy*. London: Routledge (2nd edition).

Conclusion

With the foregoing survey of social theory in mind, I would like to conclude by bringing up some broader questions regarding theoretical innovation and advancement, and by suggesting some tentative answers to these questions. First, some of the guidelines which I suggest follow on from the more philosophical discussions in this book (see especially chapter 8). In particular, I will elaborate briefly upon the relationship between theory and empirical research, and between social theory and other disciplines. Second, in line with some recurrent criticisms of social theories throughout the previous chapters (see especially chapters 1, 3 and 4), I suggest a theoretical outline which acknowledges the fundamental dynamic and reflective nature of social life. In brief, social theory ought to take seriously the simple fact that individuals are able to reflect upon their circumstances, and that they might act on that knowledge as they go along.

The first issue concerns which intellectual enquiries theorists ought to focus upon. It should be clear from the discussion in previous chapters that, whilst social theory has for a long time been a divided discipline with mutually exclusive standpoints, attempts have recently been made to transcend hitherto opposing theoretical views. Bourdieu's generative structuralism, Alexander's neo-functionalism, Giddens's structuration theory and Habermas's critical theory all try to incorporate different viewpoints, and are all attempts that rest upon the assumption that one of the pivotal aims of social theory is to link various levels of analysis (see chapters 1, 2, 4 and 6). So, it is held that social theory needs to bridge the gap between, for instance, the individual and society, the micro and the macro, or agency and structure.[1] From this, social theorists tend to infer the necessity of incorporating both objectivism and subjectivism, both system analysis and hermeneutics, or both structuralism and social phenomenology. I fear that this intellectual route might encounter an impasse. It is, of course, important to be sensitive to the interconnections between various layers of the social realm whilst carrying out empirical research. Neither do I doubt that it is desirable for a theory to link the various layers, since this increases its breadth. From this it does not follow, however, as so many now assume, that social theorists ought to set themselves, as the central task, the linking of these layers. For theoretical contributions to be worthwhile, they need to be question-driven, and the questions ought to be precise. Questions regarding the link between, say, system analysis and hermeneutics or between the micro and the macro are too general and unfocused, and therefore generate vague and uninformative answers. Although the methodology of rational choice approaches has been shown to be seriously flawed (see chapter 7), it should be acknowledged that they, more than any other social theory, set an example in attempting to answer accurate and focused questions. For example, one of their recurring questions is under which conditions concerted, collective action might be jeopardized, and how the problem can be overcome. Or, they examine under which circumstances self-interested action might lead to suboptimal results. I do not wish to advocate rational choice theory, but do wish to stress that putting forward clear, focused questions, as rational choice theorists do, is a major step forward compared to any attempt at an all-inclusive theory.

The second issue concerns how theory relates to empirical research. Many still hold that the validity of a social theory ought to be decided mainly on the basis of empirical testing. Theoretical progress is then seen as the result of empirical falsification and corroboration. Very few would go as far as to claim that one falsification is sufficient to abandon a theory. Instead, they take a sophisticated falsificationist position, claiming that a sequence of empirical refutations is strong indication that the theory concerned is some-how false and ought to be abandoned. Not only do many sociologists hold this view; several philosophers of science do as well. Even realists, who claim to challenge the orthodoxies of today, basically hold this position.[2] This widespread view is, however, problematic. It is, after all, impossible to anticipate all variables which might intervene in a given empirical social research setting, and it is, *a fortiori*, impossible to be ready for all of these factors (see chapter 8). Furthermore, a finite number of empirical observations cannot be a solid base from which to decide upon the cognitive validity of a theoretical statement, since the latter refers to an infinite or unknown number of cases. Hence, the validity of empirical testing as the central medium for deciding upon the truth or acceptability of a theory is doubtful. That is not to say that empirical social research cannot inform us in any other way about the intellectual value of a theory. Empirical research might, for instance, illuminate the extent to which a theory provides counter-intuitive, novel or profound insights. There are many problems, however, with empirical testing being used as the sole arbiter of validity.

This brings me to a third, related point regarding the relationship between theory and the empirical subject-matter. I already mentioned that the reigning consensus considers theory mainly as a means for explaining and predicting

empirical phenomena, and empirical research primarily as a means for deciding upon the validity of the theory. Against this, I plead strongly for adopting
a different intellectual attitude towards the object of empirical research in
sociology. Rather than conceiving of the object of social research as solely
that which needs to be illuminated or explained, the very same object also
needs to be seen as a central source for inferring theoretical insight. For
example, rather than reducing the sociology of literature to a mere attempt to
account sociologically for literary products, the latter should also be seen as
a vital reservoir for sociological imagination and theoretical insights. Objects
of social research *can* be seen like this because, contrary to natural objects,
they are pre-interpreted by the individuals involved. It would be highly
unfortunate to close oneself off to the various ways in which 'lay people'
express insights about the social world. Given the transient nature of the
social realm, the flux of time always provides the possibility for novel
theoretical insights. Due to the remarkably fast-changing conditions under
which we currently live, the empirical realm has become more a potential
intellectual source than ever before.

A fourth question refers to how social theorists should relate to aligned
disciplines. It seems to me indisputable that theoretical innovation depends
to a large extent on the proper use of analogies with and metaphors drawn
from other fields of enquiry. Learning from aligned fields makes social theory
a highly creative enterprise with a huge reservoir of potential theoretical
innovations. Most significant innovations in social theory in the twentieth
century have been made by drawing upon insights from other disciplines.
To give a few examples: structuralist social theory drew upon analogies with
linguistics; functionalist theory relied upon analogies with biological evolution; and rational choice theory relied upon models derived from economics
(see chapters 1, 2 and 7). There are, however, still a significant number of
developments in other disciplines that have so far received hardly any attention by social theorists. I am thinking here, for example, of recent theories
regarding the selfish gene, chaos theory and dissipative structures, all of
which seem to have interesting analogies in the social realm.[3] They are,
sadly, rarely explored, and, if at all, less by social theorists than by natural
scientists or philosophers. There has, indeed, been a trend amongst social
theorists in the late twentieth century towards avoiding the employment of
knowledge from other fields. Instead, quite a number of scholars seem to
assume that theoretical progress depends solely on close scrutiny and re-
cycling of preceding social theories.[4] This intellectual strategy might facilitate analytical clarity, but, in isolation, it is unlikely to provide innovative
and penetrating social knowledge. The distrust towards using analogies
with other disciplines can be explained by the fact that two deeply fallacious
beliefs seem widely held. The first is that the gap between the social realm
and other realms of reality is so wide that analogies break down. Those who

hold this position simply miss the point. To look for analogies is not to assert identity; it implies being sensitive to differences as well. And awareness of the differences between social and other realms can, indeed, be highly informative about the workings of the former. The second belief is that to use analogies with other disciplines implies *reducing* the social to something non-social. This, again, is mistaken. For example, to use analogies with Dawkins's theory of the selfish gene is not in any way to state that the social is simply the outcome of replicating genes which find adequate organisms so to do. Rather, social rules are conceived as analogous to genes, and the analysis focuses upon the former, not the latter. The use of analogies does not entail embracing any kind of reductionism.

A fifth issue, which is central to social theory today, is the problem of social change. Remember that sociology and social theory initially emerged as a response to the socio-political and economic upheavals at the time. Several nineteenth-century thinkers thought that systematic and science-based reflections upon the workings of society would be conducive to the rational steering of society. In particular, the 'science of society' would allow for the re-implementation of socio-political order, which was thought to have been lost because of then-recent social transformations. This explains the recurrent interest in the workings of social order amongst twentieth-century social theorists, even if they abandoned the politico-practical aspirations of their nineteenth-century predecessors. This interest unites otherwise very different authors like, for instance, Durkheim, the early Parsons, Garfinkel and Giddens (see chapters 2, 3 and 4). I think that this intellectual bias towards order goes hand-in-hand with a tendency amongst theoreticians to neglect the mechanisms by which structural change is brought about. In contrast with the attention which empirical sociologists have given to change in society, social theorists tend to show less interest in the dynamics of structural transformations. It is ironic that whereas functionalism has traditionally been criticized for its emphasis on 'social statics', the later Parsons and Luhmann are amongst the few who, by sketching analogies with biological evolution and by using system theory, have attempted systematically to deal with social change.[5] One of the central tasks of social theory is to account for structural transformations. Close scrutiny of recent developments in evolutionary biology, chaos theory and thermodynamics are fruitful for the successful accomplishment of this enterprise.

A sixth point refers to the relationship between social theory on the one hand, and conditions of modernity on the other. Many contributions to social theory in the twentieth century portray people as living in an unquestioned world. In this picture, people regularly monitor their actions in accordance with implicit, shared rules. People know these rules in a practical, tacit way. In this view, people do not seem to develop discursive theoretical knowledge regarding the underlying rules and assumptions, let alone implement such reflection in their actions (see chapters 3 and 4). Quite a few of these theories claim to have contemporary relevance; they purport to say something significant about the world today. It goes without saying, however, that if the picture presented can ever be found to be applicable, it is far more representative of so-called traditional types of society. What is characteristic of conditions of high modernity is precisely the tendency of people not to take things for granted, and regularly to reflect upon previously tacit rules and assumptions.[6] It follows that modern social theory is not only out of synch with the cultural formations of advanced modernity. It also fails to take into account systematically the more general proposition that people, whether or not they are modern, are in principle able to develop 'reflection of the second order'; that is, to acquire theoretical, discursive knowledge *vis-à-vis* previously tacit, shared rules. Social theory tends to acknowledge this form of second-order reflection only in so far as it attributes this ability to the theorist or researcher – not to the individuals involved. The only type of reflection attributed to the individuals is 'reflection of the first order'. This refers to people's reflection upon the meaning and effects of their (real or imaginary) actions – not upon the underlying rules and assumptions. In short, self-reflection of the second order should play a central role in any social theory, especially one which aspires to contemporary relevance.

On the same theme, most theories in the twentieth century overestimate the extent to which people disregard novel or unanticipated experiences. In Garfinkel's documentary method of interpretation, for instance, people draw upon interpretative procedures in order to account for reality such that the procedures remain the same (see chapter 3). The procedures indeed remain intact, even if the encountered reality potentially contradicts these procedures.[7] Be that as it may, people often *do* re-assess the rules and assumptions which they had hitherto drawn upon in the light of unexpected encounters. People might develop such reflection of the second order because, for example, they encounter different forms of life, or because they are confronted with unanticipated effects of previous actions. To come across Azande conceptions of causality and witchcraft, or to read about Renaissance notions of science – both experiences might force one to reflect upon previously tacit rules and assumptions in science and philosophy. Likewise, to be confronted with the suboptimal collective effects of myopic self-interested actions might make us become aware of the limitations of our instrumental rational actions so far. All these experiences thus force people to reflect upon previously unquestioned rules and assumptions. It follows that, to develop a social theory with current significance, one ought to deal with the question: under which conditions might self-reflection of the second order emerge?

Finally, my appeal for paying attention to self-reflection of the second order ties in with the earlier request for accounting for structural transformations. Once reflection of the second order is not merely carried out individually, but also enters the public-collective realm, it can become an important source of co-ordinated collective action, and thus for intentional transformation or deliberate maintenance of structures. For example, a public-collective awareness and discussion of the free-rider problem can lead to people's attempts to transform the shared rules of the game according to which they have operated until now. To give another example, confronted with the collapse of the Soviet Union, several ethnic groups started to reflect upon their lost culture, language and political autonomy, and tried to revitalize these.[8] This example shows the extent to which collective reflection of the second order often goes together with a symbolic reconstruction of the past. That is, a different sequence of past events is selected, new values are attached to the same events, and a new ordering is attributed to that past. In this example, the Russian presence is now seen in a different light, and local political events have gained enormous significance. This reconstruction of the past is an essential motivating factor for the making of collective and co-ordinated action. To conclude, to develop a social theory with contemporary value, one should pay attention to the relationship between reflection of the second order, collective action and symbolic reconstruction of the past.[9]

References

Alexander, J. 1982a. *Theoretical Logic in Sociology; Volume 1, Positivism, Presuppositions and Current Controversies.* London: Routledge.

Alexander, J. 1982b. *Theoretical Logic in Sociology; Volume 2, The Antinomies of Classical Thought: Marx and Durkheim.* London: Routledge.

Alexander, J. 1983. *Theoretical Logic in Sociology; Volume 3, The Classical Attempt at Theoretical Synthesis: Max Weber.* Berkeley: University of California Press.

Alexander, J. 1984. *Theoretical Logic in Sociology; Volume 4, The Reconstruction of Classical Thought: Parsons.* London: Routledge, Kegan and Paul.

Archer, M. 1995. *Realist Social Theory: The Morphogenetic Approach.* Cambridge: Cambridge University Press.

Baert, P. 1992. *Time, Self and Social Being: Temporality within a Sociological Context.* Aldershot: Ashgate.

Beck, U., Giddens, A. and Lash, S. (eds) 1994. *Reflexive Modernization; Politics, Tradition and Aesthetics in the Modern Social Order.* Cambridge: Polity Press.

Garfinkel, H. 1967. *Studies in Ethnomethodology.* Englewood Cliffs, NJ: Prentice-Hall.

Giddens, A. 1977. *Studies in Social and Political Theory.* London: Hutchinson (reprinted, 1979).

Giddens, A. 1979. *Central Problems in Social Theory.* Cambridge: Polity Press (reprinted, 1993).

Giddens, A. 1984. *The Constitution of Society; Outline of the Theory of Structuration.* Cambridge: Polity Press (reprinted, 1993).

Giddens, A. 1993. *New Rules of Sociological Method.* Cambridge: Polity Press (2nd edition).

Habermas, J. 1987c. *The Theory of Communicative Action, Volume 2: Lifeworld and System: A Critique of Functionalist Reason.* Cambridge: Polity Press (originally in German 1981; reprinted, 1991).

Habermas, J. 1991. *The Theory of Communicative Action, Volume 1; Reason and the Rationalisation of Society.* Cambridge: Polity Press (originally in German, 1981).

Harré, R. 1993. *Social Being.* Oxford: Blackwell (2nd edition).

Kiel, D. and Elliott, E. (eds) 1996. *Chaos Theory in the Social Sciences.* Ann Arbor, MI: University of Michigan Press.

Knorr-Cetina, K. and Cicourel, A. V. (eds) 1981. *Advances in Social Theory and Methodology: Towards an Integration of Micro- and Macro-sociologies.* London: Routledge, Kegan and Paul.

Lawson, A. 1997. *Economics and Reality.* London: Routledge.

Luhmann, N. 1982. *The Differentiation of Society.* New York: Columbia University Press.

Luhmann, N. 1990. *Essays on Self-Reference.* New York: Columbia University Press.

Parsons, T. 1966. *Societies: Evolutionary and Comparative Perspectives.* Englewood Cliffs, NJ: Prentice-Hall.

Parsons, T. 1977. *The Evolution of Societies.* Englewood Cliffs, NJ: Prentice-Hall.

Rothschild, J. 1993. *Return to Diversity: A Political History of East Central Europe since World War II.* Oxford: Oxford University Press (2nd edition).

Schieve, W. C. and Allen, P. M. 1982. *Self-organization and Dissipative Structures: Applications in the Physical and Social Sciences.* Austin: University of Texas Press.

Notes

Chapter 1 A Timeless Order and its Achievement

1   I very much recommend Lukes (1973) as a semi-biographical introduction to Durkheim.
2   Durkheim (1982, pp. 63 ff.). See also Lukes (1973, pp. 67 ff.).
3   Durkheim (1984, pp. 31–87).
4   Durkheim (1982, pp. 64 ff.).
5   Durkheim (1984, pp. 149–75).
6   Durkheim (1952; 1982).
7   Durkheim (1984; 1982, especially pp. 119–46).
8   Durkheim (1915).
9   Durkheim (1982, p. 59).
10   Ibid. (pp. 60 ff.).
11   Ibid. (pp. 40 ff.).
12   Lukes (1973, pp. 6–7).
13   Durkheim (1982, pp. 50–51).
14   Ibid. (pp. 51–2).
15   Ibid. (pp. 52 ff.).
16   Ibid. (pp. 119–46).
17   See, especially, Durkheim (1915; 1963).
18   For an excellent discussion, see Lukes (1973, pp. 435–49).
19   Saussure (1960).
20   Ibid. (pp. 71–100).
21   Ibid. (pp. 7–23).
22   Ibid. (pp. 65–7).
23   Ibid. (pp. 67–70).
24   Culler (1986, pp. 28–33).
25   Saussure (1960, pp. 68–9).
26   See, for instance, Harland (1988, p. 13).
27   Saussure (1960, pp. 88 ff., 110–11).
28   Ibid. (pp. 120–2).
29   Ibid. (pp. 79–81).

30 Ibid. (pp. 79–100). See also Culler (1986, pp. 46–57).
31 Saussure (1960, pp. 122–7).
32 For example, Barthes (1972; 1983).
33 Braudel (1972, preface; 1980).
34 For an overview of history of the *Annales* school, see, for example, Burke (1990).
35 Althusser (1972); Althusser and Balibar (1970).
36 Althusser and Balibar (1970); Poulantzas (1968).
37 Lévi-Strauss (1994, pp. 5 ff.).
38 This is not to say that Durkheim's methodology is necessarily without criticism.
39 Lévi-Strauss (1993, pp. 206–11).
40 Ibid. (pp. 211 ff.).
41 Ibid. (pp. 214 ff.).
42 Ibid. (pp. 213–15).
43 Ibid. (p. 216).
44 Ibid. (pp. 215 ff.).
45 Ibid. (1993, pp. 1–27; 1994, pp. 312–362).
46 See Derrida (1973; 1976; 1978), Lacan (1989). I am referring here to Foucault's genealogical writings. See, for example, the interviews and articles in Foucault (1977; 1980).
47 Cixous (1981), Irigaray (1985), Kristeva (1982). See also Marks and de Courtivron (1981).
48 Bourdieu (1993, pp. 29–30), Bourdieu, Chamboredon and Passeron (1991) and Bourdieu and Wacquant (1992b, pp. 158–62). See also Wacquant (1992, pp. 26–35).
49 Bourdieu (1977, pp. 1–30; 1990, pp. 25–51).
50 Ibid. (1977, pp. 3–10; 1990, pp. 30–51).
51 Ibid. (1977, pp. 10–16, 22–30).
52 See, for example, ibid. (pp. 164–71).
53 With regard to the notion of *habitus*, see, for example, ibid. (1969; 1977, pp. 78–86; 1990, pp. 52–65).
54 With regard to the relationship between field and *habitus*, see, for example, ibid. (1971).
55 Obvious examples can be found in ibid. (1969; 1971; 1973; 1977, pp. 171–82).
56 For a comparison with rational choice theory, see, for instance, Wacquant (1992, pp. 24 ff.).
57 Compare Bourdieu (1977; 1990) with Giddens (1984) and Bhaskar (1989).
58 See, for example, Bourdieu and Passeron (1977).
59 Bourdieu (1984).
60 Willis (1993).

Chapter 2 The Biological Metaphor

1 Durkheim (1982, pp. 119–46).
2 Ibid. (1984, pp. 11 ff.).
3 Ibid. (1982, pp. 85–107).
4 Ibid. (1984, pp. 31–67).

5   Ibid. (pp. 68–87).
6   Ibid. (pp. 200–88).
7   Ibid. (pp. 291–309).
8   Malinowski (1944).
9   Ibid. (pp. 73–4).
10 Ibid. (p. 26).
11 Ibid. (pp. 26–35).
12 See, for example, ibid. (pp. 69 ff.).
13 Ibid. (pp. 7–14).
14 See, for example, ibid. (pp. 39, 83).
15 Ibid. (pp. 75–144).
16 See, for example, ibid. (pp. 120 ff.).
17 Radcliffe-Brown (1958, pp. 16 ff.).
18 See, for example, ibid. (1977, pp. 49–52).
19 Ibid. (1958, p. 8, footnote 3). Radcliffe-Brown was far more sympathetic to-
    wards French sociology (1958, pp. 85–6).
20 Ibid. (pp. 16 ff.).
21 Ibid. (pp. 52 ff.).
22 Ibid. (pp. 108–29).
23 Ibid. (pp. 67 ff.).
24 Ibid. (pp. 66 ff.).
25 Ibid. (pp. 90–5).
26 Ibid. (1952, pp. 182–3).
27 Ibid. (1977, pp. 19–21, 25–42).
28 Ibid. (1952, pp. 3–4, 191 ff.).
29 Ibid. (1977, pp. 21–4, 43–8).
30 Ibid. (1952, pp. 180 ff.).
31 Malinowski (1944, p. 150). Italics are mine.
32 Ibid. (p. 171). Italics are mine.
33 Radcliffe-Brown (1952, p. 181).
34 Parsons (1937).
35 Ibid. (1951).
36 Ibid. (1937, pp. 89–94).
37 Ibid. (pp. 473–694).
38 Ibid. (pp. 3–470).
39 Ibid. (pp. 697–776).
40 With regard to the pattern variables, see, for example, ibid. (1951, pp. 46–51,
    58–67).
41 With regard to the functional prerequisites, see, for example, ibid. (pp. 26–35).
42 Ibid. (1966, chapter 2).
43 Ibid. (1960).
44 See, for example, ibid. (1966; 1977).
45 For a similar argument, see Homans (1961, pp. 10 ff.) and Rocher (1974,
    pp. 164–5).
46 For a similar argument, see Cohen (1968, chapters 2, 3 and 7).
47 Merton (1968).
48 See ibid. (pp. 39–72).

49   Ibid. (p. 39).
50   Ibid. (pp. 40–1).
51   Ibid. (pp. 79–91).
52   Ibid. (pp. 84–6, 90, 105).
53   Ibid. (pp. 79–84, 90, 106).
54   This increased solidarity is often orchestrated so that the mobilization of forces can take place more smoothly.
55   Merton (1968, pp. 91–100, 106–8).
56   Ibid. (pp. 114–36).
57   Ibid. (pp. 185–214, 215–48).
58   With regard to this third point, see Giddens (1977, pp. 106 ff.).
59   E.g. Althusser (1972); Althusser and Balibar (1970); Marcuse (1968).
60   Elias (1970); Giddens (1979, pp. 198–233; 1981).
61   Giddens (1977, pp. 96–134; 1984).
62   Luhmann (1982, pp. 37 ff., 139 ff.).
63   Ibid. (pp. 213–17).
64   Ibid. (1990, pp. 21–85).
65   Ibid. (pp. 1–20).
66   Ibid. (pp. 123–74).
67   Ibid. (1982, pp. 232–8).

Chapter 3 The Enigma of Everyday Life

1   Mead (1934).
2   Ibid. (1938).
3   Ibid. (1959).
4   Ibid. (1936).
5   Take, for instance, Mead's article 'A behaviorist account of the significant symbol' which can be found in his *Selected Writings* (1964, pp. 240–7).
6   Harré and Secord (1972).
7   Mead (1934, pp. 136 ff.).
8   Ibid. (1934, pp. 1, 48–51, 140, 222 ff.; 1964, pp. 105–13, 243).
9   See Baert (1992, pp. 56–7).
10   Mead (1934, pp. 61 ff., 81 ff.)
11   See, for example, Mischel and Mischel (1977).
12   Mead (1934, pp. 173–8, 192 ff.).
13   See, for example, ibid. (1907; 1936, pp. 503–10).
14   Ibid. (1934, pp. 152–64; 1964, pp. 245–7, 284 ff.).
15   The term was first introduced by Blumer in an article in *Man and Society* in 1937.
16   Blumer (1969, pp. 62–4).
17   Ibid. (pp. 65–8).
18   Ibid. (pp. 68–70).
19   Ibid. (p. 17). See also pp. 70–7.
20   Ibid. (p. 18).
21   See, for example, Giddens (1993).

22 Compare with Durkheim (1982, pp. 50 ff.). See also chapter 1.
23 Mead (1929) and Maines, Sugrue and Katovich (1983, p. 163 ff.).
24 Mead (1936, pp. 264–91, 507 ff.; 1959, pp. 13 ff.).
25 Related notions are Maturana's notion of 'social- or self-consciousness' and Giddens's concept of 'institutional reflectivity'. See Maturana (1980) and Giddens (1989, especially pp. 36–44; 1992).
26 This issue is taken up in chapter 5. See also Giddens (1984).
27 See also Baert (1992).
28 Goffman (1969).
29 Ibid. (1981).
30 See also Manning (1992).
31 Simmel (1950, pp. 307–78).
32 Goffman (1963, pp. 24 ff.; 1972a, pp. 7–13).
33 Ibid. (1969, pp. 28 ff.).
34 Ibid. (pp. 32 ff.).
35 Ibid. (pp. 36–7).
36 Ibid. (pp. 83–108).
37 Ibid. (pp. 109–40).
38 Ibid.(pp. 203–30).
39 Ibid. (1972b, pp. 48–56 ff.).
40 Ibid. (pp. 56–95).
41 Ibid. (1963, pp. 24, 193–7, 216–41).
42 Berlin (1967, p. 4).
43 Garfinkel (1952).
44 Ibid. (1967).
45 Parsons (1937, pp. 3–470).
46 Garfinkel (1967, pp. 3–103).
47 Garfinkel and Sacks (1970).
48 See, for instance, Parsons (1937, pp. 708–14, 719–26).
49 Garfinkel (1974).
50 Ibid. (1963; 1967, pp. 76–185).
51 See Schutz's paper: 'Concept and theory formation in the social sciences' (1962, pp. 48–66).
52 See Schutz's papers: 'Commonsense and scientific interpretations of human action' and 'On multiple rationalities', ibid. (pp. 3–47, 207–59).
53 Garfinkel (1963, pp. 210–11); Heritage (1984, pp. 52 ff.).
54 Garfinkel (1963, pp. 212–13), Schutz (1962, pp. 11 ff.).
55 Garfinkel (1974).
56 Ibid. (1967, pp. 7–9).
57 Ibid. (pp. 116–85).
58 Ibid. (pp. 4–7).
59 See, for example, ibid. (1963).
60 Heritage (1987, 226–40).
61 The term was coined by Mannheim in his essay 'On the Interpretation of *Weltanschauung*' (1952, pp. 33–83).
62 Garfinkel (1967, pp. 77 ff.).
63 Kuhn (1970).

Chapter 4 The Skilful Accomplishment of Social Order

1   Elias (1978).
2   Giddens (1971a).
3   Originally published in 1972. For a revised edition, see ibid. (1981a).
4   Ibid. (1971b).
5   Ibid. (1972; 1978).
6   Originally published in 1976. For a revised edition, see ibid. (1993).
7   Ibid. (1977; 1979; 1982).
8   Ibid. (1981b; 1985).
9   Ibid. (1984).
10   Ibid. (1990).
11   Ibid. (1991; 1992).
12   Ibid. (1994).
13   Ibid. (1993, p. 26).
14   Ibid. (1984, pp. 229–43).
15   Ibid. (1993, pp. 163–70).
16   Ibid. (1987, pp. 109–15).
17   Ibid. (1984, pp. 51–60).
18   Ibid. (1981b, pp. 33–4).
19   Ibid. (1981b, pp. 29–41).
20   Ibid. (1984, pp. 110–19).
21   Ibid. (1979, pp. 9–48; 1984, pp. 207–21).
22   Ibid. (1984, pp. 34–7; 1981b, pp. 19–20).
23   See, for example, ibid. (1984, pp. 288 ff.).
24   Ibid. (1979, p. 55).
25   Ibid. (1984, p. 9).
26   Ibid. (1993, pp. 78–82).
27   Ibid. (1984, pp. 14–16; 1993, p. 118; 1985, p. 7).
28   Ibid. (p. 16).
29   Ibid. (p. 21).
30   Ibid. (pp. 31 ff., 258 ff.).
31   Ibid. (1984, p. 33). See also Craib (1992, pp. 46–7).
32   Giddens (1984, pp. 16–25).
33   Ibid. (1984, pp. 185 ff.).
34   Ibid. (pp. 28–30).
35   Ibid. (1989, p. 204).
36   Ibid. (1984, p. 36 ff.).
37   Ibid. (1979, pp. 70–1).
38   Ibid. (1977, pp. 294 ff.; 1984, pp. 26–7).
39   Ibid. (1984, p. 174).
40   Ibid. (p. 25).
41   Ibid.
42   Ibid. (1979, p. 70).
43   Ibid. (1984, p. 28).
44   Ibid. (1979, pp. 78–9).
45   Ibid. (1990, pp. 17–21).

46 Ibid. (pp. 4–35).
47 E.g. Thompson (1989).
48 Archer (1982; 1988; 1990).
49 E.g. Callinicos (1985).
50 E.g. Bernstein (1989).
51 Giddens (1982).
52 E.g. Bhaskar (1981); Harré (1981); Wright (1989).
53 Wright (1989).
54 See also Archer (1990, pp. 77–8).
55 Mouzelis (1989).

Chapter 5 The History of the Present

1 Foucault (1990a, pp. 3–16).
2 Ibid. (1954).
3 Ibid. (1989a).
4 Ibid. (1989c).
5 Ibid. (1989d).
6 Ibid. (1989b).
7 Ibid. (1977a).
8 Ibid. (1979; 1990b; 1992).
9 For example, Smart (1988, pp. 41 ff.); Sheridan (1990).
10 Foucault (1989b, pp. 15 ff; 1989d, p. xiv).
11 Ibid. (1989a; 1989d).
12 Ibid. (1989b).
13 See also ibid. (pp. 3–30).
14 Barthes (1983).
15 For a discussion of the stratified conception of reality in realist philosophy, see Baert (1996).
16 Braudel (1966, preface).
17 Foucault (1989b, esp. pp. 3–17).
18 Ibid. (esp. part 2).
19 Ibid. (esp. pp. 3 ff.). See also Bachelard (1984) and Canguilhem (1978).
20 Foucault (1989b, p. 8).
21 Ibid. (p. 9).
22 Ibid.
23 Ibid. (1989d, p. xiii).
24 For example, Saussure (1959, pp. 88 ff., 110 ff., 120–2).
25 Foucault (1989d, p. xv).
26 Ibid. (1977a; 1979; 1990b; 1992).
27 Ibid. (1989b, pp. 12–14).
28 Ibid. (1977b, pp. 140–64). The article appeared initially as 'Nietzsche, la généalogie, l'histoire' in a volume in memory of Jean Hyppolite.
29 See especially ibid. (1980).
30 With respect to genealogy, see the excellent contribution by Geuss (1994).
31 Foucault (1977b, p. 146).

32 Ibid. (1990a, p. 37).
33 Ibid. (1977b, pp. 142 ff.).
34 Ibid. (p. 146).
35 Ibid. (1980, p. 115).
36 Ibid. (1979, p. 82).
37 Ibid. (1990a, pp. 104–5).
38 Ibid. (1979, pp. 84–5).
39 Ibid. (pp. 92–5).
40 Ibid. (1980, pp. 97–8).
41 Ibid. (1979, p. 83).
42 Ibid. (1980, pp. 120–4).
43 Ibid. (1979, pp. 95 ff.).
44 Ibid. (1977a, pp. 3–69).
45 Ibid. (pp. 57–69).
46 Ibid. (pp. 135–69).
47 Ibid. (pp. 170–94).
48 Ibid. (pp. 170–7, 195–228).
49 Ibid. (pp. 177–84).
50 Ibid. (p. 304).
51 Ibid. (1990a, p. 37).
52 Ibid. (1977a, pp. 3–7).
53 Ibid. (pp. 73 ff.).
54 Ibid. (1990a, p. 37). Italics are Foucault's.
55 Ibid.
56 Ibid. (1977a, pp. 293 ff.).
57 Ibid. (p. 151).
58 Ibid. (pp. 192 ff.; 1980, pp. 107 ff.).
59 Ibid. (1990a, p. 36).
60 Ibid. (1980, p. 62).
61 Ibid. (1990a, pp. 263–4). Italics are mine.
62 Ibid. (1979, p. 93).
63 Layder (1994, p. 107).
64 For a similar argument, see Poster (1990, pp. 161–2).
65 Foucault (1979, p. 94).
66 Ibid. (p. 95).
67 Ibid.
68 See also Poulantzas (1978) and Layder (1994, pp. 106–8).
69 Foucult (1979, p. 95).
70 Ibid. (1980, p. 119).
71 Ibid. (1979, p. 86).

Chapter 6 The Spread of Reason

1 Adorno et al. (1976), Habermas (1987b; 1987c, pp. 1–49; 1987d), and Habermas
   and Luhmann (1971). For an overview of Habermas's participation in public
   debates, see Holub (1991).

2 Habermas (1989) Like the French *D'octorat d'État*, the German *Habilitations-schrift* refers to an extensive doctoral dissertation.
3 Habermas (1987d).
4 Ibid. (1987a; 1973b; 1988).
5 Ibid. (1976; 1979).
6 Ibid. (1987c; 1991).
7 Ibid. (1987a, pp. 25–63).
8 Ibid. (1987b).
9 Ibid. (1993).
10 Outhwaite (1994).
11 Habermas (1991, pp. 339–99).
12 Ibid. (1987b, pp. 51–122; 1987a, pp. 71–90).
13 Adorno (1973, pp. 146–61).
14 Compare Adorno and Horkheimer (1973, pp. 1–119) with Habermas (1987b, pp. 106–30).
15 See also Dews (1986, pp. 101 ff.); Wellmer (1985, pp. 52 ff.); McCarthy (1985, pp. 176 ff.); Honneth (1987, pp. 356–76).
16 Habermas (1987c, pp. 113–97; 1976, pp. 1–7).
17 Ibid. (1987a, pp. 196 ff.). For a critical overview of Habermas's theory of cognitive interests, see, for example, Ottmann (1982).
18 Habermas (1987a, pp. 308–15).
19 Ibid. (pp. 71–90, 308–9).
20 See also Giddens (1985a, pp. 125 ff.), Bernstein (1978, pp. 188–9).
21 Habermas (1987a, pp. 140–60, 309–10; 1988, pp. 89–170).
22 Ibid. (1987a, pp. 310–11).
23 Ibid. (pp. 220 ff.).
24 Pusey (1987, p. 74; 1973, pp. 29 ff.).
25 See also Bernstein (1985b, pp. 12–15).
26 Ibid. (pp. 15 ff.).
27 Habermas (1991, pp. 1–141).
28 Ibid. (pp. 328 ff.).
29 Ibid. (pp. 236 ff.).
30 Ibid. (1979, pp. 1–59; 1991, pp. 286–328).
31 Ibid. (1979, pp. 59–68; 1973b, pp. 1–40).
32 Ibid. (1970a; 1970b).
33 See also Giddens (1985b, pp. 114–16).
34 Habermas (1979, pp. 69–129).
35 Ibid. (pp. 69–177).
36 Ibid. (1976, pp. 68–92; 1979, pp. 178–205).
37 Ibid. (1987c, pp. 332–73).
38 See also Roderick (1986, pp. 158–9).
39 For a similar argument, see also Held (1980, pp. 397–8) and Giddens (1985b, pp. 114–16).
40 For a related discussion, see Lukes (1982).
41 Habermas (1973b).
42 See also Held (1980, pp. 397–8). For a more comprehensive critique of Habermas's contribution to philosophy of science, see Hesse (1982).

Chapter 7 The Invasion of Economic Man

1   See, for instance, Boudon (1982); Elster (1985). Serious objections have been raised to the reconstruction of Marx along these lines (e.g. Cohen 1982).
2   See, for example, Arrow (1951); Downs (1957); Olson (1965); Becker (1976); Coleman (1990).
3   See, for example, Kreps (1990).
4   See, for example, Elster (1979; 1983; 1986a; 1986b; 1989); Hollis (1988; 1994).
5   Scholars familiar with RCT might wish to skip this section.
6   Elster (1978, pp. 106 ff.; 1989, pp. 95 ff.).
7   Sartre (1960, pp. 232 ff.).
8   Elster (1978, pp. 122 ff.).
9   Arrow (1951, pp. 13 ff.).
10 Keynes (1921); Knight (1921).
11 Obviously, in cases of uncertainty, where Pi is incalculable, expected utility is likewise indeterminable.
12 Kreps (1990, pp. 9 ff.).
13 Ibid. (pp. 9–25 ff.).
14 Nash (1950).
15 Axelrod (1984).
16 For a more elaborate account of the applications of game theory in this area, see, for example, Jervis (1978). For an overview of the relevance of game theory to political science in general, see, for example, Riker (1992).
17 Downs (1957); Olson (1965); Becker (1965); Coleman (1990).
18 Olson (1965, pp. 6 ff.).
19 Ibid. (pp. 14 ff.).
20 Ibid. (pp. 22–52).
21 Becker (1976, pp. 3–5).
22 Ibid. (p. 14). Becker's italics.
23 Ibid. (pp. 5–7, 14).
24 Compare Parsons (1951), Merton (1968), Giddens (1984) and Coleman (1990).
25 Coleman (1990, pp. 6 ff.).
26 Ibid. (pp. 8 ff.).
27 Ibid. (p. 14).
28 Ibid. (pp. 18–19).
29 Ibid. (pp. 19 ff.).
30 See, for instance, ibid. (p. 18) and Becker (1976, pp. 13–14).
31 Brown (1965). See also Coleman (1990, pp. 203–11).
32 Becker (1976, pp. 39–88, 205–50).
33 Elster (1986b, p. 24)
34 Hardin (1982, pp. 115 ff.).
35 Riker and Ordershook (1973, pp. 62); Hinich (1981); Schwartz (1987); Coleman (1990, pp. 290 ff.).
36 Becker (1976, pp. 5 ff.).
37 Ibid. (p. 5).
38 E.g. Coleman (1990, p. 19).
39 See e.g., Bhaskar (1979); Cartwright (1989); Hacking (1983).

40 See Lawson (1989).
41 See, for example, Friedman (1953); Becker (1976); Posner (1980).
42 Becker (1976, p. 7).
43 Bourdieu (1977; 1990).
44 Becker (1976, p. 10). My italics.

Chapter 8 Eroding Foundations

1 See, for example, Comte (1969).
2 See Kolakowski (1972, pp. 11–13) and Bryant (1985, pp. 2–4).
3 Hempel (1965; 1966) is the most vocal representative of this view.
4 Compare, for example, Ayer (1946, pp. 5–16) and Carnap (1959) with Popper (1989, pp. 33–41).
5 'Humean' because it relies upon Hume's views on causality, See, for example, sections iv to vii of Hume's *Enquiry Concerning Human Understanding* (1975, pp. 25–79).
6 For example, Bhaskar (1978; 1989); Cartwright (1989); Hacking (1983); Harré (1975).
7 Weber's views on this matter are explored in two papers, 'The meaning of "ethical neutrality" in sociology and economics' (1949, pp. 1–50) and 'Objectivity in social science and social policy' (1949, pp. 50–112).
8 This is to some extent applicable to Giddens (1977, esp. pp. 80–9).
9 Durkheim (1952).
10 Comte (1969); J. S. Mill (1891, especially book vi); Spencer (1961).
11 Ayer (1946) contains a clear summary of the logical positivist view.
12 See especially Hempel's paper, 'The function of general laws in history' (1965, pp. 231–44).
13 See, for example, Homans (1964; 1967).
14 Winch (1990).
15 Bhaskar (1989, especially pp. 25–70, 120–59).
16 See, for example, Giddens (1993, especially pp. 50–6, 163–70).
17 The major disagreements between positivists and critical theorists were recorded in the so-called *Positivismusstreit*. See Adorno et al. (1976).
18 Keat and Urry (1982, pp. 3–45).
19 Harré (1985, pp. 56–8).
20 For an example of the inductivist method, see Mill (1891). For an accessible summary, see Chalmers (1976, chapter 1).
21 The problem of induction was first introduced by Hume in his *Treatise of Human Nature* (1978, book i, part iii, section vi). See also Russell (1967, pp. 33–8).
22 Compare Kuhn (1970a) with Popper (1968).
23 Some basic problems of inductivism are listed in Chalmers (1976, chapter 2). For Popper's treatment of inductivism, see, for instance, Popper (1968, pp. 27–30, 262–5, 311–17; 1989, pp. 42–55; 1992, pp. 141–7).
24 Compare Popper (1968, especially pp. 27–30, 32–4) with Duhem (1954) and Hempel (1965, 1966).

25 See, for instance, Popper (1968, pp. 59, 106–7; 1970, pp. 51 ff.).
26 For the intellectual background to Popper's notion that science proceeds through 'trial and error', see ibid. (1992, pp. 44–52).
27 Ibid. (1968, pp. 40–2, 78–92).
28 Ibid. (pp. 119–23).
29 Ibid. (1992, pp. 31–8).
30 Ibid. (1986, p. 3).
31 Ibid. (pp. 115 ff.).
32 Ibid. (1950; 1986, pp. vi–viii).
33 With regard to Popper's critique of utopianism, see, for example, ibid. (1966, especially pp. 157–68).
34 Kuhn (1970a; 1970b).
35 Popper (1970).
36 Feyerabend (1975, especially pp. 69–164, 171–80).
37 Bhaskar (1978, pp. 63–142).
38 Lakatos (1970).
39 Harré and Secord (1972); Keat and Urry (1982); Bhaskar (1989).
40 Harré and Secord (1972).
41 Keat and Urry (1982).
42 Bhaskar (1989).
43 For instance, Layder (1992).
44 For the relationship between economics and realism, see Cartwright (1989).
45 Bhaskar (1989, pp. 1–70).
46 See, for instance, Lawson (1994, pp. 262 ff.).
47 Ibid. (pp. 262–6).
48 Bhaskar (1978, especially chapter 2).
49 Ibid. (pp. 125 ff.).
50 With regard to the realist views on social theory, see ibid. (1989, pp. 31–54).
51 Durkheim (1952).
52 Bourdieu published his ideas on this matter in 1972, Giddens in 1976. See Bourdieu (1977); Giddens (1984; 1993).
53 Baert (1992).

Conclusion

1 Alexander (1982a; 1982b; 1983; 1984); Giddens (1977; 1979; 1984; 1993); Habermas (1987c; 1991). See also Knorr-Cetina and Cicourel (1981).
2 Lawson (1997).
3 E.g. Schieve and Allen (1982); Harré (1993); Archer (1995); Kiel and Elliot (1996).
4 E.g. Alexander (1982a; 1982b; 1983; 1984); Giddens (1977; 1979; 1984; 1993).
5 See, for example, Parsons (1966; 1977); Luhmann (1982; 1990).
6 See, for example, Beck, Giddens and Lash (1994).
7 Garfinkel (1967, pp. 77 ff.).
8 See, for example, Rothschild (1993).
9 For a further development of these ideas, see Baert (1992).

Index